CAPTURED!

CAPTURED!

CAROLYN PAINE MILLER

CHRISTIAN HERALD BOOKS

Chappaqua, New York

Copyright © 1977 by Carolyn Paine Miller
First Edition
CHRISTIAN HERALD BOOKS, Chappaqua, New York 10514
ISBN NO. 0-915684-17-9
Library of Congress Catalog Card No. 77-81401

Manufactured in the United States of America

PREFACE...

"I cannot tell you how I shared in your captivity," a college friend wrote just after our release. "I guess part of what I felt was in hearing you sing a song we sang together that had much meaning for you, 'Make Me a Captive, Lord, and Then I Shall Be Free....'"

I smiled, remembering. My real captivity, as well as my real freedom, had begun simultaneously when I, like the Apostle Paul, had been "apprehended" by Christ Jesus (Philippians 3:12). Compared with that event, our recent experience was merely an incident.

This story is not mine alone. It belongs to all of the "Banmethuout 14," and I am grateful to others of the group who have read the manuscript and offered suggestions. It also belongs to the thousands of people who stood with us in prayer.

I am grateful to Hugh Steven of the Wycliffe Bible Translators and others who encouraged me to write and gave guidance at various points along the way. I am especially grateful to my husband John who pushed and encouraged me, typed and evaluated the manuscript, and without whose loving support I would have never persisted. Above all I am grateful to God with whose help and for whose glory the story is told.

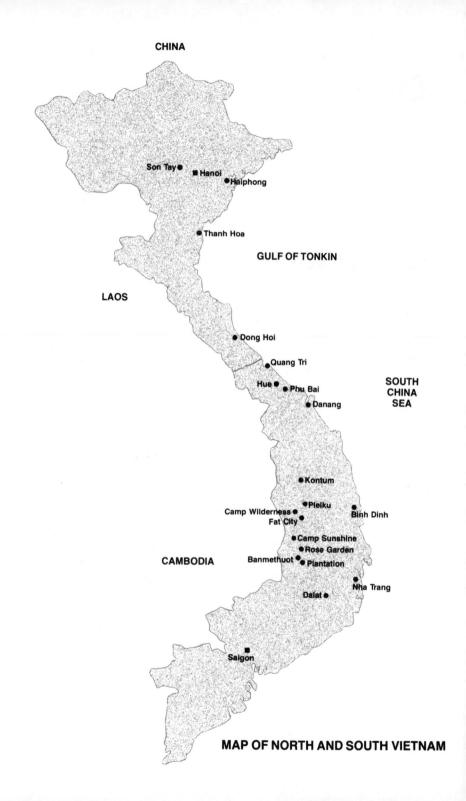

CHINA

Son Tay ●
■ Hanoi
● Haiphong

● Thanh Hoa

GULF OF TONKIN

LAOS

● Dong Hoi

● Quang Tri

Hue ● ● Phu Bai
● Danang

SOUTH
CHINA
SEA

● Kontum

● Pleiku

Camp Wilderness ●
Fat City ●
● Binh Dinh

● Camp Sunshine
● Rose Garden

Banmethuot ●
● Plantation

CAMBODIA

Dalat ●
● Nha Trang

■ Saigon

MAP OF NORTH AND SOUTH VIETNAM

ONE

Countdown

The nerve-shattering whine and crash of incoming rockets had stopped, but the pop of outgoing mortars and the explosion of artillery shells continued, interspersed with the rat-a-tat of small arms fire. Was the battle still in progress? Or were the soldiers in the nearby South Vietnamese army camp just edgy and shooting into the shadows?

I shifted my weight on the cold cement floor and looked up. The faint gray tinge at the windows promised the dawn of a new day and a new week in the South Vietnamese highland city of Banmethuot. "Thank God the night is ending at last!" I thought.

"John," I whispered to my husband, "do you think we should try to go now?"

"Yes, I think we should," he said, getting awkwardly to his feet. He walked over to the window and peered out. "Maybe this is all we'll get this time," he said, "but if there should be a ground attack we don't want to be here."

I knew what he meant. The Christian and Missionary Alliance (C&MA) property on which we'd been living as guests for the past five months was on the south edge of town directly adjacent to a large South Vietnamese army base. A few yards from our house was the grave site and memorial for six missionaries who had been killed here in 1968 by Communist forces pushing to take over the city of

Banmethuot (pronounced "Ban me to it"). Vietnamese and tribal friends had warned us not to stay here should there be another attack.

John moved toward the door. "I'll go see if the Phillipses and Betty want to go with us," he said. Christian and Missionary Alliance missionaries Richard and Lillian Phillips and Betty Mitchell were the only other foreigners living on the property.

Our five-year-old daughter LuAnne was sleeping peacefully on the floor beside me but woke immediately when I sat up. I marveled at her ability to sleep through all the racket. I had held my breath in suspense with the whine of every rocket that passed overhead and flinched with each accompanying crash. Some landed close enough to throw dirt on the roof of our house. Many shook the house with a violence that rattled windows and caused bits of plaster to fall from the ceiling—and LuAnne had slept through it all.

She woke briefly at the outset of the barrage when we got her out of bed to dress her and move her to the floor of the hallway where there were no windows or outside walls. When I stretched out beside her she snuggled up close and was asleep in an instant.

Only once during that long noisy night did she waken. When I got up and felt my way to the bathroom at the end of the hall, LuAnne immediately sensed my absence. "Mommy!" she called. "Where are you?"

"I'm right here, LuAnne," I answered. "It's all right."

Now I got to my feet and began a hurried check of the house. LuAnne clung to the long black tribal skirt I was wearing and followed me from room to room.

"Mommy, where are we going?" she asked.

"We're going to Mr. Struharik's house," I said. "He'll tell us what to do and help us to get out of Banmethuot if there's going to be more fighting." Paul Struharik was the official representative of the U.S. Consul in Banmethuot, and we had been instructed to contact him in an emergency.

The suitcases containing most of our belongings were already in our Land Rover. John had put them in during the night. In the kitchen I grabbed a woven plastic market bag and opened the refrigerator door. The electricity had gone off very early during the shelling and the freezing compartment was already defrosting.

I took a canned ham and a box of cheese we had brought back with us from a recent trip to the coast to visit our three older children. They were in a mission school in the city of Nha Trang. I closed the refrigerator door, put the ham and cheese into the bag along with a loaf of local French bread and hurried into the study.

I looked around. "Nothing in here to take," I thought. We had already packed the corrected manuscripts of the Bru New Testament and our other language materials in what we called our "Priority Number One Bag."

Monday, March 10, 1975, would become a date for us to remember. After years as missionaries in Vietnam we were now about to begin an eight-month ordeal that would test every spiritual principle I'd ever learned.

THURSDAY

The first real indication we'd had that serious trouble was imminent came on Thursday, March 6.

John and I and two Bru language helpers had been deeply engrossed in cross-checking for consistency the rendering of certain key Greek words and phrases in the Bru translation of the New Testament. We were eager to finish this one last procedure and send the manuscript to Saigon to begin the printing process. This would mark the culmination of fourteen years of painstaking work in learning the Bru language, working out a writing system for it, preparing literacy materials and training teachers to use them. All of this had been toward an eventual goal of giving them the Word of God in the only language they could understand—Bru.

I looked up in surprise to see Dick Phillips at the door. "Dick," I said, "it's good to see you out. How are you feeling?"

It was the first time he'd been out of the house since he'd collapsed a week earlier. A local doctor had diagnosed it as "nervous exhaustion."

"I wondered if you knew Route 19 has been cut?" he said.

"No," John answered, "when did that happen?"

"Day before yesterday," he said. "Apparently Communist forces are holding one of the mountain passes between here and the coast."

"I guess that means no more gasoline until the government opens the road again," John remarked.

"No more fish or market supplies from the coast either," I added.

After Dick left we discussed this piece of news. It was not particularly alarming. The road to the coast passed through long stretches of rugged and isolated terrain. It was not uncommon for traffic to be temporarily suspended when bridges were blown up or government convoys ambushed. At the same time, we didn't like to be so completely dependent on the uncertainties of air travel in the event of an emergency. We thought we should be prepared to leave at a moment's notice but as yet we felt no sense of real urgency.

SATURDAY

By Saturday the situation had worsened. That evening we were invited for dinner to the home of Canadian missionaries Norman and Joan Johnson. After supper Norm got out the carroms board and we were looking forward to relaxing after a hard week of language work. But before we could get started, a Raday tribal student from the Bible school where the Johnsons taught came to the door.

"Mr. Phillips wants to see you right away," he said to Norm. Norm and John left at once.

Joan and I agreed to play a game with LuAnne while we waited for the men to return. We were tense. Ironically the game she selected was called "Trouble."

"What do you suppose is the matter," Joan wondered. "Do you think Dick could have had a relapse?"

When Norm and John returned an hour later they brought sobering news. Dick had just had a visit from a Vietnamese friend in the government, a member of the Evangelical Protestant Church in Banmethuot. The report

10

was that the North Vietnamese army had recently moved two divisions into the area reenforcing the division already there. It seemed likely that they would attempt to take over the city. The friend was sending his wife and children out, and advised Dick to leave as soon as possible.

But how could we? Road travel out of the area was impossible and the only commercial airline, Air Vietnam, was booked solid for weeks ahead. Paul Struharik, the only U.S. government representative in the area, was in Saigon but was expected back the following afternoon. We would try, we decided, to ask for seats on the U.S. government courier plane on Tuesday, its next scheduled flight. Time and opportunity seemed to be slipping away.

SUNDAY

We debated whether or not we should drive out to the Bru village. It was in that area that the recently arrived North Vietnamese army division was supposedly located. It was a big area, though, extending a long way back into the jungle, and the Bru village of Buon Jat was near the district center and near the highway.

We felt an obligation to the two young Bru men who were staying with us. They had come to help us with the understanding that we would take them back to the village. And if there was going to be trouble, they would want to be with their families. We decided that unless the soldiers at the military check point should advise us not to go, we would drive out.

The morning was clear and the vehicle loaded as we started out of town. A number of Bru high school students from the boarding school in Banmethuot were taking advantage of this chance to go home to the village for a few hours. At the edge of town John pulled over to a guard post and stopped. I pushed back the window and addressed the soldier on duty.

"Is it all right to travel on this road as far as Buon Jat?" I asked.

"Yes, you can travel as far as Buon Jat with no problem,"

11

he replied. "But you can't go down to the coast. The road is closed just beyond Kilometer Sixty-Two."

When we arrived at the village, we found the Bru people quite apprehensive and filled with foreboding. "We're meeting a lot of the 'jungle ones' these days when we go out to look for firewood or work in the rice fields farther from the village," one man reported. "They tell us to buy up lots of salt and rice," he added, referring to the two commodities most essential to Bru life, "because they say there's going to be much fighting soon."

It was time for the morning worship service. We walked into the simple unpainted board structure that served as a church. LuAnne and I took our places on the right-hand side with the other women and children. John sat across the aisle with the men and boys. Mandõ, the young Bru lay-pastor, had charge of the service. We sang a few hymns and had a time of prayer.

It was Communion Sunday. Mandõ took out a dog-eared typewritten copy of the Gospel of Luke that he and so many others had helped us translate. Opening it to Chapter 22, he read the following words: "I feel very strongly wanting to eat and drink with you remembering the day God helped the people of Israel come out of the land of Egypt. I want to eat this before I meet great difficulty. I tell you truly, I will never eat and drink again with you as I am at this meal until the day comes that the things remembered by eating and drinking this meal are fulfilled. That will be the day God reigns."

As Mandõ read on, I looked at the people sitting on the low hand-hewn benches around me and listening intently to the reading of God's Word. I felt a great surge of gratitude to God for allowing us to share in the lives of these people, many of whom we had known intimately for fourteen years.

"What if," it crossed my mind, "this should be our last opportunity to share this feast of remembrance with our Bru brothers and sisters until 'the day God reigns'?"

When Dick and Lil met us on our return home that afternoon with news that radio contact with Banmethuot had been lost and Communist troops were positioned on roads leading to the town, we all decided to pack and be ready should there be an opportunity to leave. Norm Johnson had heard that Air Vietnam was putting on a special flight to Nha Trang the following day. Perhaps we could get on that. We would get in touch with Paul Struharik as soon as he came back to Banmethuot. If the situation seemed critical, he could even ask the U.S. consulate in Nha Trang for immediate evacuation.

John gathered up the translation materials and language notes and put these into one small suitcase. If we could take only one bag, that would be the one. The other suitcases we also packed in order of priority. The second bag contained tapes, tape recorder, radio, toilet articles, money, mementoes, and a few sets of our better clothing. The third and fourth contained more clothing, books, my portable sewing machine, tennis racquets and balls, Texas-ware dishes, tools, and bathing suits. These things would be good to have if we were to set up housekeeping in Nha Trang and were not restricted in the amount of baggage we could take out.

It was early evening before Norm and Dick finally made contact with Paul Struharik. They stopped by our house to report on their visit.

"Paul has checked with Vietnamese authorities responsible for the security of Banmethuot," Norm said. "They are expecting some military activity in the area but are confident they can handle it. Paul says we're welcome to spend the night at his house if we'd feel safer there."

"Paul's house is built more strongly than these are," I said, "and it isn't near any military target. But I'd hate to descend on him if it isn't necessary, especially when he has company." Norm had mentioned that an Australian visitor had just arrived in Banmethuot and was staying with Paul.

"Betty told me she doesn't feel she can leave until someone comes to take care of Ba Tu," Dick said. Betty Mitchell, in addition to teaching at the Raday Bible School and doing village visitation, had been caring for an elderly Vietnamese woman who was almost completely blind and deaf.

"In that case," John said, "we had better stay here tonight. I don't think we should go without Betty."

LuAnne's bedtime evasion tactics lasted longer than usual that evening. During the afternoon she had been very happy. Packing to go somewhere was one of her favorite activities, and the prospect of a trip to Nha Trang to see her brothers and sister filled her with joy. But she had not missed the implications of the adult discussions going on around her.

"Mommy, can't I sleep in your room?" she asked. "What if the fighting comes here?"

"If there's any fighting, we'll come in and get you," I promised, sitting down on the couch to read. With this assurance she finally went to sleep.

I read till about midnight and then got ready for bed. I put my clothes right beside the bed where I could get into them quickly if I needed to and crawled under the mosquito net, being careful not to wake John.

I fell asleep immediately, but it seemed no time at all before I was jolted awake by a series of thudding explosions. Both John and I sat up in bed.

"That's incoming!" John said. "Better get LuAnne and get into the hall."

"What time is it?" I asked.

John looked at the luminous dial on his watch. "Two-fifty," he answered.

I had my nightgown off and my clothes on in an instant. Slipping into a pair of sandals, I hurried across the hall to LuAnne's room. She was still asleep.

"LuAnne," I said gently, reaching into her net and pulling back the covers, "there's some shooting outside, and we want you to sleep in the hall where it's safer. Here, put these clothes on."

Her head bobbed sleepily as I put on her slacks and shirt and slipped on her light blue sweater. John took the pillow and a blanket from her bed and led the way into the hall.

Outside the house the sounds of war increased. The noise of mortars and artillery being fired from the nearby army camp added to the din of continuous explosions of incoming rounds. Flares which lit the skies for miles around caused the house to glow with an eerie, shifting light even

14

after the electricity flickered and went off. But the sound I dreaded most of all was the whine and crash of the incoming rockets.

"You're out of practice," I chided myself as I lay and listened. During the war years when we were living in the northern part of the country, nighttime mortar and rocket fire had been so frequent as to be almost monotonous. Nights had always been noisy. But since the 1973 cease-fire, we had heard very little nighttime firing.

A particularly loud crash brought bits of dirt and plaster down on my face. I shifted uneasily. I could imagine the whole ceiling falling down on us.

"John," I said, "don't you think we should try to go to Paul's house?"

"No," he replied. "It's too risky to move around at night. We'd probably get shot at by both sides. But I'll go check with Betty and with Dick and Lil."

He left the house and was gone about ten minutes. "Wow!" he said as he hurried back in, "stuff is landing on all sides of us. Betty and the Phillipses are okay and don't want to leave till it gets light. I don't know about the Johnsons. There sure is a lot coming in over that way."

"I think," he added, "I'll move our Land Rover over between our house and Betty's so it will be more protected and put our bags in. That way we'll be ready to go in the morning."

I thought the night would never end. I remembered that an American soldier had told me one time, "If you hear the whine of a rocket you can be thankful. You know you don't have to worry about *that* one, because it's already passed over you."

But with rockets coming in all the time, I found the thought not particularly encouraging. Besides, how could one feel thankful about being missed when in a populated area like this every one of those crashes quite possibly meant death or injury for someone.

"Oh, God," I prayed, "please make them stop." But the explosions continued.

I thought about the Psalms I had been studying lately

15

and all the verses I had read about waiting. "I waited patiently for the Lord; and he inclined unto me, and heard my cry."
"Rest in the Lord, and wait patiently for him." "Wait on the
Lord: be of good courage, and he shall strengthen thine
heart: wait, I say, on the Lord."

"Funny," I mused, "how in a situation where there is
absolutely nothing you can do, it's the hardest thing in the
world just to wait."

MONDAY

With daybreak there was a temporary lull in the fighting.
I hurried through the house with my market bag, feeling
relieved to be able to do something. I went into our bedroom
and changed into a pair of slacks. These would be easier to
walk in should this be required. The tribal skirt I stuffed into
the market bag. Then looking at the unmade bed, I decided
to take the net, a thin cotton blanket, and the pillows.

I heard the outside door open. John had gone out earlier
and was back. "Betty and the Phillipses are going with us,"
he said. "Come on, let's go."

I had no time to go into LuAnne's room and so neglected
to take her little flight bag of toys and books I had prepared.
How she missed them later!

Bullets whistled overhead as we ran to the Land Rover
and got in. The pastor of the Raday church next door stood
by the vehicle and watched Betty and the Phillipses put in
their suitcases. Betty handed him the keys to her house and
he agreed to look after the old Vietnamese lady until her
family could come to get her.

"Would you send someone down the hill to Johnsons'
house to tell them we have gone to the American compound?" she asked him. "There is nowhere to turn around if
we drive down there, and they can come in their own
vehicle."

"I'll send someone right away," he promised.

The street leading into town was deserted except for
clusters of soldiers at some of the intersections. Several tanks
were positioned at the entrance to the province headquar-
16

ters. Soldiers inside the tanks stared at us in surprise as we drove quickly past. Driving past a large military installation I felt terribly exposed and hunched down in the seat, covering LuAnne with my body. But no one shot at us, and in a short time we pulled up to the U.S. government compound.

John honked the horn. A startled face appeared at an opening in the gate. A few seconds later the guard opened the gate and we drove in. I breathed a sigh of relief.

Paul Struharik walked out of the long low office building. He didn't appear surprised to see us.

"Go on into my house," he said, indicating the building on our left. "You can take your things upstairs to the living room and make yourselves comfortable. I'll be up shortly. I'm trying to find out what's going on."

We walked into the unfamiliar house, spotted a stairway over to the left at the end of the hallway and proceeded up. The stairway opened into a spacious living-dining room with a small kitchen just beyond. We all sat down and waited.

A Vietnamese man wearing a long woman's overcoat walked into the room. "Don't worry," he told us, "it's nothing very serious."

"Oh?" I said. "That's good."

I barely had time to feel encouraged about that piece of news before two or three other men rushed through the room and headed for some stairs leading to the roof.

"The V.C. are in Caritas!" one of them said as he dashed past. Caritas was the Catholic compound just a block or two down the street.

A few minutes later he came back. "False alarm," he said. "Someone must have seen some civil defense troops in their black pajama outfits and *thought* they were Vietcong."

I sat there feeling bewildered.

When Paul came in we all asked him how serious it was.

"I don't really know," he answered. "My big radio is out, so I have no way of contacting Nha Trang or Saigon. We're trying to monitor the local Vietnamese military frequencies to see what's going on. But no one seems to have a very clear picture of the overall situation."

TWO

Captured!

Flashes of red and blue ascended and descended like exploding flares in the semi-dark room.

LuAnne had picked up her light blue sweater and rolled it into a ball. Then with a quick glance to see if Harry, her new-found Vietnamese friend, was watching, she threw it toward the ceiling and giggled softly as she caught it.

Harry had caught the idea and had also rolled his red sweater into a ball. Before I knew it, they had started laughing with excitement.

Sternly I placed my finger to my lips and shook my head at them to be quiet. It was 8 A.M. Outside by now the sun would have begun to warm the crisp morning air around the city. But none of its freshness was reflected in the stale air of the room. We had been in the room for two days. The longer we could keep our presence unknown, the greater might be our chances of survival.

Another giggle, this time from Harry, demanded action. I motioned for LuAnne to come over to the corner of the room where I was sitting on the floor.

"Why don't you and Harry draw for a while?" I whispered.

LuAnne frowned and shook her head. "Harry doesn't like the way I draw," she said.

I reached into my purse and took out a tiny cereal-box

puzzle—a remnant from our last furlough in the United States. "How about playing with this?"

Immediately Harry came over to investigate, intrigued with the challenge of fitting the pieces together. For a moment both children were quiet, and I leaned back against the wall to reflect.

It was hard to keep track of time, but I figured that this must be Wednesday. We certainly hadn't thought when Paul Struharik ushered us into his bedroom on Monday morning that we'd still be sitting here two days later.

Shortly after we had arrived at the U.S. government compound that Monday, the tempo of fighting had picked up. A strange-sounding staccato burst had erupted from somewhere close by.

"What on earth is that?" I had asked Paul.

"That's an anti-aircraft weapon," Paul answered, "and it sounds as if it's been set up right down the street from here." Then as a series of explosions shook the house, Paul had said to us, "I think you'd better go downstairs to my bedroom. That room has reinforced concrete on all sides and should withstand anything but a direct hit."

Paul led the way down the stairs and opened the door into a completely dark room. He lit a candle on a dresser by the door. Then he motioned us into the roughly twelve foot square room. It was furnished simply but comfortably. Dick Phillips stretched out gratefully on the large bed and Lil sat down beside him. Dick had managed the exertion of the trip, but it left him pale and exhausted. John, LuAnne and I put our pillows down on the floor in the corner and sat there. Betty joined Lil on the bed.

We were not the only ones to take refuge in the bedroom. When we first arrived, Paul had introduced us to Peter Whitlock, a short, wiry man with a dignified-looking moustache, a courteous manner, and a proper Australian accent.

"Peter is with the Australian Broadcasting Commission," Paul had explained. "He is interested in tribal language broadcasts. I was going to take him to visit the Banmethuot radio station this morning."

Shortly after that we were joined in Paul's living room by a tall, blonde, curly-haired young American. He was wearing blue jeans and rubber thonged sandals and brought with him only a small blue Air-France shoulder bag. Quiet and withdrawn, the only indication he gave of being under tension was the rapid succession with which he was lighting up cigarettes. He introduced himself to us as Jay Scarborough and said he had arrived in Banmethuot just the day before.

"I came to visit some friends who are attending the Banmethuot Normal School," he said. "I guess I couldn't have picked a worse time. I spent last night at the school and it was awful. One round came right into the courtyard."

Several employees and members of their families who lived on the compound also shared the room from time to time. We had already met Enrique Tolentino, one of the employees. A slightly built Filipino with a pixie haircut and a friendly smile, he was popularly known as Ike. His expertise was in agriculture and he worked closely with Paul on community development projects in many of the tribal villages. Occasionally John had chatted with him when he had gone to the U.S. office building to pick up mail or request permission to travel on chartered Air America flights.

It was while we were sitting in the bedroom during that first morning that Paul and some of his Vietnamese employees had spotted Russian tanks rumbling along a nearby street. A short time later they saw North Vietnamese soldiers standing leisurely in the street only a few yards from the house. That was when the regimen of silence had been imposed.

How much LuAnne and Harry understood about the reason for silence was hard to know, but they had cooperated beautifully. Only once or twice, when LuAnne had hurt her arm or become unhappy over some restriction, did I have to put my hand quickly over her mouth and quiet her. I knew how important Paul felt it was to keep from making noise when I saw him give some tranquilizing tablets to the father of the only other child on the compound. The child was too small to understand the reason for this unusual confinement and was inclined to be fretful.

21

The small candle flickering on the dresser was the sole source of light for the room. There were no windows, and without electricity the air conditioner on the opposite wall was useless, leaving the room dark and stuffy. I had scanned the contents of Paul's bookcase, but the poor light, the need to entertain LuAnne and keep her quiet, and the general feeling of tension and uncertainty were not conducive to reading.

On the far wall to the left was a big wooden closet and next to it was the door into the small bathroom. Quiet was especially important in there because it was on the outside wall, and its tiny high window opened on the street side. During the first two days we flushed the toilet under cover of the frequent air strikes and accompanying anti-aircraft barrages. But when the fighting moved further from the city we had a problem.

On the floor was an object on which everyone's attention was riveted for a few moments every hour throughout the day. It was an olive-green, battery-operated field radio, our only contact with the outside world. Knowing the signal from this small radio could not reach more than a few miles, Paul had tried periodically all Monday morning to make contact with any American plane flying over the area.

We waited hopefully every time he said, "Any Air America station. Any Air America station. This is Foxtrot. This is Foxtrot. Over." But all morning the only reply had been static.

"If we could just get through to Nha Trang," I thought, "surely they would send someone to take us out."

Finally in the early afternoon our weak signal was picked up. A small plane was sent up from Nha Trang to make contact with us. Because of the heavy South Vietnamese bombing strikes and the intense anti-aircraft fire, the pilot had to maintain a high altitude. But his voice came through clearly.

Paul identified the people who were with him in the house and gave a brief rundown of the situation as he saw it from his roof.

"We have two helicopters in Nha Trang standing by to

come in and get you," said the voice on the radio. "Can you get somewhere where you can be picked up?"

"There's a large coffee-drying area right next to my house," Paul replied. "Can you identify my house?"

He put a large brightly painted sheet of plywood on the roof to help them spot it, but it was to no avail. The pilot was unfamiliar with Banmethuot and too high to see the plywood. Paul didn't want to pinpoint its location over the radio because he knew the information could be heard by North Vietnamese soldiers in the area.

The plane circled overhead for the rest of the afternoon. Every hour Paul reported in. It was frustrating to have help so near and yet so totally unavailable. Yet at the same time it was encouraging to know that people on the outside knew where we were and were concerned about us.

I became aware of the gravity of our situation late Monday afternoon. Paul was talking on the radio for the last time that day.

"We're going back to Nha Trang for the night," the voice on the radio said, "but we'll be back at 0600 tomorrow morning."

A look of panic crossed the face of one of the Vietnamese employees as it dawned on him what was being said. "Aren't they coming in to get us?" he asked.

"They can't," said Paul. "The only way they could possibly attempt it would be to come in with a helicopter. If the pilot knew exactly where to go, he could come straight down without circling and go straight back up. That's the only way he could even hope to make it without getting shot. But from that altitude they can't identify my house, so they don't know exactly where to come down."

The Vietnamese man's eyes showed genuine fear as he said, "But this is our last chance!"

Monday evening the tension was high. A young Vietnamese girl sat near me on the floor praying quietly. She began to sob and Lil reached out to comfort her. Lil spoke of God's love and care for his children, and the girl stopped weeping.

That night Dick, Lil, Betty and I all slept on Paul's bed.

23

Paul, with some of the employees from the office and their families and the rest of his unexpected houseguests slept on the floor. The bed was comfortable, but the heat from sixteen bodies and one candle made the room unbearably hot and airless. Betty, Lil and I took turns keeping a prayer vigil through the long, hot, noisy night. Throughout the night the words of Psalm 46, which I had learned as a child, kept going through my mind. "God is our refuge and strength, a very present help in trouble. Therefore will not we fear . . ."

Toward morning the sounds of war became fewer and farther away. I was inclined to view the change with relief, but I soon sensed that the men didn't share my optimism. Paul could tell from cautious observations from the roof that the cessation marked the retreat of the city's defenders.

It was a somewhat subdued group that sat in the bedroom that Tuesday morning. No one had much to say. Dick Phillips was still resting quietly on the bed. Lil sat beside him, reading her Bible. John, who was sitting by the bathroom door on the only chair in the room, glanced at the little pocket calendar in the back of his New Testament and observed in a whisper, "Today is my anniversary." Lil looked over at me. She knew from my puzzled expression that John couldn't be referring to his wedding anniversary.

"Sixteen years ago today," John went on, "I arrived in Vietnam for the first time."

Lil smiled and whispered back, "In that case, let me give you an anniversary verse." She flipped the pages in her Bible for a moment and then said, "Here's the verse. It's Psalm 91:15. 'He shall call upon me, and I will answer him: I will be with him in trouble; I will deliver him, and honor him.' "

How little John could have known when he got off the ship in Saigon sixteen years earlier, young and single, what the coming years would bring into his life. And how little he knew at this point what even the next few days would bring. Yet, as we were reminded by Lil's "anniversary verse," the presence of God and the availability of his resources were just as much a reality now as they had been sixteen years before.

That afternoon we had discussed our options. "As I see

it," Paul said, "we have two alternatives. We could try to walk out of the city to an area where we could be picked up by helicopter. Or we could wait to be discovered by the North Vietnamese forces taking over the city."

We discussed option one. It didn't look too promising. Since we had no idea where the attacking forces were coming from, we didn't even know what direction to go. Our size and coloring would make us very conspicuous during the daytime. And trying to go quietly through unfamiliar jungle territory at night with three children seemed impossible.

"Chances are," John said, "we wouldn't get much farther than the front gate."

"If we are caught trying to get out of the area," said Paul, "I think it's more likely we'd be shot immediately than if we're discovered here in the house after the battle is over."

"If we weren't here would you try to walk out?" I asked Paul.

Paul shrugged. "I don't know," he replied. Paul would have the best chance of any of us, I thought, to get out. He knew the area well and had friends in all the surrounding villages.

"Why don't you, Peter and Jay try to make it out tonight?" I suggested. Paul shook his head.

This left option two. Paul looked around the room at the rest of us and asked, "Anybody heard how they are treating prisoners these days?"

The unspoken question in all of our minds took me by surprise. We discussed it briefly and dispassionately. Someone mentioned the Catholic sisters who had been held for a few weeks after the battle for Phuoc Long and then released unharmed to return to Saigon.

But in the back of our minds most of us were thinking about our friends who had been in Banmethuot in 1968, who were either killed immediately, or died in the jungle, or experienced years of imprisonment. I've no doubt that Betty was thinking about her husband, Archie, who with two other missionaries had been taken into the jungle thirteen years earlier and had not been heard from since. The discussion lapsed into silence.

In the quiet room there was abundant time for thinking. Up until then I had confidently felt that somehow God was going to get us out. He had delivered us so many times in the past from threatening situations, often just in the nick of time. I recalled the 1968 Tet offensive and how we had been taken from the Wycliffe center in Kontum by helicopter only minutes before it was overrun by attacking forces. I thought about the helicopter we had gotten off just moments before it slammed into a mountain, of the land mine that hadn't gone off, of the many mortar and rocket attacks we had come through unscathed. It seemed inconceivable that God was not going to get us out again. I knew he had the power to reverse our situation even at this point, but for the first time I faced the hitherto unthinkable possibility that he might not choose to do so.

My thoughts went to our three older children, Marjorie, Gordon and Nathan in a boarding school in Nha Trang. Two weeks earlier we had left them with reluctance, promising them we would be back down to see them at the end of the month. Did they know what was happening in Banmethuot now? Whose task would it be to tell them that their mom and dad and little sister had been taken captive or killed.

And what of our own parents? I knew our director would keep them informed, but what would a protracted period of uncertainty and concern about us do to them? And what about our director and the other Wycliffe workers in Vietnam? How would this affect them? The list grew as I thought of others whose lives would be touched by what was happening to us.

Several times since the outbreak of fighting Sunday night I had prayed what had become my customary "prayer-while-sitting-out-an-attack": "Lord, if there is anything I ought to do now, help me to know what it is. And if there isn't, help me to wait quietly, knowing that nothing can touch me except what you in your love and wisdom allow."

John and I opened our two suitcases, and as well as we could in the dark and crowded room we went through them. From the suitcase of books and manuscripts we took only the corrected manuscripts of the Bru New Testament, the Greek

Interlinear New Testament, and some lists of concordant words we were working on.

From the big suitcase I selected an extra set of clothing for each of us and a few items of sentimental value. I took the handwoven skirt some dear Bru friends had given me, the pearls John had given me years ago for my birthday, the ring that matched the ones my two sisters wore, and the watch that had been my engagement gift. These I put into the roomy plastic market bag along with the thin blanket and a mosquito net we had brought from our house. I decided to wear both sets of my clothing. It was uncomfortable in the hot room, but it would make the market bag easier to carry and would perhaps lessen the chance of the clothing being taken away.

John came across a packet of South Vietnamese currency in the suitcase and held it with a questioning look. "Should we take it?" he asked.

"Why bother," I replied. "It would only be taken away from us."

John hesitated a moment and then slipped the packet into the market bag. "If they take it, they take it," he said, "But I'm not going to leave it here."

During the following months I would sometimes think back on these days and wonder why I had not done things differently. Why hadn't we checked through our things more carefully? Why had we brought toothbrushes but not toothpaste or soap? How could we possibly have overlooked the manuscripts for Matthew and Mark?

But it is exceedingly difficult to prepare for the unknown. And even while we were making what preparation we were, there was, for me at least, a feeling of unreality and almost of futility about the whole situation.

Others were also making preparations. Paul walked into the room, took one of the pillowcases from his bed and tied it to a bamboo pole. A little later when I slipped out of the room to sit on the stairs and get a few breaths of fresh air, I saw the makeshift white flag standing ready in the hallway, and Paul opened the door to show me the big sign one of the Vietnamese employees had made to post on the door: "Don't shoot! In here are foreigners who have taken refuge from the fighting." It couldn't be seen from the street, but anyone coming into the compound would surely see it.

Throughout the day my thoughts had centered around what our capture would mean to other people and most particularly to our families, but that evening as I settled LuAnne down for the night on the floor and heard her whispered prayer, I began to think about what might lie ahead for her and for us. How would we manage long walks in the jungle? Would any special consideration be given to LuAnne? Would we be separated from each other, or would she be taken away from us?

Later as John and I stretched out on the welcomely cool but hard tile floor, we clasped hands and committed these uncertainties and fears to the Lord. And our hearts were quieted by the awareness of his power and his loving concern for us. Before going to sleep, I asked the Lord for LuAnne, as I had done for our other children under similar though less desperate circumstances, that he would take her to be with himself rather than allow her to grow up in an environment where she would have no opportunity to know and understand his love.

That night I slept well. In the morning someone jokingly complained about Peter's loud snoring, but that kind of noise didn't bother me at all! Sitting on the floor I watched the two children play.

At 8:30 A.M. Paul came into the room, closed the door into the hall tightly, extinguished his cigarette, and sat down on the floor by the radio. All of us watched him fiddle with the dials and listened as he reestablished contact with the plane. This time the radio conversation didn't last long. They had nothing new to report. Earlier they had told us that attempts were being made "at all levels" to get us out. Paul reported on our end that our immediate area was quiet and that it appeared the city had been "liberated."

"Who's in control?" was the rather startled query.

"The guys with the red stars," said Paul.

Radio contact over, Paul looked up at us. "I think it

would be a good idea if we took an inventory of our supplies," he said. "I think I have enough rice in the house for a couple of weeks. And the water supply from the tank on the roof should last if we are careful. But I don't know what other food I have in the house."

I welcomed the opportunity to get out of the stuffy room and do something. Whispering to John that I was going to help, I slipped out the door and tiptoed up the stairs to Paul's living-dining-kitchen area.

Betty was already in the kitchen looking through the cupboards. I stooped down and waddled across the living room to the kitchen. Because of the possibility of snipers on rooftops and in buildings nearby, Paul had cautioned us not to allow ourselves to be seen through the window.

Betty was shaking her head. "One pound of grits, a box of beans, a jar of Wesson oil, and some popcorn," she whispered.

I went back to the living room, crawled over to the sideboard, and inspected its contents. Peter helpfully produced a pen and yellow legal pad and began to record the contents of the cupboard. Two cans of tuna, a jar of caviar, mustard, cocktail onions, smoked herring. . . . I smiled to myself over the strange assortment. Living by himself, Paul probably never had a great quantity of food in the house. And of course he had just returned from Saigon the night the fighting began.

We moved all the food supplies downstairs and gave Paul the list. It was time for radio contact again. Paul reported that we had enough food and water to last for ten days. The reassuring word from the plane was, "Plan to spend one more night."

Harry's mother brought a pot of freshly cooked rice into the room, and we fed the children rice with a little tuna fish. The rest of us reheated the beans and ham we had cooked up the night before and ate that with rice.

It was 12:25 P.M. when Peter came into the room and quietly said, "Paul and Jay are talking with a soldier at the gate. I guess this is it."

My stomach tightened, and the room seemed very still.

29

We sat and listened. I could periodically hear faint voices from outside the house, but not clearly enough to have any indication of what was going on. I thought about the plane flying around overhead. It was almost time for a radio contact.

"Don't you think we should try to make contact and tell them what's happening?" I asked Peter. He shook his head, and Ike Tolentino reached over and scrambled the dials. Later Peter explained that he was afraid the soldiers might come in while we were talking in the radio and be angry about it.

It couldn't have been more than a few minutes, but it seemed forever before Paul opened the door and said, "We are to walk out in single file and go out on the street. We are permitted to take one small bag apiece. The keys to all the vehicles are to be turned over to them. If you'll give me the keys to your Land Rover," he added, turning to John, "I'll turn them over with mine." John reached into his pocket and gave Paul the keys.

I lifted LuAnne and put her Bru-fashion into the tribal skirt slung over John's shoulder, then put my purse over my own shoulder. We picked up the market bag, our yellow one-gallon Wesson oil jug of water, and the foam rubber pillow we had been sitting on and walked out.

As I stepped from the room through a few feet of hallway and outside, my eyes were dazzled by the brightness. When they adjusted, I could see a soldier standing a few feet away in the courtyard with his eyes on us and his gun held ready. "So this is what a North Vietnamese soldier looks like," I thought irrelevantly, taking in the red star on the broad brimmed helmet, the youthful face looking at this moment edgy and suspicious, the plain green uniform and green canvas boots, and the strange looking rifle. Other soldiers were looking around the compound and watching us curiously.

I was surprised at my feeling of detachment. It was as though a part of me was surveying a scene which was of no personal concern. As we walked out of the courtyard into the street, I saw Paul put a handful of keys into the hand of the soldier standing by the guard-post at the gate.

A guard walking around the compound motioned for Paul to come and shouted a question. Paul shrugged his shoulders to indicate he didn't understand and turned to me.

"What did he say?" he asked. I turned and followed Paul back into the courtyard and interpreted the question and Paul's answer.

"How many people are in this building?" the soldier asked pointing to the office.

"None," Paul replied.

"And this one?" pointing to another wing of the building.

"No one," said Paul.

The guard tried one of the locked doors and asked Paul what was in there. Paul stepped back and with a well placed kick broke open the door. The guard looked startled, but walked over and looked in at the files and office equipment.

"The only people in all of these buildings are the eighteen people who came out onto the street," Paul said. An apparent discrepancy in the number of people who had come out was cleared up when it was understood that Paul was counting the children, while they were not.

The soldier who had been given the keys came over and asked if any of the vehicles in the compound used diesel fuel. We told him our Land Rover was the only one. The soldier then held out the handful of keys and asked which ones belonged to that vehicle. I looked through the keys in his hand, but those for the Land Rover were not there! Puzzled, I told him that none of these keys went to that vehicle.

"These are the only keys I was given," he said suspiciously. We looked on the ground where he had been standing, but found no keys. What to do? It seemed we had reached an impasse between our assuring him that we had given him the keys and his insisting that we had not. Suddenly I remembered I had a duplicate ignition key in my purse and produced it. The crisis was averted.

Betty asked and was given permission to go back into the house for her sweater, and I was allowed to get a large blue container of drinking water. Paul, who was still following

31

the key man around matching keys to the U.S. government vehicles, called over to me. "In my closet there are two cartons of cigarettes," he said. "Would you bring those? And ask the soldier if we should bring any of the food."

The soldier shook his head impatiently when I inquired about bringing food. I walked back into the house. The contents of Paul's dresser drawers and our suitcases had been dumped out all over the floor. It was difficult to see anything in the darkness, and the guard was telling us to hurry up and get out. Betty couldn't find her sweater, but we got the other items.

I walked back out onto the street and joined John and LuAnne. I looked down the street and saw a few people standing outside their houses, but the usually busy street seemed almost deserted. A three-wheeled Lambretta passed by with a coffin in the back, a sad reminder that not everyone had come through the bombardment unscathed.

The soldiers backed all the vehicles in the compound out onto the street. Then one of them told the Caucasians to get into the Land Rover. Ike Tolentino and the Vietnamese were loaded into one of the U.S. government vehicles. We crawled into the back of the Land Rover with the suitcases and watched the soldiers scurrying in and out of the gate.

Paul chuckled as he saw one of the soldiers carrying off his AM/FM and shortwave radio. "I hope he enjoys it," he said. "That thing hasn't worked for two years." One of the office typewriters perched precariously on a corner of the guard post where it had been temporarily set. A soldier emerged from the compound and walked toward the vehicle carrying a bottle which Paul recognized as coming from his wine cupboard.

"Well look at that!" Paul marveled. "That fellow has good taste. He picked the only valuable bottle in the cupboard."

A man in civilian clothes took the driver's seat and an armed guard climbed in the other side. The guard was giving directions but seemed a bit uncertain as to where to go. Once he stopped to ask directions of a civilian who was walking along the road before he settled on a route leading out of the city that I had never been on before. We had no idea where we were being taken or what would happen when we got there, but as we rode along I almost had a feeling of relief. We had passed the first hurdle of being discovered without being killed, and it was so good to be out of that stuffy room and be able to talk aloud again.

The Land Rover pulled off the road, bumped along the edge of a field and stopped. Up ahead were parked an assortment of vehicles, camouflaged with tree branches. The jeep nearest us was marked ICCS (International Commission for Control and Supervision), the international group appointed to oversee the cease-fire agreed upon in 1973. We were told to get out and take everything with us. No small task, we discovered, as we tried to gather it all up. Besides the personal bundles we had set out with and the water containers, we had acquired by virtue of their having been left in the Land Rover a large suitcase of Betty's, one of the Phillipses, and two of ours, a portable electric typewriter, and two more pillows.

I tucked the pillows under LuAnne's arms and picked up a suitcase and the market bag. The soldier who had brought the bottle was standing beside the Land Rover, head tilted back, enjoying his recent acquisition. "Enjoy it," Paul said to him in English as he started after another soldier who was beckoning us to follow. "That bottle cost twenty-five dollars." The soldier looked at him without comprehension and passed the bottle to a comrade.

We lugged our possessions through a field of manioc over to the edge of a heavily wooded ravine where we were told to stop and sit down on the ground. The hillside was swarming with soldiers and littered with trophies of battle. We had just time to note the motorcycles and bicycles strewn around the trenches dug into the side of the hill when the scene was blocked off by the excited, gesticulating crowd of soldiers pressing in on us on all sides.

An officer shouted for them to leave and go back to their places. They backed off a couple of paces, but didn't leave. The officer again ordered them to leave with the same result. I was surprised. Somehow I had expected the North Vietnamese soldiers to be perfectly disciplined men who would respond immediately to a command. But this curious, shoving, disorderly group didn't fit that picture.

Frightened by the close proximity of so many soldiers, LuAnne began to cry. The officer spoke to the men again telling them if they wanted to stay and watch, they must at least stand farther back. Then he turned and spoke to a soldier, who left and returned a few minutes later with a can of South Vietnamese military issue sweetened condensed milk and a package of North Vietnamese combat rations. LuAnne stopped crying when the officer spoke kindly and gave her the milk and the package of what appeared to be crumbled up biscuits pressed into a bar. I thanked the officer and opened the packet for LuAnne.

Then he spoke to the rest of us. "You are now in the custody of the Liberation Armed Forces of Vietnam," he informed us in Vietnamese. "As long as you obey all regulations and do exactly as you are told, you have nothing to fear." He went on to inform us that the Liberation Armed Forces maintained a policy of humane treatment for all prisoners. "Don't worry," he said, "you will see your families again. Even the American pilots who were guilty of grave crimes against the Vietnamese people were allowed to return to their families."

He asked us about the other Americans in Banmethuot and was frankly disbelieving when we told him we were the only ones there. "We know there are 24,000 American military men in Vietnam masquerading as civilians," he said accusingly. Our answer was that while we couldn't answer for the rest of the country we were certain there were none in Banmethuot.

LuAnne was a bit confused about what was happening. "Mommy," she asked looking up at me, "are these men keeping us so we won't be captured?"

Torn between the need to be truthful and the desire to reassure her, I replied, "No, Honey, we *are* captured. But the man told us not to worry because they will let us go back to our families. Besides, we know that God is with us and will take care of us."

34

Another officer came over and told us he wanted any maps, photos, cameras or military equipment we had. Paul asked permission to go through a survival pack he had brought, since it had been given to him by someone else, and he didn't know what was in it. We all watched with curiosity as he pulled out a mosquito net, a nylon poncho, fish hooks, insect repellant, et cetera. But there were also some items which were contraband. "Oh, no!" Paul muttered as he sheepishly handed over a small package of bullets. The guard seemed puzzled over a small pocket flare, but decided to keep it, along with a map of the area and a tiny chain which could be used as a saw.

Inspection of the rest of us resulted in the taking of several cameras, a package of negatives and family photos of the Phillipses, and a couple of cards from the International Protestant Church in Saigon which had a small map showing the location of the church.

The officer asked for something in which to put these things, and we gave him a pillowcase from one of the pillows. Before putting the cameras and photos into the pillowcase, he assured us that these items would be returned to us after they were checked, and very carefully made out a receipt for them.

Jay Scarborough, the most fluent speaker of Vietnamese in our group, had been singled out by the guards to interpret for those who spoke no Vietnamese. The officer now handed him the receipt and left with the pillowcase. "I hate to tell you this," Jay commented, "but the last thing the Nazis did before sending the Jews to the gas chamber was to give them a receipt for all their possessions."

"Thanks a *lot*, Jay," I retorted.

As we sat waiting, Betty made some comment to Lil, and they chuckled. A soldier immediately walked over and spoke to them angrily. "You should behave meekly as prisoners," he said. "From now on you are not to speak English anymore. If you have something to say to each other you must say it in Vietnamese."

"But we don't all speak Vietnamese very well, and some of us don't speak any," they gasped.

"Then they must keep still," he said, "and speak only when absolutely necessary."

An uncomfortable silence settled over the group, and we waited without talking except for an occasional request to "pass the water jug, please." LuAnne needed to relieve herself, so a guard led us behind a clump of bushes and turned his back. All the while we were there we could see lines of South Vietnamese prisoners filing by behind us, hands tied behind their backs, some in military uniform, some in civilian clothing. Someone brought a few packages of the combat rations and told us, "Eat these. After you have eaten you will leave." We found the bars rather pleasant to taste, but very dry and thirst producing. We nibbled at them for a while and then just sat.

Finally someone came over and said, "Bring your things. You are going to be taken to another location." We struggled back through the manioc patch with all our gear to wait near the place we had been dropped off. There must have been a shortage of fuel because soldiers were running around with hoses and siphoning fuel from one vehicle to use in another.

The sun was setting when the Land Rover was finally driven up and we were loaded in. Lil Phillips sat in front between the driver and an officer who was to accompany us. Another soldier brought a rope up to the back door to tie the arms of those of us in back. Paul asked if he could get a drink before they tied him. After a brief consultation with another soldier the man decided it wouldn't be necessary to tie us, but he warned us sternly, "Keep all windows closed and be very quiet. If people are aware of your presence, they might seek to do you harm."

This thought was unsettling. We had never done anything to hurt anyone. Who then was going to seek to do us harm?

ThREE

The Rose Garden

The young man chosen to drive the Land Rover had obviously never driven one before. "How do you turn the headlights on?" he asked.

John showed him the switch. He then asked how to operate the gears for the low range and four-wheel drive. "The road is very bad," he explained.

"Very bad! That doesn't begin to describe it," I thought as the trip progressed. Black top turned to grass, and then we plunged into what seemed to be virgin jungle through which a trail had recently been hacked. A few times as we lurched down into a gully through a stream, then labored up the opposite bank, we could see soldiers standing in the stream still working to pile up branches and rocks at the place where the vehicle forded. Several trucks seemed to be following us.

The drone of an airplane sounded above the noise of the Rover engine. The driver immediately switched off the headlights and brought the vehicle to a stop until the plane could no longer be heard.

LuAnne put her head on my shoulder and went to sleep. Several times we stopped briefly at what appeared to be checkpoints, and North Vietnamese soldiers stared at us with surprise and curiosity. Once when the Land Rover was surrounded by a group of shouting, gesticulating soldiers, I recalled the words of warning at the outset of the trip.

"Look!" one of them shouted pointing at us, *"Thằng*

37

Mỹ!" The term indicated contempt and derision for Americans. Faces pressed closer.

The officer accompanying us jumped out. "Please don't cause any trouble," he pleaded.

My heart constricted in fear as one of them pushed open the window by my shoulder where LuAnne was sleeping. I sat there without moving as he reached in and touched her. But LuAnne didn't stir, and to my great relief the vehicle started up again. Somewhat shaken I reached up, closed the window and locked it.

It was nearly midnight when we passed through another checkpoint, drove slowly through an area which appeared to be a military camp of some sort, and then pulled off the trail into some high grass.

"Get out and wait here," the officer said. The trucks which seemed to be following us now pulled up and stopped. I noted they were filled with South Vietnamese prisoners.

As I shifted LuAnne's weight and stepped to the ground, I heard our driver say to the driver of one of the trucks, "This vehicle is terrific! Sure beats any Russian vehicle I've ever driven!" I smiled and thought to myself, "If I ever get out, I could certainly write a convincing commercial for the Land Rover company after tonight's ride."

We sat in the grass for a few minutes until a soldier emerged from the thickly forrested area behind us and motioned for us to follow him. Leaving some of the baggage, we stumbled uncertainly along a trail. The soldier had a flashlight and moved it back and forth along the path occasionally to reveal obstacles. The rest of the time we felt the way with our feet. Ten or fifteen minutes of walking brought us to a clearing. The women were told to wait while the men went back for the rest of the luggage.

On one side of the clearing a soldier sat at a rude table fashioned by placing a board across bamboo posts sunk into the ground. A small wick protruding from a can of kerosene threw a flickering light over a sheaf of papers lying on the table. We watched as first one group of South Vietnamese prisoners and then another was led into the clearing and ordered to sit in rows in front of the table.

38

"Give me your name, military rank, unit and occupation!" ordered an older man standing near the table. After the information was recorded, the men were marched off into the darkness on the opposite side of the clearing. Some were wounded and walked with difficulty, supported by comrades. A few had to be carried in and lay motionless and unresponsive on the ground.

Our men returned, perspiring heavily, grumbling at the weight of our luggage. I noted that one of the items in our large brown suitcase had been taken out and was being carried separately—my portable electric sewing machine! The incongruity of having all this equipment in the jungle struck me forcibly, but not the humor. We were too tired for that.

The older man walked over and looked at us sitting on the ground. All of us were tired, but Dick appeared ready to collapse. LuAnne was asleep on my lap.

"We will question you in the morning," he said.

A guard led us to a spot a short distance from the clearing where we could just make out a cache of crates.

"You can sleep here," he said.

Paul spread out the nylon tarp from his pack and most of us crowded onto it. Jay stretched out on the ground a few feet away. Seeing that he had nothing under him, a guard brought him a piece of plastic. LuAnne barely stirred when we put her down on two suitcases beside us. They weren't flat, but then neither was the ground. Moving my shoulders and hips to avoid the worst bumps, I stretched out and looked up into the sky.

The giant trees around us reached up an incredible distance with their leafy tops. And in the black sky the brilliant stars appeared to be suspended just a few feet above them. Before I drifted off to sleep I barely had time to note the beauty of that sight and think uneasily, "I wonder if these crates at our heads are explosives." But even in sleep I was conscious throughout the night of the muted voices of still more and more prisoners being brought in, and of the sound of footsteps crackling through the underbrush all around us.

When daylight came I sat up, curious to see this place to which we'd been brought. I was astonished to see a vast number of people all around us. They were also beginning to stir in the early morning light. A guard noted that we were awake, came over and asked us to move our things to a spot on the other side of the crates at the edge of what I could now see was a large clearing.

Spotting a little stream near the place we were assigned, I went to it and tried to splash away some of the dust and perspiration from yesterday's trip. I combed my hair and then sat watching the activity going on around us.

Behind us, across the stream and separated from us by piles of brush, the job of processing new arrivals continued. For a while I scanned the faces of each new group, looking for any that might be familiar, but I found none. I wondered about the Johnsons and about our Bru friends in the large resettlement village east of Banmethuot. How had they fared in the heavy fighting?

Looking at the crowded clearing in front of me I saw to my left a man in priest's clothing. At one point Betty managed to get close enough to talk to an intense-looking young man she knew well. He was a Raday lay-preacher who had been picked up while walking back to Banmethuot after conducting a service in a nearby village. He was tired, hungry and discouraged. He worried about his family, and what they would feel and do when he didn't return home.

A short heavy-set man walked through the crowd in front of us following a guard and nodded briefly to Paul. "That's the province chief of Darlac Province," Paul told the rest of us. Paul and Betty recognized the European manager of the large rubber plantation complex in Banmethuot and several of his half-Vietnamese sons. His was the only Caucasian face to be seen outside of our little group of nine.

We were all concerned about Norm and Joan Johnson. I knew that the week before some tribal friends of theirs had said that if fighting broke out, they would take Norm and Joan to a safe place. As I committed them to the Lord's care again and again, I wondered whether their tribal friends might not be able to get them safely through the jungles and down to the coast.

A couple of guards came over to the pile of crates in front of us and began opening them. Their contents proved not to be ammunition, but dried combat ration bars in large olive-drab tins, about the size of five-gallon kerosene cans. The guards began to open tins, break open packages and distribute the bars to the throngs of people sitting around. We ate the bars issued to us with more appetite than we did the day before. But they were so dry. And we were concerned about our dwindling water reserves.

We began to talk about our pre-attack activities and the strange providence that threw us together in this situation.

"Peter," I asked, turning to the now rumpled and disheveled looking man sitting next to me, his mustache blending into the dark stubble of several days chin growth, "do you have children?"

"Yes," he replied, "I have four, three girls and a boy."

"How old are they?" I asked.

"Nineteen and twenty," was the reply.

I was still trying to figure that out when Peter helpfully added the information that they were two sets of twins.

Peter, we learned, had been in Vietnam only five days when he was caught up in the events preceding his capture. Some months before he had been given a leave of absence from his position as the Australian Broadcasting Commission's Program Director for Western Australia. He had been sent by the Australian government to help the Thai Broadcasting Company with radio programming for ethnic minority groups in Thailand. His tour of duty in Thailand was almost over when he had finally been given permission to visit South Vietnam to see what was being done in that country in terms of ethnic minority broadcasting.

"I'll be back in a fortnight," he assured his wife, Peg, as he kissed her goodbye and left her in the lovely mountain town of Chieng Mai, Thailand.

"Be sure you go to Banmethuot and look up Paul Struharik," a friend had encouraged him. "Banmethuot is one of the primary areas for ethnic minority groups and Paul really knows the area."

Now Peter found himself sitting on the ground in a Vietnamese jungle trying to think of a suitable way to thank this helpful friend for his advice should the opportunity ever present itself.

Paul's grievance was with the national airline, Air Vietnam. "After all the times they cancelled flights I was scheduled to go on," he complained, "why couldn't they have cancelled that one?" He had gone to Saigon for medical help the week before and returned to Banmethuot on what proved to be the last flight into the city airport. Yet Paul had had no sense of foreboding as he flew back to the highlands that day. He was anticipating a visit the following week from his wife and children, who were living in Bangkok, and wanted to have everything ready for them.

Paul's lovely wife, H'lum, whose dark eyes had looked at me from her portrait on the bookcase in Paul's bedroom, was a native of the Banmethuot area. Her father held the prestigious position of judge among his own Raday people and was greatly respected by them. The Raday people, although an ethnic minority group in respect to the overall population of South Vietnam, were the majority group in this area of the central highlands, and Paul's rapport with the Raday people had been enhanced by his marriage to H'lum.

"Do you have any pictures of your boy?" I asked Paul. He took out a wallet and showed me several snapshots of a healthy looking baby. "These were taken several months ago," he said. "He's six months old now." He also had school pictures of his two step-daughters, Guillene and Marie France, who were attending an American school in Bangkok. Paul frequently visited the family in Thailand, but it had been some time since H'lum had been to Banmethuot. The entire family had been looking forward to the proposed visit, and H'lum's parents were anxious to see their grandson for the first time.

Lil Phillips was intently studying the printing on a package of the dry combat rations. Besides proclaiming the contents to have been made in China, the package had a breakdown in English of the food ingredients it contained: milk, sugar, vitamins A, B, and C, protein. . . . Lil had taken her Merck Manual out of their suitcase and was trying to compute how much of this substance we would have to consume in a day to meet our minimum daily food requirements. Dick was looking on over her shoulder.

We had known Dick and Lil the longest of all in the group, and had a great deal in common with them. They had been married in Vietnam only a year or so before we were, and their four children were roughly the same ages as ours. They worked under the auspices of the Christian and Missionary Alliance (C&MA) but because of Dick's training and competence in the field of linguistics they had been involved in many of the same programs we were, and had cooperated with our organization in starting literacy and educational programs for the Mnong people.

I first met Dick in 1962. John and I had been working on the Bru language for several months, attempting to use the linguistic methods and skills we had learned to analyze the sound system of the language. But when we showed our director the results of our analysis, he looked a bit dubious.

"There's no language in the world that's been reported to have that many vowels," he said, looking at the forty-one contrasting vowel nuclei we had discovered. "I wonder if you haven't over-differentiated. You know," he added, "Dick Phillips did some work on a related language and found something he called a 'register contrast.' I wish you and he could get together and go over some of your material."

At our director's request, Dick had flown to the city of Hue, and we drove down with our Bru language helper. We spent several days working with Dick and were impressed by his quiet competence and by the thorough way he went over our material. The Bru language did, indeed, have all the contrasts we had noted, he assured us.

He helped us organize our material, suggested alphabetical symbols for these sounds, and helped us write a linguistic description of the sound system.

Our paths crossed again in 1968 two days before Tet, the Vietnamese New Year. I arrived at the Wycliffe Language Center in Kontum with our children and a Bru language helper. John planned to follow us in a few days. The Phillips family had left their home in Banmethuot and were attending a literacy workshop at the Kontum center. In the ensuing days they, like the rest of us, lost most of their possessions

43

through emergency evacuation from Kontum and the destruction of their home. But this was nothing compared to the blow of learning that all of their fellow workers in Banmethuot had been killed, severely injured or captured.

In September 1974 when we were in Banmethuot looking for a place to live near a large number of resettled Bru so we could finish up the final work on the Bru New Testament, the Phillipses had suggested that we rent one of the homes on the C&MA property which was currently not being used. We moved in October and the five intervening months had been very productive ones for us. The Bru believers had taken upon themselves the task of making sure a Bru committee was always available. Each Sunday when we went out to the village, they would select the individuals who would go back and work with us that week. If someone were busy, he might send a brother-in-law or son in his place. Sometimes the young high school students would fill in during the hours they were not in school. This gave us a wide range of ages and backgrounds for our checking and we felt the resulting translation well represented a cross-section of Bru culture.

One of the unexpected side benefits of the five months had been the friendships established with our missionary neighbors. Each Wednesday evening we would gather in one of the homes for a time of fellowship and sharing in prayer one anothers' concerns. During Christmas vacation our children had played together, and we'd pooled our resources to share in special Thanksgiving and Christmas dinners.

Though none of the soldiers wore any indication of rank, an older man with the bearing of an officer walked over to us, bringing my attention back to our present situation. With him was a young soldier carrying a handful of papers. The young man, it seemed, was an interpreter. But it soon became obvious that his knowledge of English was meager, and Jay was again pressed into service.

"I have here a list of questions for you to answer," the officer stated. "You must answer every question carefully and truthfully. Don't think you can lie about anything," he continued, fixing us with a stern look, "because the Revolution knows everything and it will certainly be exposed."

The young man handed Jay the blank papers along with a sheet of handwritten questions and went over the questions with him. Some of the questions were straightforward and easy to answer: name; place of residence in Vietnam; place of birth; nationality; parents' names, ages, addresses and occupations; organization and job description; religion; political party; education. Some reflected distinctions important in the Vietnamese culture but either unimportant or non-existent in ours. We were all asked to list our aliases, to indicate our ancestral place of origin (this as distinct from place of birth, or home of parents), and our ethnic stock.

Some questions were more subjective, such as, "What were your thoughts before capture? What treatment have you received since capture? What are your opinions and aspirations?" One question they seemed particularly concerned about was, "Did you have any previous knowledge of the attack?"

"Do they think," Paul retorted, "that we'd have been there if we had?"

A question that caused John and me no small trouble was the one that said, "When did you arrive in Vietnam? List all the places you have lived since that time, the dates you lived there, and what you were doing while there." We had moved so often during the course of our fourteen-year marriage.

The first part of the question was easy. John had arrived in Vietnam on March 11, 1959, and I on the 19th of June in 1961. Not reflected by that simple statement were more than two years of uncertainty, prayer and patient encouragement on John's part and indecision on mine.

When John left for Vietnam I was a junior in college, deeply engrossed in my college career and in the production of the various student publications. I was not yet sure what I wanted to do with my life, and was alternately thrilled and scared at the thought of the quiet, serious man seven and a half years my senior who had recently expressed his love for me.

I felt I hardly knew him, though I had been acquainted with him for four years and knew a great deal *about* him. John was from Allentown, Pa., of Pennsylvania Dutch extraction, and number seven of thirteen children, all but two of them boys. Neither family precedent nor financial consideration encouraged him to consider higher education. So after graduation from high school he got a job in an office.

The Korean War changed this. In 1952 John was drafted into the army, went through basic training and truck driver's school, and spent the remaining eighteen months of his time in the service driving a water truck at Fort Jackson, South Carolina. When he was separated from the army in April, 1954, he was eligible to receive government help for further education. One of his younger brothers had enrolled in a small, church-related college in Western New York and was encouraging him to study there. These two considerations were major factors in his decision to attend Houghton College, and it was at that point that he entered my life.

I had been raised as the middle of three girls in a warm, supportive family. The year I was born, my father, Stephen Paine, had at the age of twenty-eight become the youngest college president in the United States. Before assuming the presidency of Houghton College he had earned his Ph.D. degree from the University of Illinois, taught Greek and Latin at Houghton, and served as Academic Dean. His involvement in higher education was not without family precedent. His great-grandfather had been founder and first president of Wheaton College in Illinois, of which he and both his parents were graduates. His great-uncle had been president of the same institution and his maternal grandfather had taught German there. Dad met Mother while in graduate school. They had married, and she finished her college career at Houghton after the birth of my older sister.

A man of deep spiritual commitment, my father maintained a strong interest in the church on local, denominational and national levels. At one time he served as president of the National Association of Evangelicals. As a child I was unimpressed by Dad's position, but I enjoyed traveling with him when he represented the college. I appreciated the wide variety of cultural and entertainment programs available in a

46

college community and was delighted to be able to rub shoulders with, or serve cookies to, leaders in the political, educational and religious fields when my parents entertained them in our home.

Because of the shortage of available dormitory space for men when John came to Houghton in 1954, many of the men students roomed in the homes of faculty, staff and other townspeople. John's brother, Ron, had for two years been one of four students living in my parents' home. John requested and received assignment to be his brother's roommate. And assignment to live at the Paine House brought him into frequent contact with the members of our family.

The year before John came, two things happened which greatly affected the life of our family, and to a lesser degree the lives of the "Paine House Boys," as our student-roomers called themselves. The first was the birth, in June, of my brother, Steve, who became the object of lavish attention and affection on the part of three jubilant older sisters, ages eleven, fifteen and seventeen.

Four months later the attention and jubilation diminished when my sister, Marjorie, a sophomore in college, contracted both bulbar and spinal polio. For weeks which stretched into months she lay in an iron lung under constant nursing care. My parents tried to carry on their regular responsibilities and yet be with Marge in the hospital sixty miles away part of every day. Consequently my younger sister Miriam and I often had to assume responsibility for the care of baby Steve as well as certain household chores.

By the fall of 1954 when John came to live at our house Marge's condition had stabilized to the point where she was able to be brought home occasionally for short visits using a portable chest respirator. But she never recovered use of lost muscle functions, and in March 1955 during my junior year in high school she developed kidney complications and died.

When I first met John, my initial reaction was one of surprise that he was so much different from his brother. Ron was short, jaunty, with dark wavy hair. John was taller, more casual, and with a short blonde crew-cut. Ron was an extrovert, strongly assertive, involved in every social activity on

47

campus to the point where sometimes, as he put it, he couldn't fit his classes into his schedule. John was quiet, withdrawn, conscientious in his studies and involved in few campus activities.

John regularly attended Foreign Missions Fellowship, and in his senior year served as president of that organization. Though raised in a formal Protestant church, it was not until his late teen years that he had realized the need to make a personal commitment of his life to God. Over the succeeding years the Word of God became increasingly meaningful to him. When a representative from the Wycliffe Bible Translators spoke to the student missions group presenting the need to make the Word of God available to more than two thousand language groups still without it, John became very interested. To be an instrument in bringing the Bible to one of these groups seemed a project to which he could gladly devote his life.

When John graduated and left Houghton in June 1957, I had no reason to believe he regarded me in any other way than as a slightly mixed-up, but tolerated, kid-sister figure. That spring when I was debating whether to take a summer job in the same town as the fellow I was currently dating or accept another offer to work on Cape Cod, John listened sympathetically, went over the pros and cons with me, but refrained from expressing an opinion.

John left Houghton to study at the Summer Institute of Linguistics (SIL) at the University of Oklahoma, and I went to Cape Cod to work as a waitress in a summer resort. I was surprised and flattered to receive several letters from him that summer. These were merely accounts of his summer activities, but the Scripture references at the end of one of them puzzled me.

"Alfreda," I said to my roommate and close confidante, "what would you think if someone put these verses in a letter to you?" I read the verses alluded to, beginning with, "I thank my God upon every remembrance of you," and ending, ". . . because I have you in my heart."

Alfreda's eyes grew big. "Wow!" she replied. "Sounds like more than brotherly interest to me."

John visited briefly in Houghton that fall and I dated him

a few times, but when he wrote me just before leaving for Wycliffe's Jungle Training Camp in Mexico that fall that his feelings for me grew stronger every day and he felt God might be bringing us together, I was floored. This sounded like a serious commitment, and I wasn't ready to even think about that.

By the time John received assignment to Vietnam I was at least considering the possibility that God might lead us to work together somewhere in the world. My knowledge of world geography, however, did not extend to the country of Vietnam.

"Where's that?" I asked John.

"It used to be part of French Indochina," John answered. "Wycliffe is just beginning work in that country and I've been asked if I would accept an assignment there."

"Well at least you're not being assigned to Alaska," I quipped. "If you were, you'd have to count me out. I don't think I could hack the cold weather. At least Vietnam ought to be warm."

In the following months it became evident from John's letters that the climate in Vietnam was "hot" in more ways than one. He wrote about the bombing of President Diem's palace only a few blocks from the house where he was living, and the American press reports of terrorism in the rural areas of the country. I noted that the response to my statement, "My boyfriend is in Vietnam," had changed from a rather puzzled, "Let's see, Vietnam. . . ?" to an emphatic, "Oh no! Not Vietnam!"

After graduating from college I attended the SIL sessions at the University of North Dakota. I found the scientific procedures involved in transcribing and analyzing an unwritten language both challenging and fascinating. After three months of Jungle Training Camp in Southern Mexico, I realized that living in a primitive setting is not exactly glamorous, but neither is it impossible. And somewhere along the line I became certain that I did indeed want to join John and work with one of the thirty-some-odd minority language groups of South Vietnam.

June 16, 1961, was my brother Steve's seventh birthday. My youngest sister, Kathy, had just turned four. "This is the worst birthday I ever had," Steve complained as my family drove me to the Buffalo airport to see me off for Vietnam. In my suitcase was Grandmother Paine's hand-stitched batiste wedding gown, but neither she, nor any other member of my family, would see me wear it.

How difficult this parting was for my parents I never even suspected. They had taken pains to see that I should not. Not till years later did my sister, Mim, tell me that Dad had charged them strictly, "I don't want any tears, do you understand? It will be hard enough for Carolyn to leave home without our making it harder by crying." They had certainly done their best.

For me the tears didn't come until the big plane had lifted off the ground and was heading west. "By the time I see my family again," I thought, "Mim will have finished college, Steve will be in junior high school, and Kathy a grownup schoolgirl." I was leaving my family and the pleasant, secure life I had known, and going to a strange country to marry a man I hadn't seen for two and a half years. "For someone who has all her life done the conventional and predictable," I told myself, "you sure are acting out of character!" But though I felt sadness, I felt no uncertainty. I *knew* I was doing what God wanted me to do.

By the time I reached Hawaii I was thinking not so much of the people I had left as about the one to whom I was going. Although John had written faithfully, I still wondered how well I knew him. We had had so little opportunity to be together before he left. Expressing his feelings and emotions in words had never been one of John's strong points and his letters were quite reserved. Yet through them all was an undercurrent of quiet hope, persistent love and urgent need to which I had responded.

Now I wondered what it would be like to spend the rest of my life with this man. Would I be able to respond to his love enough to make him happy? Would I be accepted by the other Wycliffe members with whom he lived and worked so closely?

The loudspeaker in the Honolulu airport was calling my name. I hurried over to the counter. Earlier the agent from the airline had been reluctant to let me check in for the flight to Saigon because I had no visa for Vietnam stamped in my passport. At my insistence he checked his book and found that a seven-day tourist permit could be obtained by a U.S. citizen at the Saigon airport if that individual had a ticket to leave Saigon for some other country. I was glad my father had insisted I carry traveller's cheques. I purchased a ticket to Bangkok and hoped I would not have to use it. Only then had he allowed me to check in.

As I approached the counter I wondered if some new obstruction had arisen. "Miss Paine," the girl at the counter said, "we find we have overbooked this flight. Since you do not have a visa for Vietnam we wondered if you would like to spend two days in a hotel on Waikiki Beach at the expense of the airline? This might give you opportunity to apply for a visa."

"Wow!" I thought. "Who in the world wouldn't like two days on Waikiki Beach at someone else's expense?"

Yet I hesitated not more than a second before declining the offer. I could just imagine trying to explain two days on Waikiki at the other end of the trip! After waiting two and a half years for this occasion, I knew John would be bitterly disappointed to have it delayed by so much as a day.

Besides John had specifically instructed me not to apply for a visa. All applications for visas by new members of Wycliffe were at the time being denied by the government of Vietnam. But even immigration officials seemed unwilling to stand in the way of romance. They told John I should come without applying for a visa, taking advantage of the seven-day permit. After my arrival he could bring me to the immigration office, and they would grant an extension of the permit.

"This will not work for any other members of your organization," the official cautioned. "It is a special exception for your fiancée only."

When I stepped out of the plane into the hot humid sunshine of Saigon, I could see a row of smiling people waving from an upstairs balcony. Some of them I recognized from photos John had sent. My eyes sought out a familiar blonde head with a crew-cut as I entered the building to begin the lengthy immigration and customs inspection.

51

He was waiting beside the door to the restricted section. I emerged somewhat uncertainly and found myself caught up in a tight embrace, heedless for the moment of time, place or the rest of the welcoming committee. I had arrived!

The following month John and I were married in the little yellow stucco French Protestant Church in Saigon. The missionary community in Saigon as well as Vietnamese and Chinese friends came to help us celebrate the occasion. A Vietnamese friend took us to and from the church in his bright red car. Red, I learned, was the color of happiness and very appropriate for weddings.

On one item we clung to American tradition. A local baker expressed disapproval when one of the Wycliffe women ordered a completely white wedding cake. "We want a white cake with white frosting and trim. White leaves, white flowers, white everything," she stipulated.

"I can make it that way," he said dubiously, "but it won't be pretty."

"That's the way we want it," she insisted. The man shook his head in bewilderment. There was no accounting for the strange tastes of foreigners. But he made it white. And to us it was beautiful!

We had lived in so many places since then. It was in trying to list them all that John and I had some problem.

"We'd better make sure our papers agree," John said, "in case they cross-check." We talked it over and finally came up with a list of fifteen moves we had made since our marriage.

To the question about our treatment I responded gratefully and truthfully, "We have been treated with courtesy by the officers of the North Vietnamese Army."

As to my "aspirations," I stated that I wished "to be reunited with my three children who are studying in Nha Trang."

The officer collected the papers, but returned in a few minutes with them. He approached Jay and asked him to translate all of our answers into Vietnamese. Jay agreed without enthusiasm. He didn't know how the papers would be used and didn't want to assume the responsibility for correctly representing everything the rest of us said. Going over to the pile of crates, he upended a couple boxes of combat rations and began writing.

LuAnne was playing happily with two little satin covered pillows "Aunt Betty" Mitchell had brought in her suitcase. The pink one she promptly named Gerry after Aunt Betty's teenaged daughter, who had been in Banmethuot during Christmas vacation.

"Do you have a boy?" she asked Aunt Betty.

"Yes, I do," Betty answered. "My boy's name is Glenn and he is in America."

"Then this will be Glenn," LuAnne decided, indicating the blue flowered pillow. She took from our market bag my black tribal skirt and slipped it over her head. Then in tribal fashion she put "Gerry" into the skirt-sling. "Glenn" she gave to Aunt Betty to hold.

Betty Mitchell had been our closest neighbor on the C&MA property. LuAnne loved to visit her and look at the books and magazines Aunt Betty kept on a table near the door. I couldn't blame her. I sometimes dropped over to Betty's just to ask a question or borrow a cup of sugar, and ended up staying for an hour talking. I was impressed by her love and concern for the Raday people, and by her quiet courage in the face of a series of crushing blows life had dealt her, any one of which would have devastated most other people.

Her older brother was taken prisoner during World War II. Not until after the war and a long period of uncertainty did the family learn he had been killed while trying to escape. A younger brother and sister were killed by a balloon-borne Japanese explosive device while they were on a Sunday School picnic. Also killed in this incident was the wife of the young pastor who later became Betty's husband.

Then in 1963 Betty's husband, Archie, was taken off into the jungle by Communist guerillas while living at a leprosarium near Banmethuot, of which he had recently been appointed director. Betty was left with the responsibility for their four children and constant concern about her husband's welfare. Betty once told me she never took a shower without thinking about Archie and wondering if he had facilities for bathing. Always she prayed and hoped for his return.

As the long day wore on, Betty, Lil, LuAnne and I tried to coordinate our trips to the latrine facility. The procedure for going was a bit complicated. Next to the clearing was a burned off area where a small slit trench had been dug. By mid-morning, when that became inadequate, the entire field area began to serve as a latrine. Always twenty or thirty men were sitting on the ground waiting to go out there. The guard would allow only five men at a time to leave the clearing. When all five returned, five more men were allowed to go, or we four women.

When our turn came to use the facility we hurried as quickly as we could. It was not an area where one cared to tarry. Besides we didn't want to hold up the line. Lil had brought along her black tribal skirt, and we held it up for each other to give a bit of privacy from the gaze of soldiers and prisoners in and around the clearing.

As we returned to the clearing, we passed a place where tarpaulins had been hung on trees, shielding a small area from view. Groans and cries from the place left no doubt as to its use. Here the severely wounded were being treated.

We stepped over and around people in the crowded clearing to get back to the spot we were assigned. Jay had finished translating the papers and given them to the officer. He returned only a minute later in some agitation. Lil, it seemed, had referred to them as the North Vietnamese Army.

"We are not the North Vietnamese Army," he said emphatically. "We are the Liberation Army of Vietnam."

"Is there a difference?" I asked innocently.

"Of course there's a difference," he snapped. "The Liberation Army is engaged in the struggle to free their own country from the Thieu clique and the American imperialists."

"In that case, you'd better give my paper back too," I said holding out my hand, "because I made the same mistake."

Lil and I crossed out the offending phrase in answer to

54

the question about treatment since capture and wrote in the proper designation.

"I was afraid they'd take exception to that," Jay said as the man walked away. "But I went ahead and translated it anyway. The fact that every single soldier we have met is from North Vietnam is beside the point," he added with a smile.

"Jay," I asked, impressed by his facility in the Vietnamese language and his understanding of even political and economic terminology, "where did you learn so much Vietnamese?"

"At Cornell as an undergraduate student in the Southeast Asia Program," he said. "After I graduated I didn't feel like studying anymore and I still didn't know what I wanted to do, so I volunteered to go to Vietnam with the International Voluntary Service (IVS) for a couple of years. I was interested in Vietnam and the Vietnamese people, and figured this would be a good way to pick up some first-hand knowledge."

Jay spent several years with IVS teaching English at a boarding school in Phan Rang. Living and eating at the school, he was immersed in the Vietnamese language and culture. Visiting the homes and villages of his students, he had formed deep friendships with many of them.

Many of his students were Cham. This ethnic group, which once controlled most of South Vietnam, was now a small minority group. The Cham were fiercely proud of their language and culture, but the necessity of living in a Vietnamese society was drawing them further and further away from their old traditions.

Some of the old Cham men had shown Jay ancient manuscripts written in the Arabic-looking Cham script which had been passed down from their ancestors. Some of them were crumbling with age. The young people had never learned to read the script and valued these documents lightly. "What a shame," Jay thought, "that these documents, which must be of tremendous historical value, are not being preserved."

After finishing his tour with IVS, Jay stayed on in Vietnam for a year to work for Pan American Airways. He shared his apartment with several Vietnamese students and helped them with food, and sometimes even tuition. Even after he returned to Cornell to enter law school, he lived frugally so he could send money back to Vietnam to help these young people through school.

Still concerned about the Cham manuscripts, Jay had contacted the Ford Foundation, and was given a grant of money to return to Vietnam for six months to photograph as many of these as he could find. This would at least preserve the contents of the documents for scientific study.

The project was going well. Jay had already collected many rolls of film when he accidentally left his film loader on a bus. He wrote to the United States, requesting that another loader be sent, and decided that since he was unable to continue photographing, this would be a good time to visit some Cham friends who were now living in Banmethuot studying to be teachers. Events proved he couldn't have picked a worse time.

That afternoon we were brought rice and a can of chopped pork. We whittled chopsticks out of bamboo lying on the edge of the clearing, and dug in. It tasted delicious! We were concerned, however, about getting drinking water. Our supply was completely gone, and the little stream at the edge of the clearing was probably polluted.

"Could we have something to boil water in?" we asked one of the soldiers. "We don't want to drink unboiled water, but we would be happy to boil it ourselves." The request was transmitted to an officer who soon appeared to discuss the problem with us.

"You may use one of the dried combat ration tins to boil water in," he decided. "But you must not use a fire at night or any time there are aircraft in the area."

We readily agreed and began to look around the edge of the clearing for branches and dead wood. Both Paul and Peter possessed skill in fire building, and Paul's cigarette lighter proved very useful. By evening we had a fresh supply of drinking water, but I went to sleep thirsty. It was still too hot to drink!

That night we strung up between two trees the double

bed net we had brought from our home in Banmethuot. By squeezing together, most of us could get our heads under it and be partially protected against mosquitos.

In the morning I took LuAnne to the stream and tried to wash her with John's handkerchief. "LuAnne," I said, observing with exasperation her stringy braids and half-grownout bangs falling in her eyes, "I think we ought to cut your hair."

"Oh no, Mommy, please don't," she begged. "I want to grow it out long like Margie's."

"I used to put my little girl's hair in French braids," Betty suggested. "Let me try to do LuAnne's that way."

LuAnne borrowed Aunty Lil's little mirror to survey the results proudly. A little later Aunty Lil taught her to make a little mouse out of the handkerchief.

"My mother showed me how to do this when I was a little girl in India," she told LuAnne.

"India?" Peter questioned with interest.

"Yes," Lil answered. "My parents were missionaries in India. I was born and raised there."

"I was born and raised in India, too," said Peter. "My father was an engineer working for the British government." He and Lil discovered that though they had lived in different parts of the country they had many experiences in common.

The day passed slowly. We boiled more drinking water. We played with LuAnne, batting the handkerchief mouse back and forth across a string. Across the clearing we saw one of the Vietnamese employees who had been in Paul's house with us. With him were his wife and child.

Paul asked an officer if he knew what had happened to the Filipino who was taken the same time we were.

"No," he replied. "I don't know anything about a Filipino."

"He worked for me," Paul said, "and I would like to know what happened to him."

That afternoon a tired, dusty-looking Filipino came in with a group of men who had been brought on foot from Banmethuot. As soon as he was given permission to enter the clearing, he rushed over to where we were sitting, threw his arms around Paul and greeted the rest of us warmly.

57

"Oh boy!" he exclaimed with a big grin. "Am I ever glad to see you. I felt as if I was losing my identity as a foreigner."

Ike, we soon learned, was a good man to have around. Cheerful and sensitive to other people's needs, he was always willing to help. Cultured and well educated, he nevertheless possessed a wealth of knowledge about jungle living, and an expertise in utilizing bamboo for our simple needs that the rest of us envied. An ex-boyscout, he greatly enjoyed building fires, though Paul and Peter often razzed him about the "unorthodox" way he built them. During the Japanese occupation of the Philippines, his family had fled to the mountains and had experienced a period of jungle subsistence. Although only a young boy, he was taken in by a group of American soldiers to live and work with them.

Ike was a graduate of an agricultural college and had been employed for several years by a Philippine company to work with United States Aid for International Development (USAID) projects in Vietnam.

During that second day, Paul was taken out for questioning. When he returned we asked him how it had gone.

"Well," he replied, "they wanted to know why I came back to Vietnam after I got out of the army. I gave them my version of the old story about Boy meets Girl, Boy falls in love with Girl, Boy marries Girl."

"And what did they say to that?" I asked.

"They seemed to find it hard to believe that H'lum is my only wife, and that I don't have another back in the States somewhere. They also tried to get me to admit that I am a Colonel in the U.S. Army. I think, if I'm going to be taken for a Colonel, I ought to get a Colonel's pay when I get out of here!"

By the third day the large clearing was jammed with men. Some were being led away into the jungle in groups, accompanied by North Vietnamese soldiers, but many more continued to arrive. Guards bustled here and there trying to organize the mass of prisoners, supervise the cooking of huge vats of rice over open fires, and keep order.

The stench from the area we had facetiously dubbed "The Rose Garden" was getting bad, particularly when the wind blew from that direction.

That afternoon a North Vietnamese photographer came by to take pictures of us. It was hard to imagine a less photogenic group. We were dirty, disheveled and unshaven. But we posed very readily and hoped for a wide circulation of the photos. Maybe they would let our families know we were alive.

A fresh-faced young soldier came up to us. He carried a black leather shoulder bag which we were beginning to recognize as a mark of an officer. "I have some questions I want you to write answers for," he said brightly. We looked at him as he began to go through them: what is your name, your address, your organization . . . ?"

"Oh, we already answered those," Betty said confidently.

The young man looked slightly taken aback. "No you didn't," he said, "this is the first time I've talked with you. How could you have answered them already?"

"That officer over there had us answer the very same questions," said Lil pointing. "I'm sure he'll show you the papers."

"That was for him, this is for me," he said firmly. "You'll have to do it again."

After struggling to recall our fifteen moves up and down, to and from, Vietnam, John decided, "I'm going to make a copy of this for us to keep. That way, if we're asked to do this again sometime, we won't have to sit around and figure it out, and we can be sure of saying the same thing every time." This proved to be a wise decision, since the papers we wrote never seemed to go with us, and every time we were moved to a new location we were required to write out answers to the same questions again with minor additions and variations.

We were still writing when a guard came over to us and said very quietly, "Hurry and get done. You're being moved to another location."

We women decided to make a final trip out to the "rose garden." Coming back I was stopped by a tall thin man wearing a South Vietnam Air Force flight suit.

"My name is Phuong," he said in excellent English. "I was a Major in the South Vietnam Air Force, and received my training in Texas. These are my children," he added, pointing to two youngsters squatting beside the path relieving themselves. "My wife is with me, too, and she'll be glad to know there are other women here."

"We were told we're being moved somewhere else," I told him. "But perhaps we will meet again."

We re-entered the clearing and worked our way back to our spot.

"Bring your things and follow me," a guard ordered.

We followed him out of the clearing to the processing area where we saw an open truck with high wooden slats on the sides. Two rows of South Vietnamese prisoners were lined up behind the truck. We were ordered to form a third line. A soldier with a long rope was tying each man to the man directly in front and behind. We stood and watched uneasily.

"I have a letter that a man put into my hand as we left the clearing," Lil said softly. "He wanted me to take it to his family."

"Lil, we're not going to be released now," Paul answered grimly. "You'd better get rid of it."

"I know," Lil said rather desperately. "I told him that, but he gave it to me anyway. What do I *do* with it?"

"Chew it up!" was Paul's unsympathetic response. Lil obediently popped the note into her mouth.

"Now what?" she mumbled a few minutes later, opening her mouth to reveal a pulpy mass.

"I think you can spit it out now," Paul smiled.

The soldier with the rope approached our group. An officer with what appeared to be one glass eye and a sneering expression said to us, "We are going to tie you up for your own protection."

"Please don't tie me up," I requested. "I have a child to hold."

"You can still hold the child," he said unsympathetically. "We won't tie her, but you must be tied." The rope went from Ike's right arm to mine and on to John's.

One group of Vietnamese prisoners was already loaded onto the truck. Then our baggage was put on, and we were told to get in and sit on it. The truck seemed nearly full.

"Move back!" a soldier commanded. "Farther, farther," he added as one row after another was loaded in.

I squeezed LuAnne between my knees on the small suitcase that had the Bru New Testament manuscripts in it. My knees were poking John's back. I was pressed against the slats of the truck on my left and Ike on my right.

"Would you mind if I sat on this bag?" a voice behind me inquired courteously. I turned and found myself looking into the face of the ex-province chief of Darlac Province.

"Please do," I answered, referring to the market bag that was squeezed in between us.

As the truck bounced across the "rose garden" latrine area and set off along a track across the plateau, I reflected on the vagaries of human authority. A week ago I would never have expected to even meet this gentleman, whose authority was unchallenged throughout the whole area. Now he sat on our market bag with his knees in my back and we were prisoners together.

Dusk gave way to darkness and still we traveled. Still-burning fires showed evidence of efforts to clear patches of vegetation on both sides of us, but we didn't see any other sign of human habitation. The track could not have been well marked because occasionally one of the soldiers would get out to try to determine which way to go. A few times the driver had to back up and search for another way through a thicket of trees.

The passengers in the back of the truck shucked back and forth as the truck went up and down, each person trying to preserve his own space against the press of forty-two other bodies. John was annoyed at the way a very ill man near him was having his space preempted because he was too weak to push back.

"If some people didn't have so much gear," one man grumbled, "we'd have more room." I felt acutely conscious of all our unnecessary baggage and heartily wished two-thirds of it were at the bottom of the sea.

Ike had pushed back and away from me, and the rope that held us together was pulling on my arm. My back and legs ached with trying to keep LuAnne from being crushed between my knees. When the truck tilted sharply to the left

61

and went through a riverbed, I had a panicky feeling. "If it should tip over," I thought, "LuAnne would certainly be killed by all the weight on top of her."

Reaching up to steady myself by grabbing hold of the slats at the side I immediately saw a beam of light directed at my hand.

"Get your hands down," the guard who accompanied us ordered.

It was 1 A.M. when the truck stopped. LuAnne had slept the entire trip. I handed her down to John and discovered as I jumped down that my stiff legs would hardly support me.

Soldiers came out of a tiny thatch hut near the truck. One of them directed us to a pile of thatch some distance from the other prisoners and told us we could spend the night there.

"Yes, there is malaria in this place," he said in answer to our query. He helped us hang our two nets from a tree and a bamboo pole. We spread the thatch out so we could all lie with our heads under the net.

"I don't know where we are," I thought as I stretched out wearily on the thatch between John and LuAnne, "but wherever it is, I'm glad we've arrived!"

FOUR

Camp Sunshine

"What do you think about the Thieu government?" The question was addressed to Lil by a middle-aged senior political officer with a puckish expression, twinkling eyes and a big smile.

The rest of us sat in silence as Lil looked somewhat uncomfortable and answered evasively, "Our work in Vietnam has been religious and we do not involve ourselves in the politics of the country."

"But you must have some opinions," he pressed. "Otherwise you are like an ostrich burying its head in the sand, refusing to face problems."

The officer was squatting directly in front of me under a bamboo, thatch covered shelter, hastily put together that morning with the thatch we had slept on the night before. Now changing his line of questioning, he turned and looked at me. "Do you believe a just cause will always triumph?" he asked.

I was taken off-guard, and hesitated before answering. What did I believe? According to the Bible, God's power is absolute, and he promises ultimate vindication of righteousness and punishment of evil, but in the day-to-day confrontation of men and nations this didn't seem to be the rule. I could identify with David in the Old Testament who said, "I have seen the wicked in great power, and spreading himself like a green bay tree."

"I believe that in the end justice will triumph," I answered, "but that we do not always see this happening in the world around us."

"Of course justice will always triumph," he said beaming. "That's why the American Revolution succeeded. It was a just cause. And that's why we will succeed in defeating the American imperialists. Because ours is a just cause.

"Under the revolution we have complete religious freedom," he explained. "I myself am a Catholic, and I pray every day that God will punish Gerald Ford."

I debated whether or not to express an opinion that in following Christ's teaching he might better pray that God would bless Gerald Ford and give him wisdom and understanding. I remained silent, but John decided this would be a good time to ask about our present religious freedom. "Does this mean," he asked, "that we can read our Bibles?"

"Of course you may," the man replied.

"This morning when I took out my New Testament and began to read it, a guard ordered me to put it away," John said doubtfully.

"That was only because he didn't understand," the officer assured him. "You may read your Bible any time you want to."

"It is our custom on Sunday to get together to sing hymns, pray and study the Bible," one of the ladies said, "May we do this here?"

The man hesitated, then said, "You may, if you do it quietly so you don't disturb others."

A few days later I overheard the same man talking to a group of South Vietnamese prisoners on the subject of religion. "Under the revolution," he said, "you are free to follow any religion you choose, or none at all. But, of course, your duty to the state must come first."

"And there," I thought, "is the rub." I recalled Christ's statement that a person who puts anything ahead of his commitment to him "is not worthy of me."

From our nine by twelve foot shelter we looked around at the activity within the enclosed area to which we had been brought. In the darkness and exhaustion of the night before, I was not even aware that we had been taken inside a

64

stockade. Now I could see that interwoven bamboo poles enclosed an area roughly the length of a football field, and a bit wider. Much of the area was still covered by high grass and undergrowth. Most of the large trees inside the stockade had been cut and lay where they had fallen.

Two openings in the fence permitted entry and exit. The one at the front right-hand corner from where we sat was guarded at all times. It was through this gate that guards, political cadres and camp administrators entered from their houses outside the fence. The second gate was opened only at certain hours. It was located on the fence behind us, almost directly opposite the first. That one, we learned, opened out onto a path which led down to a nearby river. Large holes had been dug inside the corner of the stockade near that gate for building fires under huge caldrons of rice. This constituted the camp kitchen.

A path leading from the front to the back gate passed directly beside our shelter. In the far corner of the stockade a log platform with several holes over a large pit came to be known as "the throne," and served as latrine facilities for the camp.

Two thatch covered structures with bamboo latticed sides along the front fence to our left were the only ones inside the stockade. Some fifty or sixty prisoners were living in them when we arrived. The group that arrived with us was instructed to build a shelter behind ours. All the other prisoners were forbidden to talk with us foreigners.

We wondered where the other prisoners had come from, and how long they had been there. They seemed to know the routine of camp life. They got up at 5 A.M. when the unmelodic striking of metal on metal made it obvious that something was expected. Another beating of the metal wheel rim sent them to work. Some were assembled and taken out by guards on work details to gather bamboo, thatch or firewood. Some seemed to be responsible for kitchen details.

Around mid-morning we were brought a woven basket of cooked rice and a small pan of soup. The soup consisted of water, grease and salt. These items proved to be the primary ingredients of our diet for the five weeks we remained at this location. They varied only by the occasional additions to the soup of a few leaves, a little powdered fish, some wild figs or a few tiny bits of canned pork.

Several times that morning we requested permission to go to the river and bathe. Finally after we had eaten, a junior political officer appeared to take us. The women and children, he said, should go first, and then the men.

The path down to the river was muddy and slippery, but never was a bath more welcome. Lil had brought one tube of shampoo, which she shared with Betty, LuAnne and me. We knew it wouldn't last long, but as we sparingly lathered our hair and then squeezed out the suds to use on our bodies and clothing, we seemed to wash away not only the dirt, but the fear, discomfort and uncertainty of the preceding days.

The guard waited for us part way up the hill, but this did not mean privacy, we discovered. Kitchen workers could not be delayed in scrubbing out the huge rice pots, or carrying water for the next meal! We bathed quickly and hurried up the hill so the men could have their turn.

The next day our group was instructed to assemble in the cleared area near the front gate with our belongings. We were each issued a small hand towel and a plastic rice bowl. Each single person or family unit was issued a single-bed mosquito net and one jungle hammock from which the ropes had been removed. This was a piece of heavy green material four feet wide and seven and a half feet long. Then each of us was issued a maroon and gray striped shirt and trousers outfit.

"Go put these on," the young political officer in charge of distribution ordered. Betty, a regal and well proportioned six-footer, held a pair of pants up to her body and looked questioningly at the man. The rest of us laughed at the absurd sight, and the man retrieved the outfit.

"I guess you'll have to wear your own clothes," he said.

Lil and I went toward the back fence into a patch of waist high grass to change into our outfits. We joked about the spectacle we presented as we tightened the draw strings around our waists, and then paraded out in our new outfits as though modeling the latest fashion. I laughed when I saw John. His pant legs ended several inches above his ankles,

66

and the shirt was definitely on the tight side. On Paul and Jay the fit was even worse.

A senior political officer walked into the compound, looked at us standing there waiting, and frowned. "Those clothes are not appropriate for women," he muttered to the junior officer.

The next procedure involved going through all our possessions. "Everything except what you need in camp will be taken away and kept for you," the officer told us.

Since they had less baggage, the single men went first. Peter had only a small red draw-string bag he had borrowed from Lil at Paul's house. He was allowed to keep articles of clothing, but had to turn over watch, rings, money, passport, pocket knife and pen. He asked to be allowed to keep a large, brightly colored toenail clipper. "My daughter gave it to me," he explained. When the man looked unconvinced he added, "Besides I might need to cut my toenails." At this the man relented and handed the clippers back.

Betty protested when she was told to take off her wedding ring. "My husband gave this to me twenty-eight years ago, and I have worn it ever since. Now you tell me I must take it off," she said accusingly, tugging at the tight band to get it over her knuckle.

"Don't worry," the officer said, "you'll get it back again."

The silver belt that Archie had given her he allowed her to keep when she assured him it was functional as well as decorative. She needed it to hold up the tribal skirt she was wearing.

When our turn came, I resolutely dumped the contents of our two suitcases out on the ground. I was surprised myself at some of the things they contained. The man took the large brown suitcase to hold the items they were taking. These included the same things they had taken from the others, as well as a sewing machine, typewriter, papers, books, Bru New Testament manuscripts, tools, dishes and jewelry.

"You can keep these," he said, holding out a pair of tennis rackets. I looked at him in surprise.

"Why?" I asked.

"You might want to use them," he answered.

I looked around at the uneven ground with stumps and fallen tree trunks, the bushes and patches of high grass and shook my head.

"I'll keep the balls for the little girl," I said, "but I don't think we can use those." I was allowed to keep the photos of my children and one pair of eyeglasses.

As I was gathering up the clothing we were allowed to keep, LuAnne presented the little assortment of "treasures" she had collected for the officer's inspection. He smiled at her kindly and dismissed them with a wave of the hand.

"You may keep them," he said.

Back in the shelter I reorganized the few possessions we had left, and felt almost glad to be relieved of some of our excess baggage. At the same time, the striped uniform and the absence of my watch and wedding ring made me acutely aware of my prisoner status.

That evening we strung up our nets under the little shelter. The front of the shelter was just high enough that all of us except Betty could stand erect, and it sloped down to about four feet in back. John, LuAnne and I slept under the double-bed net we had brought, putting the one we had just been issued under our hips for a bit of padding. Peter hung his net next to ours. Paul, Ike, Jay and the Phillipses completed the row. Betty hung hers crosswise at the Phillipses' feet, so that the entire shelter with the exception of a few square feet next to the entrance at our feet was filled with nets.

It was beginning to get dark. I helped LuAnne brush her teeth and crawl in under the net. Then I got in beside her to hear her say her prayer.

"Aren't you going to sleep now?" she asked apprehensively.

"I'm going to sit outside the net a little while before I go to sleep," I answered. The breezes which made the nights a bit chilly had not yet picked up, and the dead stillness of the air made this the most uncomfortably hot part of the day. I couldn't bear the thought of lying under the net where our closed-in body heat would make the air still hotter.

"Mommy, I'm scared," she confessed.

"Honey, we all get scared sometimes," I told her. "But if

we remember God has promised he will never ever leave us and will take care of us no matter what happens, that helps us not to be afraid."

As I lay there talking to her I remembered a song I had taught our two oldest children when they were very small. I hadn't thought of it or sung it for years. But the words came back to me as I began to teach it to LuAnne . . .

> Father, lead me day by day,
> Ever in thine own good way;
> Teach me to be pure and true,
> Show me what I ought to do.
>
> When in danger, make me brave,
> Make me know that thou canst save;
> Keep me safely by thy side,
> Let me in thy love abide.
>
> When I'm tempted to do wrong,
> Make me steadfast, wise, and strong;
> And when all alone I stand,
> Shield me with thy mighty hand.
>
> May I do the good I know,
> Serving gladly here below;
> Then at last go home to thee,
> Evermore thine own to be.

This song became LuAnne's favorite, and quite often we would sing it together inside the net before she went to sleep. She didn't know it, but her mother was comforted by the trustful simplicity of that prayer as much as she was.

This was the beginning of a routine which was to continue throughout the months of our detainment, regardless of location. Each evening at bedtime I would crawl under the net with her and tell her a bedtime story. Sometimes we sang a few songs, and sometimes we just talked a bit. Then we would pray together. I would kiss her goodnight, and then crawl out for an hour or two.

Our arrival at the camp marked the beginning of the

influx of new prisoners. Day and night truckloads of new arrivals were brought into the stockade. Within a week or two we were told that the population inside the fence had reached a thousand. And as more and more people arrived, organization broke down, sanitary facilities became inadequate, shortages occurred and confusion reigned.

None of the camp staff volunteered their names, so we generally referred to them by their function or by some distinguishing characteristic. The smiling senior political officer we called Happy. The camp commander, by virtue of his position, became our Glorious Leader. The junior administrator was called White Shirt (everyone else dressed in regulation green). Peter and Paul derived considerable amusement from watching one young soldier try to organize work details among the prisoners. He never seemed to have the same number anytime he counted noses and scolded them in frustration for not doing what they were supposed to.

"You know who he reminds me of?" Paul remarked. "Sgt. Zero in the Beetle Bailey comic strip."

After a week or so, Sgt. Zero was seen no more inside the camp. "I'll bet he's been transferred to the 'Eastern Front,'" Paul speculated.

One young northerner with a husky voice was particularly friendly, and sometimes stopped to visit with Jay. We complained to him one day that we were confused about getting permission to go down to the river to bathe.

"Earlier today," I said, "an officer told us we could go to bathe, but when we tried to go out the gate, the guard there refused to let us go."

"You should check with me when you want to take a bath," he said, "because that is my responsibility." He walked off and returned a short time later to tell us it would be all right to go now. From that point on he became known as Bath Man.

Wednesday noon, four days after our arrival, we women were picking our way gingerly up the steep hill from the river and trying not to get dirty again in the process, when a long line of dust-covered, tired looking men approached us
70

going down. "Another batch of new arrivals," I noted without particular interest, stepping aside to let them pass.

Then over the side of the hill came two people we recognized: the Johnsons!

"Norm and Joan!" we shouted. They paused on their way down the hill, and we greeted each other warmly.

"We'll talk to you when we get back up," Norm said. "Right now I can hardly wait to get in that river."

The two returned from the river looking refreshed, but bedraggled in their wet clothes. Joan's slacks were torn, and she wore a pair of men's shoes several sizes too large.

"My sandals broke and they gave me these to wear," she said.

Norm's light-colored trousers were stained and rumpled, and neither of them had anything to change into. They brought with them only a bright pink blanket from their home in Banmethuot. They also brought a small woven mat and a dried-food can filled with drinking water, which they had been given.

"We can sure use that can to boil drinking water," one of us remarked. "We were given one to use back at the Rose Garden, but had to leave it there."

"The Rose Garden?" Norm questioned, and then laughed when we explained the term. "That's where we just came from," he said, "and it's even worse now!"

"I have no memory of carrying that blanket out of the house," Joan said, "but I don't know what we'd have done without it."

They had been taken into custody the first day of the attack. Like us they had decided to go to the U.S. government compound, but when they emerged from their house where they had spent the night in the shower stall of their bathroom, a series of explosions on the road beside the house had sent them scurrying to a neighbor's bunker. Before they had time to consider any other move, North Vietnamese soldiers had advanced into the area.

"They sounded like a football team as they advanced up our street," Norm said. "We heard them in our house going from room to room. They must have seen the Canadian flag in my office because I heard one of them say something about Canada."

"The eeriest part," Joan added, "was when one of them began to play our piano. I couldn't believe it. Sounds of fighting all around and this guy was playing the piano!"

A little later that day a soldier shot his gun into the ground at the entrance to the bunker and ordered everyone in it to come out. They all came out quickly. Norm asked to be allowed to go back into the bunker after his briefcase and a small bag they had packed, but the soldier refused to allow this.

During the days we were in Paul's house waiting to be discovered, Norm and Joan had been taken on foot from place to place outside the city by the soldiers, sometimes into areas that were being heavily bombed. One officer told them they were being led away from the fighting for their own safety. Another told them, "We're going to kill you!"

"We didn't have any idea what had happened to the rest of you until they took us to the place you call the 'Rose Garden,'" Joan said. "Someone told us you had just left the day before."

"We came here on the same truck as some International Control Commission men," Norm said, pointing to two men sitting over by the main gate. "I made it a point to introduce myself to them. I figured they would never remember our names, but I told them to please remember they had met two Canadians. I don't see how they can possibly hold those men, do you?"

Paul recognized the Indonesian man, and recalled having attended a party with him. The man spotted us at about the same time and came over. We greeted him and offered to share our small shelter with them, but one of the camp authorities came over immediately and led him away. The two men were taken back outside the stockade and we had no further contact with them. But when we heard a few weeks later they had been taken to Loc Ninh and allowed to return to Saigon, we were greatly encouraged. For the first time we had reason to hope our families would learn that we were alive.

The day Norm and Joan arrived, the camp authorities

announced they would return most of the things they had taken from all the prisoners the preceding days.

"You will have to be responsible for them yourselves after this," an officer announced. "Please be very careful to protect your belongings."

Norm and Joan were given rice bowls and a mosquito net, but supplies of the other items issued had already been exhausted. We knew they had run out of prison uniforms because a day or two earlier, Bath Man had said to Lil and me, "When you go to the river today, please wash out your uniforms and return them to us. They are not suitable for women. You may wear the clothing you had when you came."

Not spoken, but understood, was the implication that the uniforms were needed for someone else. We were happy to oblige. We also dug into our suitcases, and from all the clothing we had brought, most of which was unsuitable for the jungle, we were able to come up with a change of clothing for Norm and Joan.

We were called out into the clearing by the gate to receive back our possessions. They would not return flashlight batteries, pocket knives, and a few other items, but everything else would be returned. Back came the sewing machine, typewriter and big brown suitcase.

One soldier very carefully counted out the money we had turned over and returned it to John. Another soldier asked me to check the contents of the suitcase to make sure everything was there. I looked over the odd assortment of items, and then picked up the folders of the manuscripts— Galatians through Revelation was in one folder; Acts, Romans, and Corinthians in another; Luke and John in another. Puzzled, I went through them again and then looked through the suitcase. Where were Matthew and Mark?

The soldiers noted my worried look and asked if something was missing.

"There should be two more folders here," I said to him.

"We did not take any of them out," he said. "If they're not here, then they weren't turned over to us."

"I wonder what could have happened to them," I said. "You see," I explained to him, "these papers are the most valuable things we have as far as we're concerned. They represent fourteen years of work. We don't much care about the money or clothes or anything else we have, but we very much want to keep these papers."

The man looked sympathetic. "I'm very sorry," he said, "but I assure you we do not have them."

I believed the man was telling the truth. What possible reason would they have had for keeping those two folders. If they had wanted to take them, they would have taken the others also. I felt sick inside as I closed the suitcase and took it over to the shelter to tell John what had happened.

"Where do you suppose they are?" I asked him.

"I don't know," John replied. "We were using them on Saturday, and I guess I didn't actually check to make sure every folder was there when I gathered up the material to pack."

"I'm sure I would have seen them if they had been left in the office at home," I said, "because I checked that room carefully. We must have left them in the suitcase in Paul's house when we put the other folders into the market bag. It was dark in there and we couldn't see too well."

That night I couldn't go to sleep. "How could we have been so careless with something that was so important to us?" I asked myself. "If I had checked them when we put them into the market bag, we could have brought them all."

John sensed my restlessness and tried to reason with me. "Look," he said, "we did the best we could under the circumstances. Maybe we should have been more careful, but there is nothing we can do about it now. There are earlier copies of Matthew and Mark in Saigon. If we get out with what we have now, we could get a lot of the corrections by checking parallel passages from the copy of Luke. Besides," he added, "I'm not sure we'll get out with any of them. In any event it's pointless to worry about it. Let's just commit it to the Lord and go to sleep."

We had begun the practice of praying together before we went to sleep each night since the attack. Sometimes, as John pointed out, I had a tendency to fall asleep before he finished praying on the nights it was his turn to pray.

74

"It's all right," he teased. "It shows you trust me to pray about the right things."

On this night, however, I had no trouble staying awake as John committed our puzzlement and concern about Matthew and Mark to the Lord. He promptly fell asleep, but I lay on the green tarp listening to the breathing of the others around me and thought.

I remembered talking to Lil on the way back from the river the day after our belongings were taken away. She had expressed sadness that the Mnong people had so little of God's Word, and that there would now be no way for them to get more, even though there were many portions that Dick had already translated.

"I know how you feel," I agreed. "The Bru people were so eager to get God's Word in their own language that they sometimes neglected rice fields and other important projects to help us on the translation."

It was true. The Bru Christians had felt a sense of urgency and responsibility about getting the Scriptures. During the last year of checking the manuscripts, John estimated twenty-five people had been involved in helping us. When the rice harvest ripened it was hard to get a committee together. One week we thought we would have to stop for a while since only two people were able to go with us, and for the type of checking we were doing we needed at least three.

Thom had already told us he'd not be able to go with us that week. He had to work with his wife harvesting their rice field. But when he learned that we were short one person to be able to continue working, he told us to wait while he went to talk with his wife. A few minutes later he came back with a little flight bag, saying he would go with us.

"Did your wife think she could harvest the field without you?" I asked him.

"No," he replied, "she can't. But I told her God would help us get the rice in later, and if not, he would take care of us some other way. 'There will be other rice crops,' I told her, 'but we have *got* to get God's Word now.'"

This same sense of priority was evident in the prayer of another young man who was helping us. We had finished

75

breakfast and were having morning devotions. John asked Sa-âm to lead in prayer. Part of his prayer brought tears to my eyes.

"Lord," he said. "We hear reports that trouble might come, and we don't know what's going to happen to our country. But *please* help us get your Word, and then whatever comes we can take it, as long as we have your Word."

All this went through my mind as I followed Lil up the hill toward the stockade. Surely God would honor the sacrifice and dedication of his Mnong and Bru children.

"But you know, Lil," I said, "I really feel that even if we never see the manuscripts again, or ever have contact with the Bru people, what we have seen God do in the lives of people would make the whole fourteen years worthwhile."

I dozed off to sleep finally, but in my dreams I was searching for the missing manuscripts. A day or so later when Happy came by to see us I asked Jay if he would inquire about the possibility of getting the manuscripts we had left in Paul's house in Banmethuot. "Could you tell us," Jay inquired, "what has happened to the things which were left in Mr. Struharik's house?"

"Oh, everything in his house has been confiscated," Happy said, "and the papers will be carefully studied."

"When we left Mr. Struharik's house," Jay continued, "Mr. and Mrs. Miller left a suitcase there containing some papers they would very much like to have. These are part of a translation of the New Testament into a mountain language. Do you think it would be possible for them or someone else to get these papers?"

Happy looked doubtful. "If you will give me a complete description of the folders and the suitcase they are in, I will see what I can do," he promised. Jay helped us formulate the request. But Happy left the camp a week or two later not to reappear, and we never heard anything more about the request.

In one of the early groups to arrive at what we now referred to as Camp Sunshine was Major Phuong, the Vietnamese Air Force officer I had met just before leaving the Rose Garden, his wife and two children. Mrs. Phuong came over to the shelter where we were sitting shortly after their

76

arrival. She carried a two year old boy in her arms, and an attractive little girl of seven followed her.

"My little girl, Thuy, would like very much to get acquainted with your daughter," she said to me. "It is very difficult for the children to find things to do," she continued with a sigh, "when they have no toys or playmates."

I agreed with her and said that we would be very happy to have Thuy play with LuAnne. I expressed surprise that she and the children should have been taken captive, when no other military dependents were, and learned that she was there at her own request.

"You see," she explained, "we were living in a government house right next to the city airfield in Banmethuot. During the fighting our house was burned to the ground. I had no place to live and no relatives living in the highlands I could turn to, so I asked to be allowed to go with my husband."

Thuy proved to be an outgoing, self-confident child, and spent a major part of every day playing with LuAnne. Since LuAnne was reluctant to be very far from us, the two generally played inside our little shelter or close to it.

In my purse I had brought a tiny pair of scissors, a pencil, four colored pens and a glue stick. LuAnne and Thuy spent hours drawing, coloring, cutting and sticking paper that they got from Aunty Lil. When Lil's supply of mimeographed Mnong material and old correspondence dwindled, I had to ration them to one sheet apiece per day.

The fact that Thuy spoke no English and LuAnne almost no Vietnamese didn't seem to hinder the two from communicating. At the beginning they managed with gestures, but before long they had begun to learn from each other the words and phrases they needed in their playing. Sometimes they would come to ask me to explain something or interpret.

"Ma'am," Thuy might say, "would you ask LuAnne if she wants to use half of her sheet of paper and half of mine to make a paper chain?"

Or LuAnne might say, "Mommy, how do you say scissors in Vietnamese?"

Sometimes Thuy was a bit overbearing, and when she

77

pushed too far, LuAnne would refuse to play. This always seemed to take Thuy by surprise.

"What's the matter with LuAnne?" she would ask, puzzled.

"LuAnne says she doesn't want to be the one to go to market every time you play house," I would say, or whatever the latest grievance was.

"Oh!" Thuy would say, comprehension dawning on her face. "You tell her that this time I will go to market and she can cook the rice."

"Okay?" she would say turning to LuAnne.

"Okay." LuAnne would agree. And off they would go again.

Lil had brought a set of Pit cards in their suitcase, and she devised a game like "Sorry" which could be played with the cards and a board she made of paper. She also taught them to play Snap and Concentration. Peter taught them to play a game called Donkey, but thereafter generally turned a deaf ear to Thuy's entreaty, "Uncle Feet! Uncle Feet! Don-key? Don-key?"

Peter was heard to express his agreement with W.C. Fields' statement that a "man can't be all bad, if he hates dogs and children."

I was very much aware of the fact that twenty-four hours a day of constant exposure to any child was apt to be irritating, particularly one as loquacious as LuAnne. So I tried as best I could to keep her occupied and out of their way—no small job in living quarters as close as ours. The siesta hour was particularly difficult. LuAnne never slept, but everyone else wanted to. Generally she tried to be quiet during those hours, but her carelessness would sometimes bring expressions of annoyance from others in the group.

LuAnne was acutely sensitive to adult disapproval or criticism by anyone other than John or myself. Even from us she found it rather devastating to receive discipline or correction under the watchful eyes of so many.

Often the concern for LuAnne's health and happiness weighed heavily on me, and I knew that Mrs. Phuong was also feeling the strain. One day when we were down at the

78

river bathing and washing clothes, she said to me, "I appreciate so much the way you women have been kind to Thuy. I know it isn't easy to have her around so much, but she enjoys being there."

"It's perfectly all right for her to be there," I assured her. "Thuy is always obedient and well-behaved when she is with us."

"If she is ever in the way," she said, "please send her back over to our shelter."

Then suddenly she began to weep as she said, "I worry so about the children. It's one thing for us adults to put up without adequate food or shelter, but the children shouldn't have to go through this. Sometimes I feel I can hardly bear it."

I nodded sympathetically and she went on, "It's different for you, because you have faith in God. But I have nothing."

I stepped over closer to her and said, "You are right. We do have faith in God and this helps us a great deal. But you can have faith in God too. God loves you, and he is just as concerned about you and your children as he is about us."

My heart went out to her. I wanted to share with her my own gropings toward God, and his promise of love and care, but I felt so tongue-tied and inadequate to express myself in Vietnamese. I could get by in polite conversation or market transactions, but to really express the things of the heart I was at a complete loss.

It wasn't only in discussing spiritual truth that I found myself completely out of my depth in Vietnamese. The first political lecture we had to sit through might as well have been conducted in Chinese as far as I was concerned. The only one who understood it was Jay, and he was not eager to translate it in any great detail.

"Oh, they just gave their version of the history of the Vietnamese conflict," he said offhandedly.

A few key words had occurred over and over again, and I asked Jay about them. "What does *giai phong* mean?"

"That means liberation," he said.

"Oh! And how about *de quoc My.*"

"That means American imperialists."

Given a few more terms like capitalism, socialism, revolution, etc., I could go a long way toward getting the drift of future lectures.

After the lecture Jay protested one point. The speaker had made reference to a great number of American military advisors, who had remained in Vietnam after the war, and pointed to our little group to illustrate his point. Jay reminded him that every one of us was a civilian, and that under the terms of the Paris agreement, which had been signed by his government, American civilians were not forbidden to be in the country. The man immediately withdrew the accusation, but as far as I was concerned the harm had already been done.

After the first few lectures, our group of foreigners was no longer required to attend. This was a relief for it meant we no longer had to sit on the ground in the sun for long hours listening to White Shirt or Glorious Leader discourse on the progress of the revolution. But sitting in our shelter, we had a grandstand view of the proceedings anyway.

Most of the time the "American Imperialists" figured heavily as the villains of the story. The former South Vietnamese soldiers were told they had been used by the Americans to fight an American war.

"Do you know how much it cost to keep one American soldier in combat for one day?" White Shirt asked them. "It cost ten dollars a day. And do you know how much it cost to keep one Vietnamese soldier in combat? Ninety-seven cents. That is why the Americans got you to fight their war for them. They were buying cheap blood!"

"Boy!" I said to Peter during one of the lectures, "the only time they let up on the Americans is when they're running down the French."

After the lectures started, I began to be very conscious of the fact that there were so few of us, and that the Vietnamese prisoners were like a great sea surrounding us on all sides. A couple of times I felt particularly conspicuous when I happened to be walking around the lecture area as the lecturer was sounding forth on the evils of the American imperialists. I felt as though a thousand pairs of eyes were on me as I made my way to the latrine.

80

Sitting in our shelter one evening I mentioned to John my feeling of uneasiness. "I can't help wondering what the Vietnamese prisoners think about us," I said. "I'm sure they don't believe all that business about our being military advisors. A few of them knew us in Banmethuot. Besides they know none of the military men had families over here. Still, I wonder how they feel about Americans in general right about now. Some of them undoubtedly think the U.S. abandoned them, and it would be easy for them to blame the Americans for their present plight."

"I know," John replied. "I've been thinking, too, what an easy thing it would be for the North Vietnamese to incite mob action against us. The other prisoners don't owe us anything, and if it were suggested to them that it would be to their advantage to do away with us. . . ."

"Maybe the camp authorities would step in at the last minute to 'protect' us," I said. "Or maybe they'd see it as a good solution to the problem of what to do with us. Either way, think what propaganda value they could get out of it."

Over succeeding days these fears began to dissipate as our fellow prisoners consistently demonstrated nothing but courtesy and consideration toward us. Not once did anyone express to me a feeling of bitterness toward America. When I questioned one man about what had happened in Banmethuot, he shrugged his shoulders and said simply, "We lost. They won."

When the camp authorities ordered a group of former South Vietnamese officers to construct another shelter for us, however, they protested. "You accuse us of having worked for the Americans," one of them was overheard to say, "but now you are asking us to work for them."

"Yes, but this is different," the soldier assured him. "These Americans are under the control of the revolution, so you are working for the revolution."

We were delighted at the prospect of having a new shelter, and hoped this one might protect from the rain as well as the sun. Bath Man had assured us emphatically that it would not rain at this time of the year, but we were learning to expect this impossible occurrence on an almost daily basis!

The first time it happened we were taken completely by

surprise. We were awakened during the night by water splashing down on us through the mosquito net. Before we could get anything under cover, everything was soaking wet. John and I sat on the log in front of the shelter with LuAnne between us, with our soaking wet tarp around us to hold in a little body heat.

Bath Man came into the camp enveloped in a sheet of plastic. He walked over to us and shone his flashlight directly on us. The rain was running down our faces and splashing off our noses as we looked up at him. No words seemed appropriate on either his part or ours. He clicked his tongue and shook his head sympathetically, then turned around and left.

We soon learned to keep a wary eye on the sky. At first sign of rain we rushed to put all our belongings in the middle of the shelter under Paul's tarp, the only one that was water repellant. "Never mind if *we* get wet," was the thought, "as long as we can keep our stuff dry." Also under the tarp went whatever firewood we had been able to collect. It wasn't so bad to get wet, if we could warm up around a fire when the rain stopped.

In addition to the discomfort we experienced sleeping on wet ground, we had to put up with some of the less desirable forms of wild life the rain seemed to bring out. Norm got very edgy when he heard the Vietnamese prisoners next to the shelter talk about seeing a snake go by. Then one night as John was spreading our tarp for the night, he suddenly cried out in pain and clutched at the fingers of his left hand. Paul hurried over with his cigarette lighter and found the source of the trouble—a scorpion.

John was already suffering from fever and a sore throat. The throbbing in his hand in addition didn't make it easy to sleep. Then the next day as he lay on the ground listless and feverish, a little spider crawled into his ear! John shook his head and thumped it with his hand, but the spider was not to be deterred. It merely crawled back and forth across the eardrum causing a crackling in John's head that drove him nearly to distraction. Help arrived when Lil returned from bathing. She poured a little warm water into John's ear, and the spider decided to seek lodging elsewhere.

The new shelter was completed on what we judged to be

Easter Sunday. A discrepancy between John's calendar and Betty's had made us a bit uncertain as to which Sunday was Easter. We had planned to have an Easter service that morning, but delayed holding it when Paul was taken out for interrogation. By the time he returned we had been instructed to tear down the shelter we were sitting under so that the bamboo and thatch could be used to complete the new one.

We moved into it that afternoon with a feeling of relief. It was along the fence, about halfway between front and back gates, but out of the direct line of traffic—a much quieter location. Furthermore, it had a bamboo platform two feet off the ground for us to sleep on. Even the discovery that it was more crowded than the first shelter, and that the roof leaked badly in places, did not completely deflate us. We had a housewarming celebration that evening. Betty opened a small can of macadamia nuts she had brought in her suitcase, and we each had three nuts.

Though feelings of apprehension about our fellow prisoners had disappeared by now, the sense of "us" and "them" had not. A number of little incidents and problems contributed to this feeling. We discovered to our annoyance that all sorts of little things were disappearing.

One last bit of cheese we had brought in the market bag we were saving for Peter's wedding anniversary. But when that day arrived, the little piece of hoarded cheese was not to be found. Peter was not without an anniversary celebration, however. He was called out for interrogation that day, and after the session was given a welcome meal of rice, greens and fish.

When Jay's sandals were taken at the river while he was bathing, and his tarp disappeared while he was drying it after the first rain, he merely shrugged his shoulders and said, "Someone must have needed them worse that I did." The rest of us, though, found it hard to be that philosophical.

At first we readily loaned our pens to other prisoners, who wanted to try to send notes out, and furnished them with paper. But we learned by hard experience that the pens often did not return. The same thing happened with needle and thread. As our supplies dwindled and pens began running out of ink, we became less willing to lend them.

One man asked us for a drink of water, and then disappeared with the Melmac cup. A few days later, however, a buddy of his made the mistake of coming back with the same cup to ask Paul for a drink. Paul took the cup, said "Thank you" to the man, and dropped it into our bag. Startled, the man looked over to where his friend was sitting. The friend rather sheepishly admitted that it was our cup.

One man particularly annoyed us, and we began to refer to him as "the Moocher." He had come to Lil and Joan with a large carbuncle on his face. They had lanced it and treated it for several days. Every time we made a fire, he came over to use it, rearranging it to best reach whatever he wanted to heat. He also helped himself to the firewood we had collected to replenish the fire. Neither of these acts was enough to cause resentment, but combined with the man's rather smug and complacent acceptance of these things as his due, they did irk us.

We had been given several cans of powdered milk by camp authorities, and discovered that the empty cans were almost as useful as their contents had been. In the absence of cooking pots, they could be used to make leftover rice into rice gruel, or a beverage we called "rice coffee" by drying and roasting the grain. On one occasion Paul managed to catch two tiny fish while he was down bathing. We used the cans to cook these up with rice for a tasty soup. Another time we used them to cook some edible greens Ike found down by the river.

We had given away a few of the cans to other prisoners, and had upon request loaned one to "the Moocher." The following day this man came over with a canteen cup and asked whether we would trade the can for the cup. We were discussing among ourselves whether we needed the can and if the cup would serve as well, when Jay said to the man in Vietnamese, "As far as I'm concerned, you can *have* the can, but I can't speak for the rest." Then Jay turned to us and said disgustedly, "You people are always thinking of yourselves! We already have much more than anybody else, and yet you're not willing to share even what we don't need." With that he stalked off, leaving the rest of us sitting in rather stunned silence.

The Vietnamese man stood there uncertainly waiting for an answer. He seemed somewhat surprised at having set off a situation which he could sense was explosive, even though he couldn't understand the exchange of words.

"Go ahead, take it," someone told him, and the man hurried off quickly, pleased to have come out so well in the matter.

"I don't really think we deserved that," one of the group said defensively, "after all we've done for that man."

"Actually," said another, "I was impressed that he was offering to exchange something, instead of just asking us to give him the can."

"It's true we do have other cans," someone else commented, "but we did use that one to keep leftover rice in."

"What I object to most," said another, "was the way Jay put the rest of us in such a bad light. After that we couldn't do anything but give it to him, whether we wanted to or not."

For a while Jay was nowhere to be seen. This was not unusual because increasingly he had been spending his time with the Vietnamese prisoners. It was inevitable that in a group differing as widely as ours in backgrounds, personalities and life styles there would be points of friction. And in the twenty-four hour a day "togetherness" enforced upon us in this situation, there was plenty of "rubbing" at the friction points. Lately, I had been making it a special matter of prayer that God would give us a spirit of love for each other, and keep us from quarreling.

I looked over and saw Jay sitting alone on a fallen tree by the front fence, and my heart went out to him. I also had a growing feeling that much of what he had said was true. In our concern for survival, and our uncertain fears about the future, we had become introspective and self-protective. I wanted to go over and tell Jay this, but was uncertain about what to say and afraid of being misunderstood or rebuffed.

Finally though, I screwed up my courage, got up, and made my way over to the log. Jay looked up when I put my hand lightly on his shoulder.

"Jay," I said, "please don't give up on us. I know we've

85

got a long way to go, but we're trying. You're right, we have been pretty self-centered. But try to be patient with us and pray for us because God isn't through working on us."

All the hurt and disappointment he felt was in his voice as he burst out, "Carolyn, I just don't understand it. You people are supposed to be missionaries here, but sometimes I get the feeling you don't even *like* the Vietnamese people."

"Hey, wait a minute," I said. "We are here in Vietnam because we feel that God sent us to share his Word with the people here, but just because we're what you might call 'professional religionists' doesn't make us any better than anybody else. We're just *people*, Jay, with the same hang-ups and failures as anybody else." I was thinking as I spoke of all the critical comments and unloving attitudes we had been guilty of during the preceding days.

"And yet, of course," I went on, "we all do have a responsibility to demonstrate love. I'm glad you said what you did this afternoon, Jay, because I needed it.

"As for not liking the Vietnamese people, I'd have to say I don't really feel that I understand them. I've lived in Vietnam for fourteen years, but my involvement has been almost entirely with the Bru people, and they're completely different from the Vietnamese in both language and culture. With the Bru I feel completely at home. They are generally open and straightforward. They say exactly what they think and feel. But I've always felt the Vietnamese operate on two levels. The Bru say of them, 'the Vietnamese have two gall bladders.'"

"I think if you ever had a chance to get to know the Vietnamese people in a rural community setting, you'd really like them," Jay said.

"You're probably right," I agreed. "I wish I'd had the opportunity."

We sat in silence on the log for a few minutes, and then I said, "Jay, I'm concerned that we have harmony and unity as a group. We're a 'mixed bag' in terms of backgrounds and personalities. But I'm praying that God will give us love and understanding toward each other."

"That's all very well," he replied, "but what about *them*," as the sweep of his arm took in the whole compound. "There are a thousand people in this camp, all of them worse off than we are. We at least have the hope that some day we'll get out of here and go back to a country where there is freedom. These men don't even have that hope. One of these men saw his wife and all his children killed in the fighting. Most of the others have no idea where their families are, or whether they'll ever see them again."

"The way I see it," he continued, "these may be the last weeks of my life. I'd like to spend them in a way that would do someone some good. These people are being fed a constant diet of anti-American propaganda. Maybe in some way I can counteract that by showing them that some Americans really care about them."

That night under our mosquito net, I related the conversation to John. "You know," I said, "I am really ashamed to think how defensive my attitude has been, and how unloving."

"I know," John agreed, "and if anything, my attitude has been even worse. Lately God has really been speaking to me about that as I've been reading the book of Philippians. Those prison epistles have come alive for me in a new way." Together we asked God's forgiveness and help for the days ahead.

The following Sunday, when we held our little service, John shared with us some of the verses that had particularly spoken to him.

"Don't just think about your own affairs, but be interested in others, too, and in what they are doing," he read. "Your attitude should be the kind that was shown by Jesus Christ, who, though he was God, did not demand and cling to his rights as God, but laid aside his mighty power and glory, taking the disguise of a slave and becoming like man."

As God began to work in my heart, I found my attitude toward our Vietnamese fellow prisoners changing. I began to see them as individuals, each one with needs and concerns, hopes and fears, many of which I also shared.

At first we listened with skepticism to the glowing reports of the advance of the revolution. But new prisoners, who were brought in confirmed the report that first Pleiku, then Danang, Hue, Dalat and other cities were capitulating to the Communist forces. The prisoners were expected to cheer enthusiastically each time it was announced that another place had been entirely "liberated."

One morning Bath Man came into the compound all smiles, and told us, "I just heard the news that Nha Trang has been liberated!"

My heart constricted as I thought about our three children, and wondered what had happened to them. Probably Wycliffe officials would have had sufficient warning of the deteriorating situation to get the school children and other personnel out of the area before the fighting overtook them. But camp officials had told us that in Danang panic conditions had made evacuation so difficult that "hundreds of American military advisors in civilian clothing were left standing on the beach." Could this have happened in Nha Trang, too?

We had left a will on file in Saigon designating my parents as guardians of our children in the event of our death. Would our director assume that we were dead and send Margie, Gordon and Nate to their grandparents, or would they keep them in Vietnam or the Philippines, hoping that we were alive and would be released? Previous experience would probably not tend to make them hopeful, I thought.

I headed for the latrine corner, mainly to get away for a few minutes. I swallowed hard to hold back the tears, worrying how the children would adjust to being cut loose from the security of the school on top of the loss of their parents.

Nate had had a hard time adjusting to being away from us for the first time. It nearly broke my heart, when he asked me as we left to go up to Banmethuot the previous September, "If you love me, why are you leaving me here?"

I had explained to him that it was because we loved him that we were leaving him there, but John and I were prepared to move back to Nha Trang, or bring him with us to Banmethuot if he found the separation too hard. On more recent visits, he assured us he was happy in the Children's Home, and gave glowing reports of all the activities there. When I referred to the question he had asked at the beginning of the year, he looked puzzled. "Did I say that?" he asked. How was he adjusting to another new situation, I wondered?

Gordon had matured a great deal over the last year. Still I was concerned about how he would make out without us. He was impulsive and often thoughtless. He didn't show his feelings outwardly, and sometimes appeared to be unconcerned, when inside he was feeling very deeply about something. Would someone be able to recognize that underneath his facade of confidence and bravado was a boy who greatly needed encouragement and approval?

Margie had qualities of steadiness, resiliency and sensitivity to others that made me feel confident she would cope. I wished now that during Christmas vacation she had not read a book about the experiences of the missionaries who had been taken captive in 1968. She could have no way of knowing that what we were experiencing, at least thus far, was quite different from what Hank, Betty and Mike had gone through. I knew she would feel a certain amount of responsibility for helping her two brothers. Sometimes though their juvenile antics embarrassed her, and I prayed she would be patient and sensitive to their needs.

Concern and uncertainty about the children was heightened when one of the camp officials complained that the U.S. imperialists were stealing Vietnamese children. "Just a few days ago," he said, "a plane carrying hundreds of children to the U.S. crashed, killing most of the passengers." I guessed that most of these children would have been orphans, being taken to the U.S. for adoption, but wondered whether our children or some of our friends' might have been on the flight. Not for another seven months did we learn that our children were by that time safely in the Philippines, where they finished the school term with their schoolmates from Vietnam before going on to their grandparents in Houghton, New York.

Up until this time, John and I were hoping and thinking in terms of being released and continuing work in other areas of Vietnam. But as one area after another was "liberated," we realized that in all probability we would never again live and work in Vietnam. In the face of tremendous

89

openness and hunger for the Word of God throughout the country, it was hard to understand why God would allow events to take this turn.

A Vietnamese prisoner voiced the same concern to me as I sat on a log visiting with a group of them one day. This particular man and I had discovered a common bond in that we were roughly the same age, and both had children in Nha Trang. When he learned I was a missionary, he asked me, "Why has God allowed this to happen to Vietnam? Is he punishing us or what?"

"I don't know," I confessed to him, "I've wondered the same thing. Maybe," I suggested, "God wants to teach the people of Vietnam something. I think sometimes God has to bring us into difficult situations before we are willing to acknowledge and listen to him."

I told him I had once heard a Bru man talking about the hard times they had experienced during the war years. He said they had lost their homes and fields when the South Vietnamese government moved them from their mountain villages into resettlement areas near Khe Sanh in Quang Tri province. Then when the Communists invaded that area, they lost livestock, possessions and even family and friends as they fled down toward the coast. At the time this man was speaking, they were living in cardboard and tin shacks in a refugee camp.

"If none of these things had happened," he said, "we'd probably still be living in the mountains with plenty to eat and with all our possessions. But we'd still be sacrificing to appease the spirits, and we'd never have heard about Jesus Christ and what he did for us." In his estimation, finding Christ had been well worth the suffering.

Escape from the camp was a tempting possibility. With so many prisoners, so few guards and a minimum of organization, it would not have been too difficult to slip away from a work detail or drift down the river while bathing. I'm sure many of the men seriously considered the various risks.

But the prospect of evading recapture and subsequent punishment, or death, was another matter altogether. By now the entire highlands was controlled by the Liberation

Army. The possibility that a foreigner without a knowledge of the area and without provisions could make it to the coast undetected was remote. The situation for an ethnic Vietnamese was almost as bad. Whatever civilian population there was in this remote area was of mountain tribespeople. Centuries of suspicion and distrust between the ethnic minority and majority groups made it unlikely that any tribesperson would undertake, at a risk to his family and village, to help any ethnic Vietnamese person escape from other Vietnamese.

It both puzzled and amused us that the guards seemed to fear we might try to escape. Once in the muggy stillness of the early evening, I stepped outside the shelter to take advantage of any currents of air that might be stirring. The ground was still wet from an earlier shower, and Peter and Paul had moved our small brown suitcase outside to sit on while talking.

"Why don't you sit here for a while?" Peter said, getting up and offering me his half of the suitcase. I sat down beside Paul and listened to their conversation. I never ceased to marvel at the breadth of Peter's knowledge. He had read widely and could discuss with familiarity subjects ranging from American popular music to natural history, political theory, modern movies or the habits and society of ants.

Paul and I stood up to change position and Peter was moving over to take Paul's place on the suitcase when a guard happened by. He stopped abruptly as the beam from his flashlight came to rest on us.

"Where are you going?" he challenged.

"Going?" I answered stupidly uncomprehendingly. "We're not going anywhere."

"It's hot," Paul said in English fanning himself to get the meaning across. Then he sat down on the suitcase to demonstrate its function.

The guard gave a darkly suspicious look and walked on. Not till he left did it occur to us what must have gone through the guard's mind when he saw the three of us standing outside our shelter at night with a suitcase. We burst out laughing at the ludicrous picture we presented.

When he could finally stop laughing, Paul said, "I won-

91

der if he actually thinks we would take our suitcase with us, if we decided to sneak off through the jungle?"

The only prisoners who could have seriously entertained the idea of escape were those few from the ethnic minority groups of the area. One morning news flashed through the camp that five of these men had disappeared during the night. Jay discovered that one of them was a young kitchen worker with whom he had become friends. "How could he do a thing like that?" Jay commented. "I was teaching him to sing 'Old Macdonald had a Farm' and he hadn't learned all the words yet!"

The escape brought about a tightening of security measures. Inspections were held twice a day, and leaders chosen from each group were responsible to see that each man was accounted for. Jay had earlier been designated as our leader because of his fluency in Vietnamese, but was not called upon to report. It was easy to see at a glance that we were all there.

At night the guards were inclined to be edgy. A night or two after the escape, I was awakened by the voice of a guard excitedly demanding to know how many of us were there. "Twelve," one of us answered sleepily.

"Is everyone there?" he persisted, shining his flashlight inside the nets.

"Yes, yes," we assured him.

"Now what would cause that?" I wondered aloud as the guard walked off.

"It's my fault, I guess," Paul said. "I walked over to the fence to answer the call of nature, and I guess he saw movement there and thought someone was escaping."

It wasn't till the next morning we discovered there had, in fact, been one of us missing when we were questioned. Jay had been outside the fence at the time, drinking coffee and discussing life in Hanoi with Bath Man and some of the other soldiers. It was a good thing the guard didn't check too closely because none of the rest of us knew he'd gone.

The only time I ever heard a guard speak harshly to LuAnne was during this rather tense period. From the time of our arrival, the guards and officers had gone out of their way to be kind to her. In the absence of toys, Happy had

92

given her a little round tin of aromatic salve to play with and a small picture calendar. He made it clear that although the rest of us were restricted to the stockade, LuAnne was free to go outside the fence if she wished.

In fact the guards consistently tried to get her to go out with them offering her whatever treats or goodies they had in their houses as inducement. But though she sorely wanted the goodies, she refused to go. At first she begged, "Mommy, you go with me." But when she learned I could not go, nothing would persuade her to go. "If they want to give me those things," she said to me once, "why don't they bring them here?"

Her little friend, Thuy, however, took full advantage of every invitation to go out with the guards. On one occasion the Glorious Leader invited both little girls to have dinner with him, but even though Thuy begged her to go and promised to take care of her, LuAnne refused. Thuy always came back with glowing reports of the good things she'd had to eat at the guards' houses, but LuAnne never weakened.

At first I tried to persuade LuAnne to go out with the guards when she was invited. I wanted her to have the things they wanted to give her, and I had no fear they would abuse her in any way. At the same time, I knew as did she that if she got into a situation on the outside of the fence which was confusing or frightening to her, there was no way I could go to help her. So I was relieved, in a way, that she didn't want to go out.

Bath Man was especially eager to make friends with LuAnne, and teased her that he was going to take her home with him to Hanoi. LuAnne liked this outgoing young man, and sensed the kindness behind his brusque manner and loud voice. "There's my friend," she would say when she saw him around the compound.

One afternoon I was lying in the shelter feeling weak and listless from infection and fever. Earlier Bath Man had stopped by to invite LuAnne to go outside the stockade with him, but by this time she had refused so many times he didn't really expect her to go. I could hear LuAnne chattering away to Joan and Betty just outside the shelter as I drifted in and out of consciousness, so I knew she was in good hands. I became aware that a guard was shouting at someone, but paid no attention until I heard LuAnne crying and Joan quietly trying to comfort her.

"Joan," I said pushing myself up on one elbow, "did that shouting have something to do with LuAnne? What did she do?"

Joan came over to me. "Yes, he was shouting at LuAnne and it frightened her," she said. "I don't think it's anything to worry about, though. You see, Bath Man was on the outside of the fence playing with LuAnne. You know, motioning for her to come out and that sort of thing. LuAnne was laughing and watching him, and she put her head and arm out through a hole in the fence. She wasn't hurting the fence and she couldn't have crawled through, but the guard at the main gate got very excited when he saw her. I don't think he saw Bath Man on the other side of the fence. Anyway, he pointed his gun at her and told her to get off the fence and stay away from it. I guess he realized afterward that he had overreacted, because he came over a few minutes later and told us quite civilly that if the little girl wanted to go out, she could go out the gate, but she shouldn't climb on the fence because she might break it."

"What a situation!" I thought helplessly. I could understand why the guard reacted the way he had, but how was a five-and-a-half-year old child to understand a situation where one soldier was smiling and waving to her, and another shouting and pointing a gun at her at the same time!

There was about the whole experience a certain feeling of unreality to me. Sometimes for no reason at all I would look around me with a feeling of disbelief, and think to myself, "Are these things really happening to me? Is this *me* sitting here inside a prisoner of war camp in the jungles? Am I actually experiencing what I always regarded as the worst thing that could possibly happen to me? And how different it is from what I would have imagined!"

One thing I had never imagined was the sense of isolation from the outside world. "You know," I remarked to John one day, "I feel as though we are in a time vacuum or that time has stopped. My mind tells me that days and weeks are

94

going by, and that for the rest of the world life is going on as usual. People are being born and dying. Decisions are being made. International crises are probably happening. People's lives are being changed in one way or another. But it is hard for me to actually believe it. I guess I'm like Rip Van Winkle, thinking life has stopped for everyone because it has stopped for me."

It was not actually accurate to say that life had stopped, because our days were filled with one thing or another. The thing that made it seem that time had stopped, I decided, was the sudden and complete cessation of responsibility. Aside from minor decisions involving LuAnne's care, there was nothing I actually *had* to do, except get up with the waking gong, go to bed at the bedtime gong and respond to the few directives we were given in between.

Each of us faced in different ways the problem of what to do with the hours between these events. John spent the time reading. With the return of our large brown suitcase had come the return of a 1500-page Bible Dictionary and some commentaries and exegetical helps that we had hoped to return to the Wycliffe Library in Nha Trang. I envied John his ability to tune out the rest of the world and spend hours reading his Bible or these other books. But though I tried, I could not seem to concentrate on reading. Jay had brought along a novel which he read so many times he could quote passages from memory, but even this failed to hold my interest. The long descriptive passages bored me and the plot didn't seem worth pursuing.

"You really ought to get hold of yourself and find some constructive way to use all this free time," my conscience nagged me. I figured that if my dad were in this same situation he would by now have memorized half the New Testament and written a couple of books beside.

Memorization seemed a good idea. I decided to add Psalm 139 to the twenty or so Psalms I had learned as a child. This assurance of God's complete understanding and concern for me as an individual encouraged me. I might not have all the answers to my questions and doubts, but I was sure of his presence. "How precious also are thy thoughts unto me, O God! How great is the sum of them! If I should count them, they are more in number than the sand: when I awake I am still with thee."

I was not the only one to receive comfort from the realization of God's presence. One evening at dusk, John remarked with a sigh to no one in particular, "Well, I'd better take one last trip out that 'lonely path' before it gets dark," and headed off to the corner of the stockade.

He started off and noticed with surprise that LuAnne was following him. Apparently she too had decided to make a trip to the latrine before it got too dark to see, he thought. But when they got out there, she just stood quietly, waiting for him. When John questioned her she said, "No, Daddy, I didn't need to come out. I just came with you so you wouldn't be lonely."

Then as they started back she took his hand and looked up at him. "Anyway, Daddy," she said, "even if I didn't come with you, you wouldn't be lonely because Jesus is with you. Jesus is always with us."

At one point John and I decided we would use the time to continue reading and checking the Bru New Testament manuscripts. For several days we worked on it diligently. He read the Bru and I followed the Greek text. But without access to the reference books we customarily used, we seemed to be raising more problems than we were solving. And with the dust and heat, John's voice was beginning to feel the strain of too much use. So we gave it up.

Deciding to combine the job of entertaining LuAnne with preparing her to start first grade, I worked on a series of lessons using the phonic principles we had used in constructing literacy materials to teach the Bru people to read and write their language. LuAnne enjoyed this and learned the sheets almost as quickly as I could make them up. But after the novelty wore off, the lessons petered out. It was more fun to march around the compound with Thuy and her little brother playing guard. The prisoners smiled to see the three of them, one behind the other, with sticks over their shoulders patroling inside the compound.

One after another all my efforts to use this time profitably seemed to fall off. My attempt to read the New Testament

Carolyn Paine with her family at the Buffalo airport just before leaving for Vietnam, June 16, 1961.

Carolyn arriving at the French Protestant Church in Saigon for her wedding to John Miller, July 28, 1961.

The Miller house near Quang Tri. Their Land Rover is in the left foreground.

The Miller family in January, 1975, two months before John, Carolyn and LuAnne, 5, were taken prisoners. The other children are Gordie, Nate and Margie.

Vietnamese woman grinding pepper on the porch of her house near Quang Tri.

Carolyn with her first child, Margie, 1963.

Bru child with pipe caring for a younger sibling, Quang Tri.

John and Carolyn working on the Bru New Testament with their language consultants.

Exhibit at the Exhibition Center in Hanoi, showing thirty years of revolution in Vietnam. The Millers visited this center in November, 1975, just prior to their release.

Norman and Joan Johnson and their children, Pat and Doug.

Richard and Lillian Phillips and their children, Ruth, Brian, John and Jean.

The Press Conference at Bangkok Airport immediately after the "Banmethuot 14" were released from prison in Hanoi. Seated left to right: Jim Lewis, Paul Struharik, Arellano "Bogh" Bugarin, Enrique "Ike" Tolentino, Betty Mitchell, LuAnne, John and Carolyn Miller, Jay Scarborough, Lillian and Richard Phillips. Not in the picture: Norman and Joan Johnson and Peter Whitlock.

LuAnne Miller at the Narai Hotel with some of the toys she accumulated while in confinement by the Vietcong.

Betty Mitchell.

Jay Scarborough.

Carolyn Miller at her desk in Houghton, New York, 1977.

through in Greek took me only through the first few chapters of Matthew. I couldn't seem to retain the things I tried to memorize. Even games failed to hold much interest.

Jay found a prisoner who was willing to trade a deck of cards for a pack of cigarettes, and the smokers in our group decided to give up one of their precious packs in the interest of entertainment. For a while this took up quite a bit of time for Paul, Ike, Peter and Jay, but after a while their interest paled.

This feeling of lethargy was not unique to me. I think we all felt it. Norm for example was delighted when he arrived to learn that Lil had brought a game of Pit. "We used to stay up half the night playing with some of our friends," he said. But I recall seeing Norm and Joan playing Pit with Dick and Lil only one time.

One activity we women never gave up. Except when we were too sick to make the trip, we continued to go to the river every day to bathe. As time went on it became harder to make the effort, and the climb back up the hill seemed longer and longer, but we persisted.

For LuAnne this was the high point of the day. After the midmorning rice meal, which might come any time between 8:30 and 10 A.M., she would start to ask me, "How much longer till we go to bathe?"

We usually went around 11 A.M. since this had been theoretically reserved for women, and there were fewer men at the river at that time. One of the guards had shown us a path leading to a beautiful shady area just down stream from the regular bathing area, and it was the closest thing to privacy we had encountered since we left home. In the cool water we could almost shed with the dirt and perspiration the tensions of the day.

LuAnne played happily in the water while I rinsed the clothes we had worn that day. If Aunt Betty would take her out to the middle of the stream and help her "swim," her day was complete.

"Do we *have* to go yet?" she would ask when I called her back to the river bank.

"Yes, come on," I would answer. As we struggled back up the hill with our wet clothes under the glare of the noonday sun I often thought, "By the time we get up the hill from taking a bath, we need another one."

We were forbidden to lie down except at night, during rest hour or when we were ill, but as time went on we began to spend more and more time sleeping. One afternoon Bath Man came by after the gong had rung for the end of the rest hour. Jay was sitting in the shelter playing solitaire, LuAnne was out with Thuy and the rest of us were all lying down.

"Why is everyone lying down?" Bath Man asked Jay.

"Some of them are sick," Jay replied, "and the others are just resting."

"Well, get them up," said Bath Man. "The rest hour is over."

"Why should I get them up?" Jay asked. "What are they supposed to do?"

"They can read or play cards or talk," suggested Bath Man.

"We have played cards till we're sick of playing cards," Jay exploded. "We've read everything we have to read and exhausted every topic of conversation we can think of. There's nothing else to do. While they are sleeping they don't have to think about being prisoners and worry about their families and children. I'm not going to wake them up. If you want them to get up, you tell them."

I peeked out through partly closed lids and saw Bath Man was as surprised by Jay's outburst as I was. It was the first time I heard Jay show any irritation toward the guards. He had, in fact, annoyed some of the others of the group by toning down strong statements of theirs when he translated them into Vietnamese so as not to antagonize camp authorities.

Bath Man retreated without further comment.

Our apathy might have been accounted for in part by poor diet, sickness and lack of physical stamina. And no doubt the distraction and tension of constant association with people and their problems contributed its share. But I think in large part it was due to gnawing uncertainty about our future and our inability to influence it in any way.

If we had no control over what happened to us today, and obviously we hadn't, how much less could we predict

98

what would happen tomorrow? We might speculate, or hope or pray, but we certainly couldn't plan or anticipate. And beyond assuring us that they were "studying our case" the officers holding us were careful not to divulge any plans they had for us.

One discussion about our future was overheard and reported to us by Dr. Ly, an obstetrician-gynecologist, who had been drafted to serve as an army doctor, and whose service in a government hospital in the highlands had been interrupted by capture and internment here at "Camp Sunshine."

I had been surprised one afternoon to be addressed by a good-looking man in his mid-thirties, who was just being brought in with a group of prisoners. As the group filed past our shelter, he stepped out of line and spoke quietly in flawless English, and with a sense of urgency I found unusual in a complete stranger. "I am a doctor, and I want to urge you to do everything you can to keep your strength up. If your health fails, nobody is going to take care of you. Get all the exercise you can." I thanked him for his advice and passed it out to the others of the group who had not heard him.

Sometime later Dr. Ly was sitting on a fallen log in front of our shelter conversing with Joan and Betty. "I think they are going to take you to Hanoi," he said.

"What makes you say that?" they inquired.

"I was in a work party cleaning up the area around the guards' houses," he said, "and I heard them talking about the 'foreigners.'"

When Joan and Betty related this conversation to the rest of us, reactions varied.

"I hope they do take us to Hanoi," was Jay's response. "It might be interesting to see what life is like in the North."

"That's all very well for you to say, Jay," Norm responded. "You don't have kids you're worried about. As for me, I couldn't care less about life in the North. I just want to get out of here and be with my kids."

"I'm not exactly crazy about being a prisoner either, Norm," Jay retorted, "but we don't have much choice about that. Since we are prisoners, we might as well make the best of it. Anyway, I figure almost anything has got to be an improvement over just sitting around here."

"I doubt if we'd see much of life in the North even if we were taken up there," was Paul's comment. "It's not as though we'd be going as tourists."

For myself, I hoped we wouldn't be taken to Hanoi. To me that would seem to indicate a long period of internment. Besides that, so long as we were in South Vietnam I felt we were in familiar territory and surrounded by friendly and sympathetic people. To be taken north would be to travel into unknown territory and among people who would probably be hostile and unsympathetic.

"I don't really think they'll take us to North Vietnam," I said to John, "because they have made such a point about being the Liberation Army of *South* Vietnam. It seems to me they're trying to play down northern involvement."

For a while I did try to take Dr. Ly's advice about getting physical exercise. Each morning after getting up and folding the net and tarps, I would go through some bending and stretching exercises in a not-too-strenuous manner. Several of the others in our group began running in place and jack-in-the-box jumping. Paul refused to be a part of the nonsense, and Peter's only concession to morning calisthenics was that on his morning trip to the place he referred to as the "tulip patch," he would jog to the corner of the stockade and back again.

Peter and I even decided one day to try to get some exercise by hitting a tennis ball back and forth to each other in the area by the front gate where the political lectures were held. The trees had been cleared from that area and the ground was hard from constant use.

"Let's go, Billie Jean," he said as we headed over to the corner with the tennis rackets.

"I look more like Daisy Duck," I laughed looking down at my feet. I had put on John's hushpuppies for protection against the rocks and stumps. The ball bounced crazily as it hit bumps in the ground and stumps of trees. Out of the corner of my eye I saw Dr. Ly watching in amusement as I dove after the ball with more enthusiasm than skill.

"So much for that idea," I thought as I put the ball back in

100

the suitcase, zipped it and shoved it under the sleeping platform.

The end of my physical fitness efforts, however, was brought about by the very thing they were undertaken to prevent—physical unfitness. On the day we moved to our new shelter, I seemed to be coming down with the same symptoms John had been suffering for several days—fever, sore throat and headache. But several days later John was feeling a bit better, whereas I was getting weaker. Dick and Norm seemed to be coming down with the same thing. Betty and Joan took over caring for LuAnne as I lay on the floor of the shack, getting up only when I needed to make the trip to the latrine and collapsing again when I got back. Lil tried several times to get help from the North Vietnamese medic, who came into the camp twice a day, but he had very little to offer. Ever since the difficult truck trip she herself had suffered from a recurrence of phlebitis for which she had been hospitalized some months earlier.

On the morning of April 3 when I got up to make the trip to the latrine, waves of dizziness engulfed me. I clutched at one of the bamboo roof supports and waited for the blackness to recede, but this time it didn't. My head was ringing and I could feel my grip on the pole loosening. I sat down and crawled back to our corner where I lay panting for breath. Never in my life had I felt so completely weak and helpless.

We had often discussed in a theoretical way the limitations of our current diet and how long one could hope to sustain life without vitamins and other basic nutrients. But on that morning the question was no longer an academic one for me. I felt that the weeks of inadequate food had already left my body helpless to cope with an infection that under other circumstances or with medication would not have been serious at all. At that point it seemed to me not just possible, but probable, that I would die there in the jungle.

John, who was sitting beside me on the floor, reached out and put his cool hands on my face. I opened my eyes and looked at him.

"John," I whispered, "I don't think I'm going to make it."

"Don't get discouraged," he said quietly. "I think you'll pull out of it in a few days."

101

"Honey, if they were to let us go today I'm too weak to go. And without proper food and medicine I think the only way to go is down. I'm not afraid to die. That really doesn't worry me at all. But I hate to think of leaving you and LuAnne here, and I hate to think I won't get to see the other kids again."

John squeezed my hand reassuringly, but his eyes were worried. We had a time of prayer together, then he moved over to the other end of the shelter to talk to Lil, and in a few minutes she came over to talk to me.

"I think your body has more reserves than you feel it has," she said. "Don't worry, you'll get to see your kids again. I will make a strong push to try to get the medic to give you something though."

True to her word, Lil pressured the medic for medicine to give me and voiced concern that some of the others seemed to be coming down with the same thing. He was sympathetic but not overly concerned. Nevertheless, Lil came back jubilant. The medic had given her three days worth of antibiotic as well as injections of vitamin C and B to give.

The syringes were old and the needles dull, but I said to John that afternoon as I rubbed my sore hip, "I never thought I would ever feel so thankful to get a shot, and especially a vitamin shot!" That afternoon I was able to make it to the latrine with John's help and over the succeeding days recovered a measure of strength.

All of the men were taken to a thatch hut outside the camp for interrogation at least once. Peter was questioned about his reason for being in Vietnam and everyone he had contacted during his five days in the country. Dick reported that the interrogator seemed most interested in the fact that he was a third generation missionary, and that during World War II he had spent time in a Japanese prison camp in China. Paul was taken out several times and on each occasion he was asked and refused to give a list of his Vietnamese and tribal employees.

"I just don't feel right about giving it to you," he told them. "Those people are not only employees, but they are friends. Do you think I want them to end up in a place like this?"

102

"If you will not cooperate with us, you must suffer the consequences," the interrogator warned.

"What will be the consequences?" Paul pressed. But the man refused to be more specific.

John and Ike were taken out on the same morning. John had been sick the day before, and I was concerned as to whether he was strong enough for a long period of questioning.

"I might as well get it over with," he said, and followed the guard out of the gate. He returned in the afternoon quite depressed.

"How did it go?" I asked.

"Pretty badly, I'm afraid," John answered. "He didn't seem to believe anything I said, and said I was lying."

"Why?" I asked, alarmed. "What did you tell him?"

"I knew as soon as I walked in I was in trouble. Happy was going to do the interview, and they had that guy from the Rose Garden to interpret."

"Oh no," I groaned, "not him!"

"Yes, him! It was even worse than I expected. Half the time I couldn't understand the question, but if I asked for clarification or said I didn't understand, he accused me of evading. One question he asked me was 'What are your opinions?' Now how was I supposed to answer a question like that?"

"You could have given him your opinions on hair styles or the price of gasoline," I suggested. But John failed to see any humor in the situation.

"Every time the interpreter translated what I was saying, he did it with a sneer as if to indicate he knew it wasn't true, but there it was. If he had actually translated what I said, it would have been one thing, but even with my poor knowledge of Vietnamese I could tell he wasn't saying the same thing."

"Why didn't you try to answer in Vietnamese?" I asked.

"I did once or twice," he said, "but any time I tried it seemed to really irritate the interpreter."

"When did Happy accuse you of lying?" I asked.

"Well, it was really strange. He kept asking me questions

103

about American military policy, and I told him I didn't know anything about that. Then he asked if I knew about the American major in the Pentagon who had become convinced of the wrongness of the Vietnamese war and divulged a lot of secret military information. I told him I didn't know about this major, and he hit the roof. 'Everybody in the world knows about that, and you can sit here and tell me you don't know! You are lying! You say you are a missionary, but you sit here and tell lies to me!' I told him, 'Everything I have said to you is true. Whether or not you want to believe it, that's up to you. I do not recall reading about this major you mention.' "

"I don't know who he was talking about either," I said, puzzled. "Why didn't you ask him the man's name?"

"I did," John said, "but he didn't seem to remember it."

"I wonder if he was thinking of Daniel Ellsberg," I mused. "He wasn't a major so far as I know, but . . ."

"Of course!" John said. "I'll bet that was what he was referring to. Happy didn't have the facts straight, but that's the only thing he would say the whole world knows about."

"I'm afraid if Happy has anything to say about it, we're going to be here a long time," he concluded. "He told me to go back and think about what he had told me, and he would talk to me again."

That night just before we went to sleep, John remembered another part of the interview, "You know, the first question Happy asked me today was, 'Why are you here?' I didn't know if he meant 'here in this prison camp' or 'here in Vietnam,' so I asked him. He said he meant 'here in this prison camp.' I think he expected me to say, 'I don't know,' and was probably all set to tell me my crime. But I didn't think of that at the time. I answered, 'I'm here because God put me here.'

"Happy looked a bit surprised at my answer, but then he got a big smile on his face and asked, 'Why did God put you in a place like this?'

"I said, 'I'm sure I don't know all the reasons, but probably he has something to teach me. Or maybe he has some-

104

thing to teach my family, or the people back in America who support us.'

"When the interpreter told him what I said, Happy just put his hands up and shook his head and changed the subject."

"He probably doesn't believe that," I said, "but I do. I feel like I've learned a lot already, but I'll sure be glad when this lesson is over!"

FIVE

Camp Wilderness

LuAnne stirred restlessly in her sleep and threw her legs over my hips. Only half awake myself, I reached down to move them off again, and was suddenly wide awake. Even through her slacks I could feel the burning heat from her body. "Oh-oh," I thought, "her temperature is up again."

I touched John on the other side of me. "John, what time is it?" I whispered.

"2:30," he answered, checking. "What's the matter?"

"It's LuAnne. She's burning up," I said. "I think we'd better check her temperature and give her some more aspirin."

Moving quietly so as not to disturb the others, I felt for Lil's thermometer in my purse inside the net. I took it from the tiny metal case, shook it hard, slipped it beneath LuAnne's shirt and held it under her arm. Reading the thermometer was a problem. John rummaged through the market bag to find the little candle we had brought for just such an emergency and lit it inside the net. Turning the thermometer next to the candle I could barely make it out.

"What is it?" John wanted to know.

"104.8," I said.

John slipped out at the bottom of the net to get some water from the Wesson Oil jug and an aspirin tablet. I picked LuAnne up and sat her on my lap. She swallowed the aspirin without protest, though it obviously hurt her throat to swallow.

106

"I think I'll just put her down by your feet," I told John. "That way her kicking won't wake Peter." Peter, sleeping only inches away, had so far not stirred with the commotion.

I lay at the foot of the net beside her and listened as she began to talk. She spoke quietly and rapidly, trying to tell me a story. I couldn't help smiling in spite of my concern, because the story was nonsensical. She was combining two or three Bible stories with elements of the bedtime fairy tale I had told her earlier. In the middle of the story she lapsed off into sleep.

Within an hour the fever broke. I felt LuAnne break into perspiration, and with a prayer of fervent thanks to the Lord, I fell asleep beside her.

When the wake-up gong sounded, I felt as if I could hardly drag myself up to the level of consciousness. I lay at the foot of the net hating the thought of waking to another cold gray dawn.

I felt someone take hold of my leg through the mosquito net and looked up.

"Oh, I'm sorry," came Peter's surprised voice from outside the net. "I thought LuAnne was there and was wondering how she was doing."

"I moved her in the night so she wouldn't waken you with her kicking," I explained.

"Did she have a bad night?" he asked.

"Her fever went up to 104.8, but it's not that high now, and she seems to be sleeping all right."

Throughout the day LuAnne did little but sleep. She refused food but took the aspirin we gave her through the day. The North Vietnamese medic seemed genuinely concerned about her and asked one of the South Vietnamese doctors to look at her. He then brought over some tetracycline tablets and told us to give them to her. Bath Man stopped by a couple of times to see how she was. Toward evening she complained of stomach problems and, leaning over the edge of the sleeping platform, vomited the last medicines she had taken.

That night was a repeat of the previous one as LuAnne's temperature soared in the night. Toward morning she called out from a feverish dream, "Mommy! Nate's got a Coke!"

107

Her own speech woke her up, and she chuckled when she realized what she had said.

"I really thought Nate was here," she explained to me. "And I thought he was drinking a Coke. It looked so good I wanted some too."

The wake-up gong sounded at 5 A.M. as usual. LuAnne woke up complaining about her stomach again. She leaned over the edge gagging and retching, though she had nothing but stomach fluids to bring up.

A guard came over at 5:30 while we were still getting nets and tarps folded and put away for the day.

"Get all your things together," he instructed. "You are being moved to another location."

We were galvanized into action and into excited expectation.

"I think they're going to release us," was Norm's opinion. "Now that they've released the ICCS men and everyone knows we're being held, they've almost *got* to let us go."

"There must have been some reason they let us make out those 'Requests for Leniency' to the Provisional Revolutionary Government last week," one of the women said.

"That would be pretty quick action," someone else said. "Maybe now that they control most of the country they've decided to take us to Pleiku or Banmethuot or some less isolated place."

I was rather concerned about LuAnne's ability to stand a long truck ride in her condition. At the same time I was hopeful that a move would mean more adequate food and medicine for her. John tied a piece of paper around one of the blackened milk tins so we could carry it for her to use when she needed to vomit.

The news spread quickly that we were leaving. A number of Vietnamese prisoners came to stake a claim on space in our shelter. Even though it leaked, it was an improvement over sleeping on the open ground. Others asked for milk tins, water-boiling cans and other equipment.

"I wish we knew where we were going," Betty said. "If we're going to be released, we could leave most of what we have for the men here."

Paul and John advised, "Until we know for sure, we'd better keep everything we have."

Bath Man came into the compound to take us out to a waiting truck. Norm grabbed him in a bear hug and swung him around saying jubilantly, "We're going home! We're going home!"

I hoped he was right, but I noticed we were not the only ones being taken out. Major and Mrs. Phuong and their children were also leaving. So was a young lieutenant who had recently arrived with a young child. So were a number of more seriously sick and injured prisoners.

Mrs. Phuong seemed happy. "I was told we are being taken to an established camp where there are better facilities," she told me.

John held LuAnne in his arms. She rested her head on his shoulder, too sick to care about anything. A short man with an air of command and wearing tinted glasses came over to us.

"She is ill?" he asked.

"Yes," I answered, "she is very ill."

"What is the matter with her?"

"The nurses say she probably has infected tonsils and her chest is congested," I said indicating Lil and Joan.

He immediately went to Lil and asked several questions. "Don't worry," he said, "a medic will accompany you. I will give him instructions to give her an injection if she needs it on the way."

We asked this "Mr. Spectacles" about the things that had been taken away from us. In addition to the cameras and photos taken from us upon capture, a soldier we had seen neither before nor since had come a few weeks later to get our typewriter and all personal papers. These included Paul's income tax records, Peter's passport, our address file, John's diary, etc. At the time Paul asked him hopefully if he didn't also want the sewing machine, but he declined, looking puzzled when we all laughed. He did, however, take from Jay a pack of letters and papers, which included the receipt for the cameras and things taken earlier.

"Don't worry about the things that were taken from

you," Mr. Spectacles said. "They will follow you and you will get everything back."

He motioned me to get into the cab of the Russian Molotova truck. We climbed in and I sat between two soldiers. LuAnne sat on my lap and leaned back against my shoulder. Forty other prisoners were loaded in the open back before some soldiers climbed in and the truck set off in a westerly direction.

We bumped along a little-traveled track through uninhabited areas till almost noon, when we came to a place where several roads intersected. The driver stopped and the soldier on the other side of me got out to look for signs. A rough, hand-lettered sign on the road we had come indicated it led to Darlac Province. A larger sign on the branch going south pointed the way to Loc Ninh. If we were to be released, it would probably be from there. Now I hoped we would turn that way!

But the soldier selected one of the two roads heading in the other direction, and my heart sank as we turned and started up the road. We were on the main Ho Chi Minh trail heading north, and release suddenly seemed a long, long way off.

A little later the truck forded a river and stopped to give the prisoners opportunity to eat the cold balls of cooked rice we had been given to take with us. Two of ours tasted terrible because a little bottle of mouthwash Lil had given us to use to clean the thermometer had leaked on them. We weren't hungry anyway, only hot and thirsty. It felt good to stand in the water, and splash water over ourselves.

Sitting on the ground watching the others eat, I suddenly realized not all of us were in the group.

"Where are Peter and Jay?" I asked John.

"There wasn't room for them on the truck," John replied, "so the soldiers said they'd have to wait for another truck."

The soldiers gave the signal to get back on the truck. This time LuAnne's friend, Thuy, also rode in front making it more crowded. My back, arms and legs were beginning to ache from holding LuAnne and cushioning her against the constant jostling of the truck. The seat was not deep enough to put her between my legs, and when I tried putting her beside me the driver protested that he couldn't shift. She was still sick and slept from sheer exhaustion most of the day.

I asked how long it would be until we reached our destination. "Before dark, I hope," was the answer. The wild, unspoiled scenery was probably beautiful, but I didn't have much appreciation for it. I longed for a glimpse of normal human life. Occasional burned-out shells of vehicles stood as mute witnesses to earlier periods when bombing interrupted the heavy travel on the trail, but we saw not one other moving vehicle the entire day.

Toward late afternoon, we met one soldier walking along the road. The driver stopped, apparently to check on our progress. I laid LuAnne on the seat and got out of the truck to stretch out on the grass for a few minutes. It felt good to get out of the stifling heat of the cab.

A short time after that we came out onto a stretch of asphalt road. We passed an old abandoned military installation, the metal covered air strip pocked with craters and strewn with debris. One of the Vietnamese passengers later told us this was Duc Co. He had been stationed there for a period before the Americans pulled out and the base was abandoned.

The vivid brick-red color of the soil made me feel we were in the general area of Pleiku. I had been in Pleiku only once, but I had never forgotten the shock of seeing the vast expanses of red earth around the town. Its fine dust blew into the house where we were staying, covering everything. It stained the baby's knees where he crawled on the floor, and turned the older children's feet and legs a dark red hue that soap and water only partly lightened. "Maybe," I thought, "we are being taken to one of the old South Vietnamese army camps around the city of Pleiku." It had been military headquarters for the entire central part of the country, and would certainly have plenty of available housing.

This hope dimmed as we turned off the road and headed back into the jungle. Branches of trees struck the windshield and scraped along the truck. I worried about the people in

111

the back. At the same time, I would have eagerly traded places. My back was so sore it hurt to touch it, and every time the truck threw me against the seat I winced in pain.

Waves of self-pity swept over me as darkness came on and the truck moved inexorably into the jungle. "God, help me!" I cried silently. "I can't stand any more!" Instantly I felt rebuked for my complaint. I thought about Hank Blood and Betty Olson, and how they had walked for days and weeks, possibly through some of the same jungle areas that I had just ridden through. Their pain must have been considerably greater than mine.

I recalled a conversation we had at Camp Sunshine. We were complaining about some particularly high-handed or irritating restriction when Jay reminded us that we had in fact been treated a lot better than most of the American prisoners in the past. "I complained because I had no shoes," he had quoted, "until I met a man who had no feet."

"I don't think we need to feel grateful to them just because they haven't killed us, Jay," Paul protested.

I could see Paul's point. As citizens of foreign countries, we were entitled by international law to be in contact with representatives of our respective countries. Peter, Ike and the Johnsons were citizens of countries which had diplomatic representation with North Vietnam, and, so we were told, had recognized the Provisional Revolutionary Government. Yet even they had been denied their rights.

At the same time I was inclined to agree with Jay. "Thinking of what others have endured doesn't change the facts about what we are experiencing," I said, "but it does help us keep a sense of perspective about our problems."

A verse from Psalm 139 I had recently memorized came to mind, "Though I take the wings of the morning and dwell in the uttermost part of the sea, even there shall thy hand lead me and thy right hand shall hold me."

"God forgive me for complaining," I prayed. "This old Molotova truck couldn't be considered 'the wings of the morning,' and this isn't the sea, but there couldn't be any more 'uttermost' place in the whole world that I can think of. Thank you that you are leading me and holding me in your hand."

The truck finally stopped and we were told to unload everything. John unloaded our stuff while I sat on the ground with LuAnne. Norm's head had been gashed by a tree branch, but Joan could not see in the darkness if slivers were still in his scalp. Another branch had ripped Paul's shirt down the middle of his back, but his neck was spared by the hand towel he had put on earlier to shield it from the sun.

Aside from the few soldiers who came to meet the truck, there seemed no sign of life in the area. Was this merely a stopping off place for the night, we wondered?

"Bring everything with you and follow me," a soldier instructed. "I will take you to your new location."

"How far is it?" someone inquired.

"Not very far," he answered, "maybe a kilometer."

I groaned. The guards had a tendency to underestimate distances. "There's no way we can take everything," I said to John. "We'll have to leave the sewing machine and 'big brown.'" We opened "big brown" and took out the mosquito nets, tarp, blanket and pillows. I carried these and my purse, and took LuAnne's hand. She would have to walk. John had the market bag and small suitcase, heavy with books and manuscripts.

The guard cautioned us to stay close together, then set off down a small path. I could understand the warning when I allowed Ike to get more than a few feet ahead. In the darkness I hadn't the faintest idea which way to go, and felt helplessly with my feet until the sound of Ike's voice ahead steered me in the right direction.

"Hurry!" I urged LuAnne. "We've got to keep up with Uncle Ike."

Footsteps sounded behind as someone moved quickly through the underbrush beside the trail. I looked up in surprise as two North Vietnamese soldiers passed us. Between them a bamboo pole was suspended from their shoulders. Hanging from the pole by their handles were our big brown suitcase and the sewing machine!

A strange rustling sound on the ground near the path made me hesitate. Could it be snakes, I wondered? Occasionally someone behind would call out for us to stop and give them a chance to catch up, and we would pause until a

113

guard impatiently came along to see what was holding up progress.

"Hurry," he would urge. "Keep moving!"

We negotiated a couple of streams, and I found it easier to go up the steep banks rather than down in the dark. Suddenly I heard Lil scream. "Snakebite!" I thought, terrified.

"Keep moving, keep moving!" the guard ordered.

"Mommy, Mommy!" LuAnne screamed. Her voice was full of terror. After a bewildered moment I understood why. My legs felt as though they were on fire as ants swarmed over them biting me.

"Stamp your feet hard!" I told LuAnne. But she scrambled up into my arms and clung to me, wrapping her legs around me and shaking with pain and fright. Nothing would induce her to put her feet down.

"Keep going!" the guard said.

"She can't keep going," I answered exasperated. "She's sick and frightened, and she won't go." John gave me the market bag and lifted LuAnne in his arm. She had lost one of the little rubber-thonged sandals she was wearing, and in the darkness we could not find it. We left it and moved on. A week or two later when he was out on a work detail, Paul found it. The rubber sole had been chewed completely through by ants.

In the struggle to escape the ants we had gotten off the path, but now we could see up ahead what appeared to be a bonfire, and we moved toward it, ignoring brush and weeds that caught our clothes. The fire had been built in the center of a long pavilion approximately fifteen feet wide and ninety feet long. Split bamboo platforms about six feet wide and two feet high ran the entire length of the pavilion on both sides with an aisle roughly three feet wide down the middle. There were no walls.

"The married couples should sleep on this side of the aisle," a soldier said motioning to one end of the structure. I put the bedding and market bag on the end of the side indicated and sat down. The building had apparently been recently constructed since the sap was still sticky on the roof support corner posts.

114

"We are cooking rice and will feed you when it is done," a soldier informed us.

"I don't think I'll wait," I told John. We hung the net and I put LuAnne inside it. For the first time we had enough room to stretch the net to its complete double bed width. That and the substantial-looking thatch roof over us were certainly two things to be thankful for, I thought.

"Whatever you do, don't touch my back tonight," I warned John as I crawled in beside LuAnne.

"Clang! Clang clang! Clang clang clang!" If they didn't have anything else in this wilderness location, they obviously did have a gong. Every muscle in my body groaned in protest as I struggled to sit up inside the net.

A very young guard stood by looking grim faced and prepared for anything. All night long he had walked around the outside of the pavilion shining a flashlight into the nets as if expecting us to disappear at any moment.

A short, squat man came up the path to the pavilion as we were putting away our nets and bedding. "Everyone who is able to work must report for a work assignment. There is much to be done. You will work until ten o'clock. At that time you may stop to eat. When the gong strikes you will resume working until four o'clock. At that time you may go to the river to bathe before the afternoon meal. No one is allowed to leave the pavilion without permission of the guard. You will be expected to treat all camp personnel with respect and to obey all camp regulations. Is this clear?"

John, Paul, Norm and Dick were given shovels and assigned the task of digging a latrine for the use of the group. The women were to clean up the ground in and around the pavilion.

LuAnne was feverish again, and she was again retching. Her face was flushed, and when she awoke she talked quickly and too brightly. Most of the time she slept.

"You sit here beside me, okay, Mommy?" she asked before drifting off.

I sat on the end of the platform-bed and stared off into the jungle. So this was the "better location" we were promised, I

115

thought glumly. One lousy pavilion surrounded on all sides by jungle. To the right where the path led past "Jumpy," the guard, and the wheel rim "gong" hanging from a tree, I could barely discern a small thatch house where the guards apparently lived. A few yards to my left was a small clearing where a temporary kitchen had been set up. Several of the prisoners were busy boiling a cauldron of drinking water. Presumably the river was beyond that. That was the extent of the camp facilities. Less even than "Camp Sunshine."

In contrast to the camp personnel we had met here so far, Bath Man, Happy and even White Shirt seemed positively cordial. When we requested permission from "Jumpy" to go get some boiled water or to step into the underbrush to relieve ourselves, he had granted it with an unsmiling nod or a brusque "all right."

That morning a tall, good-looking medic appeared in the camp to dress the wounds of some of the Vietnamese prisoners. When he finished, Lil and I spoke to him about LuAnne.

"At the last camp, the medic gave her tetracycline and she has taken it for two days. I have enough to give her today but that is all. She is still quite sick. Could you give her some more?" I inquired.

"I have none," he answered.

"Do you have something else you could give?" Lil pressed.

"I have nothing to give her," he said curtly, and walked off without so much as looking at her.

I now sat beside LuAnne and struggled with tears. Why had they brought us here? John had wondered if we had been brought here to be killed, but his logical mind had rejected the suggestion. "Surely," he thought, "if they were going to kill us, they wouldn't go to all this bother to do it." At the same time it certainly didn't look as though they had any plans to release us in the near future. And the animosity of the guards was not encouraging.

I fumbled in the market bag for John's handkerchief to wipe my eyes. I also took out my little Bible and opened it to the place I was last reading, Psalm 146. "Praise ye the Lord. Praise the Lord, O my soul," I read. That doesn't seem very appropriate, I thought.

The next verse was even stronger. "While I live will I praise the Lord: I will sing praises unto my God while I have any being." This was not glib rhetoric when it was written, or light emotion, but an act of the will by a man whose very life was in doubt.

The rest of the chapter explained how the psalmist could do this. Though human aid had failed he had the God of Jacob for his help and his hope was in the Lord his God. As I thought about the present situation I had much for which to praise the Lord, and as I began to do so the heaviness of heart lifted.

We continued to be puzzled by the attitude of the guards. After initial suspicion wore off some of them relaxed and began to talk with us. But the next day they either avoided us or were surly.

"I request permission to go to the toilet," I said to the guard after LuAnne and I got up one morning.

"Of whom are you requesting permission?" he snapped.

"Of you, brother," I said, surprised.

"Then say so!" he ordered.

"Excuse me, but what am I supposed to say?" I asked.

"When you go you should say, 'I ask permission, *brother*, to go to the toilet,' and when you return you should say, 'I ask permission, brother, to go back in the house.'"

"All right," I agreed, and LuAnne and I went out to the latrine. When we returned I repeated what I had been told to say.

"Stand at attention when you address me!" he ordered. LuAnne, who was already running into the building, stopped and looked back puzzled as I straightened to attention and repeated the formula. The whole thing seemed ludicrous, and I had a hard time keeping a straight face. Betty, who was following me, made the mistake of snickering, and the guard made her stand at attention for several minutes before permitting her to enter.

The next day we were told we no longer needed to request permission to go to the latrine except at night, and the guards were again courteous. We were encouraged.

The following day our meager food ration was cut back, and we were all disturbed and worried. It was like going up and down on an emotional yo-yo, never being quite sure what the next day would bring.

Life at "Camp Wilderness," as we came to refer to it, was busier than at Camp Sunshine. After the men had built one outhouse, complete with thatch roof and walls, they were instructed to build another one for the use of the women. This was set a short distance from the men's latrine and on the edge of a huge bomb crater. I was reminded of Meteor Crater in Arizona as I carefully picked my way around the rim to our new outhouse. On nights when there was no moon the trip was quite hazardous, but the provision of this facility took Camp Wilderness a giant step ahead of Camp Sunshine in the estimation of us women.

"You know," Paul mused one time, "if we ever get out of here, I may be looking for a job. There isn't going to be much demand for a specialist on Darlac Province. I wonder if I could make it on the outside as an outhouse builder. Just think of all the valuable experience I'm getting in the field."

"Maybe I'll go into business with you," Norm volunteered.

We were not sure what kind of recommendation we could give them when the first heavy windstorm brought the superstructure down. Betty and Joan were the first ones up to the crater, and came back laughing at what had happened.

"It's a Communist plot to discredit us," Paul maintained. "I'll bet someone went up there in the night and knocked it down just to make it look as if we don't know how to build outhouses."

"It's at times like this," Joan laughed, "that I wish they hadn't taken our cameras away!"

After the latrines were finished there were other jobs. All supplies for the camp had to be carried in—hundred pound bags of "China Rice," and slightly lighter ones of coarse salt,

118

heavy tins of lard and fish powder. A trip from the storage area a couple of miles away left the men weak and exhausted. Paul and Norm volunteered for a work detail to go pick manioc, a starchy tuber which was being added to our diet. They were sorry they had offered to go when they had to carry heavy burlap sacks of the root down a rocky creek bed to get it back to camp. Prisoners also gathered building materials to construct two more pavilions, and cleared the jungle ground where they were to be built.

Days passed and there was still no sign of Peter and Jay or the other prisoners from Camp Sunshine.

"I wouldn't be surprised if they don't bring Peter and Jay here at all," John said.

"Why?" I asked. "Where do you think they would take them?"

"I think they might release them," he answered. "After all, Peter's government has had increasingly good relations with them."

"But Jay?" I protested. "He's an American!"

"Yes," John said, "but he's also a student, and they've made quite a point of how much the student anti-war activists have helped them."

"Well," I said, "I miss them. The group doesn't seem complete without them, but I hope you're right."

He wasn't. Eleven days after our arrival the other prisoners from Camp Sunshine began straggling in. When we saw Jay come over the rise of earth by the bomb crater, we ladies ran out to meet him.

"Jay, you look all in. How are you? How long have you been walking? Where's Peter?" we asked him almost in one breath.

"Peter's coming," he said. "We've been together all the way, but he took another trail coming in here, I guess." He handed me his jeans. I couldn't understand why they were so heavy, until I noticed they were tied at the ankles and the legs were filled with rice.

"That's what's left of the rice they issued us when we left a week ago," Jay explained following us into the pavilion. "Camp Sunshine is no more. Everyone is coming here. The

119

day after you left, they told us the truck that was supposed to take us had broken down, so we would have to walk. They gave us rice and salt to cook along the way. We'd have been in bad shape because by evening we were too tired to even think about cooking, but the guards took pity on us and cooked our rice with theirs most of the time.

"I'm not in too bad shape," Jay said. "Peter's worse off than I." But as he lifted the maroon striped trouser leg, I could see that one knee was badly swollen and inflamed.

When Peter appeared over the rise I hardly recognized him. He leaned on a stick and walked like an old man. When we hurried out to meet him I saw why. He had cut the front part of his shoes off, and his toes were wrapped individually with oozing rags. His mouth had completely disappeared in his thick, bushy beard. He was dusty and drooped with fatigue. He and Jay rested for a few minutes, then headed for a long soak in the river.

With the arrival of the Camp Sunshine contingent, the authorities did some reshuffling. There were to be three separate camps in the area, we were told—one for non-commissioned officers, one for lower ranking commissioned officers, and one, ours, for first lieutenants and higher ranking officers.

Work to complete the two additional structures in our camp went ahead with new urgency. Each of the three wall-less houses would hold approximately one hundred men. Because the Westerners in our house were bigger and took more space, only eighty-five were eventually put in it, even though the platform space was extended out under the roof overhang on our end for Jay and Peter on one side of the aisle, and Paul and Ike on the other.

A real spirit of camaraderie developed among the prisoners in our house, and I grew to value them as individuals. Major Phuong was put in charge of the house, and it was his responsibility to assign people to the various jobs he was given to perform. Mrs. Phuong, Betty, Joan, Lil and I spent part of each afternoon peeling manioc when there was any to peel. Mrs. Phuong was worried about eating so much manioc since she had been told it could cause women to have cancer. Dr. Ly, another housemate, told us not to give it to

120

LuAnne for several days when she had diarrhea. "I don't know if it is contributing to the diarrhea," he said, "but I do know that manioc acts as a diuretic."

Sometimes when there was no work to be done, Mrs. Phuong would give Lil recipes for some delicious Vietnamese dishes she knew how to prepare. Thuy made friends with the Vietnamese guards, and spent considerable time over at their house. Her little brother became known as the "little typhoon." Spoiled and petted, he was demanding and destructive, and we soon learned to keep things out of his sight. He gave Peter a wide berth, since Peter made no bones about considering the little fellow a menace, and would tolerate no nonsense from him. His harried mother was often at wits end to keep him out of trouble. But it was Thuy who probably suffered most from his antics. He demanded from her anything she was playing with, and if she refused he threw a tantrum. At that point her parents would intervene and make her give in to him to keep peace.

"I really feel sorry for Mrs. Phuong," I said to John after one bad scene. "I know what it's like trying to take care of a child under the constant surveillance of eighty-four spectators. But she's buying big trouble for herself by giving in to him all the time."

Directly across the aisle from us were two quiet pleasant looking young men who were obviously close friends. One afternoon I was surprised to hear one of them whistling a Vietnamese chorus based on John 3:16. "Do you know the words to that song?" I asked.

"Yes," he answered.

"Would you be willing to write them out for me?" I asked. "I have taught my little girl to sing that song in the Bru language, and I'd like to teach it to her in Vietnamese."

"I'd be glad to," he answered with a smile. He was from Banmethuot, he told me. Before he was drafted into the army, he worked with his father as a carpenter.

"My father did the carpentry work in the homes on the C&MA property," he said proudly. "He knows that missionary lady very well," pointing to Betty.

Some time later he and his friend came back from a work detail with a bunch of leaves. I expressed interest in what

121

they were, and he divided them and gave me a part. "It's a kind of tea," he explained. "The water brewed from these leaves is very healthful. Try some." I followed his instructions, brewed some leaves in the old milk tins, and shared the result with the others. It had a pleasant herbal taste.

This young man was one of the very few in the camp who had a Bible with him. It was a continuing source of regret to me that with all the miscellaneous paraphernalia we had taken from the Land Rover, I had left behind the front seat a package of ten to twelve Gideon New Testaments in Vietnamese. If I had known how many Vietnamese prisoners would ask hopefully for a Bible, I certainly would have brought them, but at the time the possibility that we would be kept with South Vietnamese POW's had never entered my mind.

John wondered why he seldom saw the young carpenter reading his Bible, until one day he observed one prisoner return it and a few minutes later another come to borrow it.

Another time I saw a tribal prisoner in one of the other houses reading a Raday New Testament. He had some leisure time because he was recovering from a case of the mumps that had thrown the entire camp into a state of uneasy suspense!

One housemate with a colorful personality, Pierre, was a helicopter pilot who spoke idiomatic, almost slangy English. While receiving special training in the U.S. he had acquired a fondness for American food and music. Sometimes in the evening he would entertain the Vietnamese prisoners by singing humorous or popular songs in Vietnamese. Sometimes he sang American songs with us. At other times he sat moody and withdrawn and stared into the fire. Pierre was the only survivor when the troop-carrying chopper he was flying had been shot down. He was gloomy in his predictions for the future. Sometimes he wondered if his wife, who was part French, had gotten out of Vietnam. More than anything he wished he had a helicopter so he could get out.

Pierre walked by one afternoon while Joan and I were peeling manioc, she with a nail file and I with a knife Peter had made from a strip of metal strapping material he had found.

"I'm on the cooking crew this afternoon," he said. Then as he turned to leave, he said nonchalantly, "We're going to have Spanish rice for supper."

I looked at Joan, and she looked at me. I raised my eyebrows. My mind was conjuring up visions of ground beef, tomatoes, onions, green peppers . . .

"No," Joan said, shaking her head. "I don't think so."

"I don't think so either," I said with a sigh, "but I wonder what he meant."

That afternoon when the call "Time to eat!" came from the kitchen, Joan and I hurried over to collect our rations. We were handed a pan of steaming white rice, a pan of grease soup with a few pieces of manioc floating in it, and a metal lid with a little pile of fish powder to be divided into twelve portions.

"So much for Spanish rice," Joan said.

"Yeah," I agreed.

Later that evening when I saw Pierre, my curiosity got the best of me. "Pierre," I said, "about that Spanish rice for supper. . . ."

"Oh, yes," he said, "how did you like it?"

"Oh it was good," I said, the light beginning to break. "How did you make it?"

"Well," he said, "you use less water than for regular rice and steam it so that every grain is separate. It's tricky to get it completely done without burning it. But it tastes better. We call it Spanish rice."

I didn't have the heart to tell him how *we* make Spanish rice. What would have been the use?

A few days after the arrival of the main contingent of prisoners, we were given the news that Saigon had been liberated, and that the whole country was now under the control of the Provisional Revolutionary Government (PRG). Camp officials strung an amplifier up on a nearby tree and for several days we listened to a tape being played and replayed about the triumphal entry of the Liberation Army into Saigon. Occasionally too a guard who owned a radio would bring it with him and allow the prisoners to listen to Radio Hanoi, and now also the new Radio Saigon. One news item was especially encouraging. On April 28 we heard the official announcement that two ICCS men caught in the hostilities in Banmethuot had been repatriated.

The first of May was a time of particular rejoicing for the camp staff. The traditional Communist holiday had new meaning for them since their victory over the American imperialists. "We have defeated the greatest military power on earth," they told us. "We will go on to liberate the people of the earth in every place the American imperialists have been."

The prisoners had a day of rest from work assignments. John used the time to prepare a Bible study on the book of Colossians for the following Sunday. Norm had suggested when we arrived at Camp Wilderness that we take turns leading the Sunday sessions, and that we study the book of Colossians. He had led the first session, and John was to lead the second. The non-missionaries opted out, preferring to spend the time in other pursuits.

I was particularly impressed by the Apostle Paul's prayer for the church at Colossae and began to pray it for our Bru friends, for our family and for myself. It seemed to sum up what I most desired for my own life. Paul told the Colossians that he did not cease to pray for them, and to desire that they "might be filled with the knowledge of his will in all wisdom and spiritual understanding; and walk worthy of the Lord unto all pleasing, being fruitful in every good work, and increasing in the knowledge of God; strengthened with all might, according to his glorious power, unto all patience and long-suffering with joyfulness."

The guards had a special feast that day. One of them brought LuAnne and the other children a plate of meat and eggs from their dinner. I was thankful because she hadn't been eating much at all. The rest of the prisoners each had a piece of salt pork fat that day from the camp kitchen.

That evening LuAnne took a turn for the worse. She had stomach pain and diarrhea, and complained that her legs ached. Her tonsils were swollen and blotchy looking. Her fever in the night went up to 104.6. We sponged her with wet towels to try to bring it down.

The next day we again went to the medic to beg for

medicine, but he didn't seem concerned and said he had nothing to give her. Lil had seen him hand out some sulfa pills to a Vietnamese prisoner and asked specifically for some of these. "I don't have any more," he told her curtly.

Paul had a few tetracycline tablets in the survival case given him by a friend, and he offered these, but not knowing what his future medical needs might be we were reluctant to accept them unless absolutely necessary. Lil decided at this point that LuAnne's condition constituted a medical emergency and asked Paul for his tablets.

Over the next day or so LuAnne's fever receded, but the diarrhea continued and she began to vomit again, one time bringing up bloody mucous, and another time vomiting up one of the precious tetracycline tablets. Dr. Ly suggested we boil rice and give her the liquid from it to drink. It would be easily digested he felt and might help the diarrhea. Making it was no problem, but getting her to drink it was another matter. She looked at the grayish liquid suspiciously, and after one sip her lips were sealed.

I tried telling her that it didn't taste bad and was only rice and water, but that sounded unconvincing even to me.

"Dr. Ly says you should drink it and that it will help you get better," I tried pressing it to her lips.

"I don't care, I don't like it," she answered, turning her head away.

"If you don't open your mouth right now and drink this," I said quietly but sternly, "I will take you up to the ladies' bathroom and spank you."

She assessed me with her eyes and saw that I meant it. Reluctantly her lips parted. She took one swallow and gagged.

"And don't you *dare* gag on it," I added unsympathetically.

"It's a good thing she doesn't know," I thought when she had finished the bowl and lay sleeping again, "how hard it would be for her mother to carry out that threat." The thought of spanking a five-and-a-half-year-old child who was too weak and sick to even walk seemed almost inhuman. I wished I could tempt her appetite with a cool glass of ginger ale, a cup of boullion, a cracker, or a slice of toast. But though that was impossible, I would fight with everything I had to keep her going.

I seriously wondered, though, if this would be enough. She was listless and lethargic, and we had to carry her to the latrine and back. She had lost so much weight her pants would hardly stay up. We knew she had intestinal parasites, but for this too the medic had nothing to give her.

If I found it hard to do anything about my own health at Camp Sunshine, the inability to do anything to help LuAnne was even more frustrating. I returned from the fruitless visit to the medic with all manner of questions welling up within me.

Had we been wrong in bringing the children to Vietnam? I recalled the time an American nurse in Vietnam had said to me emphatically, "If people want to expose their own lives to illness and danger by coming to a place like this, that's one thing, but they have no right to expose innocent children to these things." Both times we had returned to the United States on furlough people had expressed grave doubts about the wisdom of our returning. We had always felt that if we could trust God for our own lives, we could trust him for the lives of our children. And we had tried to instill in the children this same trust in God's loving care and purpose.

I recalled the time in 1968 when I sat with our three children in a sandbagged bunker in an American military camp near Kontum. We had been brought by helicopter from the Wycliffe Center just minutes before the outset of an all-out attack. The military chaplain who had been responsible for our evacuation ducked into the bunker to check on us.

"This bunker should withstand mortar explosion. And if a rocket hits, you won't have anything to worry about—ever."

Nate was just a baby at the time, but Marge and Gordon were old enough to understand the danger in the situation. I said to them, "We have nothing to be afraid of because we know we are in God's hands. As long as he has something for us to do here, he will protect us. If we die, we will just go to be with him, and that's even better than being here. Now lie down and go to sleep."

126

The mortars and rockets rained down throughout the night. Helicopter gunships spewed noisy fire all around the perimeter, but all three children slept peacefully through it all. In the cramped space I couldn't lie down or even stretch my legs out completely, so I sat there with my knees up and alternately dozed, prayed and thought. I prayed for John, who had stayed in Danang to see if he could help the Bru refugees who were fleeing to the coast to escape the heavy fighting around Khe Sanh. He would hear over the radio that Kontum was under attack and be concerned about us. My parents were in Japan on an alumni-sponsored sabbatical trip and planned to visit us in Vietnam in a few weeks. They would be wondering what to do in view of the widespread fighting.

I remembered how God's protection for the Apostle Paul had extended to "all them that sail with thee," and I prayed for the men that were fighting to protect themselves and us. In the morning the sounds of fighting died away, and the chaplain came to tell us we could leave the bunker.

"It's incredible!" he said, shaking his head. "I have never been in a worse situation. At times the attackers were literally coming over the fence, and it seemed we couldn't hold them off. Yet in all that fighting the only injury we sustained was that one man sprained his ankle jumping into a trench."

"Well, chaplain," I said, "we were praying."

He gave me an amused look and said with a note of cynicism, "Maybe we ought to invite you over every time we get attacked."

In the aftermath of the 1968 Tet offensive friends had been even stronger in their reservations about our being in Vietnam. Not once, though, did our parents put any pressure on us to leave.

And the Lord had given us seven busy, happy, and productive years since then. We had witnessed the working of God's Spirit in many areas of Vietnam and the maturing of the body of Christ among the Bru.

Even in the face of what had happened I could not regret our decision to remain in Vietnam as a family. And I was confident that what God asked us as parents to do would also work for the good of our children.

It was difficult not to feel resentment, though, toward the medic who was, I felt, withholding help. I knew his supply of medicine was meager, but he did have injectable antibiotics, and we had seen him continue to dispense sulfa tablets to others. Yet God was not limited, I realized, by human caprice.

The entry in John's diary for May 11 records part of LuAnne's bedtime prayer. "Lord," she said, "I know we are here because you want us to be, *but* we would really like to be back with our kids and friends." Then as she finished praying she added, "Lord, help me to trust you more."

LuAnne was certainly not the only one experiencing physical problems. Even our small group of foreigners had a multitude of complaints. Lil and Joan had lanced the abcess on Jay's knee, and it was healing nicely, but Peter's toes took longer to mend. Set as it was in dense jungle, the camp received little sunshine, and as rains became more and more frequent, the dampness was more pronounced. Ike began to suffer from arthritis or rheumatism, and Paul's fungus which had seemed to be under control began to give him more trouble. He had also hurt his hand clearing the jungle and the wound had infected. John was troubled with severe sinus headaches.

Norm had come down with a fever and chest congestion, which continued to weaken him. The medic had diagnosed malaria, but his symptoms were not typical for that disease. Dr. Ly happened to be within earshot one day when Norm went to the medic for help.

"Do you cough?" the medic asked Norm.

Before Norm could answer, Dr. Ly called over in English, "Tell him you cough all the time or he won't give you any medicine!"

Dr. Ly had no reason to get involved in our medical problems. His work assignment, like most of the other prisoners at the time, was to build the bamboo fence around the camp. Yet he was always quick to help if he could, and displayed a quiet confidence and concern we came to value. Once or twice he tried to make a suggestion to the North Vietnamese medic, but the medic seemed to resent this. Still

I was intrigued by the way he always seemed to have something to suggest.

When we told him about LuAnne's intestinal parasites, he said, "I've heard that eating boiled manioc leaves is helpful in getting rid of worms."

"Do you really think there's anything to the story?" I asked doubtfully.

"I don't know," he shrugged. "Manioc does have certain toxins. Of course, it would be better to give worm medicine, but since you don't have any, it won't hurt to try the leaves."

Paul wouldn't soon forget Dr. Ly's suggested cure for fungus.

"There's a plant that grows down along the river. If you crush the leaves of it, and rub in on the fungus, it is very helpful in drying it up. Why don't you meet me down by the river tomorrow during the bathing period, and I'll show you the plant."

It took them a couple of days to coordinate bath times, but Paul finally got together with Dr. Ly, and rubbed the crushed leaves over the affected areas of his groin.

Within a day or two the skin in these areas started to burn and become violently inflamed. Paul was miserable, and could hardly sit or walk. "The next time I meet Dr. Ly down by the river, I'm going to hold him under!" he grumbled.

But as the inflammation subsided, the top layer of skin sloughed off, and the new skin was remarkably free from fungus.

One evening during the first week in May we learned that a young South Vietnamese Army captain had died. It was a very sobering thing, and the prisoners discussed it in muted voices. "What was the matter with him?" we asked Pierre. "Had he been sick long?"

"No," Pierre replied. "That is, he's been a little sick ever since he got here, but nobody thought it was serious. I don't know how to say it in English, but the Vietnamese say he was 'trung gio.' Do you know what that means?"

"We nodded. Every Westerner who has lived in Vietnam very long knows about the "poisonous wind," which is held responsible for a wide variety of complaints. In order to

129

release this wind, a person's skin is scraped with a spoon or piece of metal at certain key points. If this is not done, the person will certainly die. Pierre and the other prisoners near us were convinced this had been the problem with Captain Binh.

Dr. Ly thought exhaustion and malnutrition had contributed to the death.

Dr. Ly was called out to a little building recently constructed over by the fence, which served as a clinic and meeting and interrogation room. Even after we crawled into our net, I could hear voices carrying on what sounded like a heated discussion.

In the morning we learned that certain changes were being made in the medical set-up. It seemed that camp authorities had asked Dr. Ly to sign a death certificate for Captain Binh, and he was not happy about doing this when he had been allowed no voice in medical treatment. As a result he and the other South Vietnamese medically trained prisoners were being given the responsibility of seeing that all prisoners who were ill were reported to camp authorities. They then assisted the North Vietnamese medic in the treatment of the prisoners.

With this step it became easier to get medical help. The medic still retained veto powers, but was somewhat reluctant to use them. LuAnne and Norm were both given injections of antibiotics. LuAnne responded well to the treatment. Her first couple of shots were somewhat traumatic for the whole camp as her loud cries brought even some of the guards running to see what was the matter. When she submitted calmly to the third one, I gave her a half stick of gum I still carried in my purse. She ran proudly to show it to Aunt Betty and Aunt Lil, and broke off tiny pieces of it to share with them.

It wasn't long, however, until the supply of medicine began to fail, and it seemed no more was expected.

"Maybe the reason that medic was so miserly with medicine was that he knew when it was gone there would be no more, and he'd be out of a job," I said to John.

When diarrhea medicine ran out, Dr. Ly and a South Vietnamese paramedic went out into the jungle to gather a plant, from which diarrhea medicine could be brewed. Unfortunately, however, there was no local cure for bacterial infection, nor malaria.

Mr. Spectacles, it appeared, was in charge of the whole complex of camps in the area. With most of the prisoners and guards he had made the 100 kilometer trip from Camp Sunshine by foot. Peter found particularly galling the fact that because of problems with his feet he had barely been able to make the trip while Mr. Spectacles who was the same age as he had breezed through the trip in a jaunty manner.

Mr. Spectacles had, they reported, been courteous and cheerful, and Jay had had some long discussions with him. He had been a teacher before beginning his military career and had broader interests than most of the men we had met.

One time he asked Jay what his philosophy of life was. "I took a copy of the New Testament in Vietnamese," Jay told us, "and read to him the first three verses of I Corinthians 13. 'That's my philosophy of life,' I told him. I believe that any political or economic system in the world is of no value at all without love!"

Recounting the incident to us, Jay added, "And he agreed with me."

"Jay," I asked, "where did you get a copy of the Vietnamese New Testament? I didn't know you had one."

"I don't have one," he answered. "I used his."

"He had a copy of the New Testament?" I asked in surprise.

"Yes," said Jay. "It was one of those put out by that group that puts Bibles in hotel rooms."

I thought again about the packet of Gideon New Testaments we had left in the Land Rover, and wondered if he had somehow gotten one of these.

We saw very little of Mr. Spectacles after his arrival, though we assumed he was in the area. Once one of the guards brought over a packet of tobacco for Peter and Jay, and a small aluminum spoon for LuAnne, saying that the camp commander had sent them. The spoon was easier for LuAnne to use than the bamboo one Uncle Ike had made for her, and I was touched by the thoughtful gesture.

After Mr. Spectacles' arrival the guards also appeared

more relaxed and less afraid to talk to us. "Jumpy" and a smallish guard we dubbed "Pipsqueak" remained sullen and uncommunicative, but they were somewhat that way, we observed, even with their fellow soldiers. One afternoon when he wasn't aware that anyone was watching, I watched Jumpy practice a speech, complete with hand gestures. When someone approached he immediately stopped. I wondered what sort of unhappy, insecure person might be underneath that hard shell of unconcern, and what his aims and aspirations were.

One tall young soldier we had real admiration for. We called him "the Deputy" because he seemed to be assistant to the short, squat man directly in charge of administering our camp. He was unassuming and industrious. His way of getting a work project started was to pitch in and show prisoners what he wanted them to do. He handled bamboo with skill that indicated years of experienced jungle living. And he could turn out more work in a short time than anyone else. When the other guards had been surly, he simply avoided us. In the more relaxed atmosphere, he was quietly friendly.

He was particularly kind to LuAnne. On several occasions he brought her a small wild fruit that grew on a tree not far from the camp. Once he offered to show her where the tree was and to check for more ripe fruit. He started off, and I could hardly believe it when LuAnne followed after him.

"Look at that!" Lil exclaimed. "Bath Man tried for weeks to get her to go with him without success. Maybe that was the trouble. He came on pretty strong, while this man hasn't pushed her at all. He's much more gentle."

In a few minutes they reappeared, LuAnne happily carrying several of the yellow, sharply acid fruits. It was the only time, to my memory, that she ever went away from camp with one of the camp officials. She left once with Thuy and Mrs. Phuong, but began to cry as soon as they got out of sight, so Mrs. Phuong brought her right back. Betty reported that LuAnne was even a little uneasy when the two of them walked up to visit the farthest pavilion inside the camp.

"Don't you think we'd better go back now?" she questioned Betty.

Once or twice when John was away on a job assignment, I had gone to the latrine without LuAnne's noticing. When I came back she asked anxiously, "Where *were* you? I couldn't see you and I wanted you."

Lil had a deep appreciation for all things beautiful. She would often bring unusual leaves or stones or flowers she found to show LuAnne. She was delighted when one of our Vietnamese housemates brought her some wild orchids he'd found. But when she fastened a head net from Paul's survival pack to a long pole and began collecting butterflies to take back for her children, we all thought she'd gone a bit too far.

Paul's sympathies lay with the butterflies. "Shoo, butterfly!" he said as one flew around his bed area. "Get out of here before Lil sees you." But in spite of our disparaging comments and the fact that her sensitive soul cringed every time she pinched one to immobilize it, she refused to be deterred.

Amazingly enough the rest of us began to come around. Peter was the first to help her, demonstrating a finesse gained by previous experience in India. Major and Mrs. Phuong, and then other prisoners came for the net and added to her collection. Even some of the guards got into the act chasing butterflies outside the fence and bringing them to her. John caught one in his hands down by the river. And Paul provided amusement for the whole camp when in pursuit of a butterfly, he tripped over a root and made a spectacular flying leap through the air landing on his hands.

One of the North Vietnamese soldiers who had accompanied us on the truck from Camp Sunshine was put in charge of our pavilion. His main responsibility, besides making sure the place was tidy, seemed to be to gather the men in this house into formation each morning and evening, and to lead them in calisthenics each morning *immediately* upon waking. From these two activities, the women and children were exempt, but all the men were ordered to take part. John and Dick were the only two men from our group to participate in the wake-up exercises. The others were either ill or disinclined to do anything strenuous so early in the morning.

The complicated drills looked like a combination of Kung

Fu and ballet. These were not the simple 1-2-3-4 "daily dozen" type of exercise that John became familiar with during his army days, but four separate drills, each consisting of 15 different moves! Even "Housefather," who led the drills, sometimes had trouble keeping the order straight. On one morning the drills ended early when the men broke out in laughter.

"What was so funny?" I asked John when he came back inside the pavilion.

"You know that move where you reach out your arms and throw one leg out behind you?" he said.

"Yes," I answered.

"Well, the man next to me threw himself enthusiastically into that position without noticing he was standing right in front of a tree," he said.

"Poor guy! I said. "That must have really hurt. Why did everyone laugh?"

"I'm sure it did," John said. "But he did look funny hopping around on one bare foot and holding the other in his hands."

Housefather dropped in occasionally to look over the pavilion. He always objected when he saw firewood under our beds.

"Get it out immediately!" he ordered. "It will cause you to get malaria."

Obediently we would take it and stack it outside. But after a day or two of struggling to start fires with wet wood, we'd bring it back under the beds until Housefather noticed it again and made us take it out.

"If we can't keep it under our beds," Paul grumbled, "we may have to each take a stick to bed and sleep with it!"

Housefather was a confirmed atheist and liked to discuss this occasionally. I overheard a conversation between him and Lil when Lil said, "The Bible says that God is love. Apart from God we can never know real love."

"That's not true," Housefather objected. "You don't need to believe in God to have love. Ho Chi Minh has taught us that we must love everyone. I love you," he went on, "in spite of all that my country has suffered from the Americans."

134

Another time I heard Jay say to him, "Some people say they can't believe in God, but for myself, I can't *not* believe in God when I look at the sun and moon and the world around me."

"Yes, in the past," Housefather said, "people used to believe that God created these things, but now science is able to explain their origins. Science has done away with the idea of God."

"Yet I think science and faith cannot be opposed to each other," Jay said, "because some of the greatest scientists in the world have believed in God."

Peter had been very cautious and courteous in any observations he made to us about religion, but as we became better acquainted he became more frank in expressing his opinions.

"I think Christianity has been one of the greatest curses that civilization has known," he said one evening.

"Why do you say that?" one of us asked.

"Because no other system has matched it for holding people in cradle through grave control by threatening them with the fear of hell for disobedience."

He preferred, he said, to give people the freedom to determine their own rules and to seek any life style they wanted as long as it didn't interfere with the rights of others.

"Do you think it could ever happen in a society?" I asked him. "Do you think people would give each other this complete freedom without seeking to dominate each other or seeking their own good at the expense of others?"

"I hope so," he said.

"My observations of human behavior wouldn't cause me to be very hopeful," I said.

"Peter," I asked him later, "do you believe in a God who is righteous and holy and has certain standards for human conduct? Or do you even believe there is a God at all?"

"I'd have to say I don't know," he said. "I am of course influenced by my early church training," and he quoted an author who states that a person taught to keep the Ten Commandments is inhibited in his actions by them even if he completely rejects them.

I thought a good deal about the conversation. Why was I

a Christian? Was it because of a fear of hell? I didn't honestly think so. I felt like David when he said, "I delight to do thy will, O my God." Peter saw Christianity as a system of rules that was restricting and fear producing, but I had seen a different aspect of the gospel of Christ in Vietnam. For the Bru believers it had meant a release from fear. I remembered Mandō telling us how as a young child a hex cast on him by someone angry at his parents had nearly brought about his death.

"After that," he said, "I was always afraid. I was afraid of the evil spirits and sorcerers and I was afraid of other people. I didn't want to be afraid, but fear was always there."

Like other Bru, Mandō had a belief in Yiang Sursī, the spirit of the heavens, who was greater than all others, completely good and the creator of the universe. But it was toward placation of the spirits of the earth that all his worship and efforts were bent. When he read that Yiang Sursī had made it possible for us to become his children by faith, he gladly accepted this. And with the power of God behind him, Mandō realized a glorious freedom from fear of the evil spirits of the earth. He still believed in them, but he no longer feared them.

I was certain that for the Bru Christians the message of Christ was not one of fear but of freedom.

My birthday on the sixth of May began like any other day at Camp Wilderness. I ate a bowl of hot rice gruel as soon as we could get last night's leftover rice boiled.

John, Dick and Jay went with a crew to clear away brush from an area recently enclosed by the bamboo fence. The fence was a matter of amusement to all the prisoners. They thought it rather unusual to be asked to build their own prison fence. Norm asked one of the guards in charge of the project why the fence was necessary after all this time. When he told the rest of us what the explanation was, I thought the man deserved an award for originality.

"It is necessary to build the fence to keep out unauthorized and undesirable people who might otherwise try to come in," he explained seriously.

136

When Norm told us this we all laughed. "I've noticed," someone said, "how people are just clamoring to get in here!"

"Yes," suggested another, "it must be that rumors are getting out about the fantastic meals they serve here!"

"If they're afraid people are going to want to get in here," said another, "things must be really bad in the rest of the country!"

Ike declined a work assignment that morning. His arm and shoulder were quite painful. But with a sweater on and a handkerchief tied around his head against the cool air, he puttered around camp working, whenever he could borrow a machete from a nearby work crew, on a bamboo table he was constructing just outside our end of the pavilion.

The women in the group busied themselves in their several ways. After a period of quiet reading and devotions, Betty took the bamboo rake Ike had made and began sweeping the leaves and twigs around the pavilion. Joan was completely absorbed in caring for Norm whose high fevers left him weak and depressed. He ate almost nothing, but craved liquid. Each time the fever broke he drenched his clothing with perspiration.

Since his arrival, Peter had been exempt from work details because of his feet and generally run-down condition. His feet were greatly improved now from daily soakings in hot water, rest and clean dressings, but he saw no reason to alter his work status. The day before he and I had experimented with a new way to prepare manioc, and came up with a taste treat we all raved about. Borrowing a pan from the kitchen, Peter mashed several tubers of boiled manioc with a stick, adding just enough water to make the starchy mixture stick together. We added a little of the salty fish powder for flavor, and formed the mixture into small "cookies," which we baked on an old rusty sheet of tin he had found and cleaned up.

Today Peter was repeating the process, but in honor of my birthday, in a few of the patties he substituted for fish powder some of the precious hoard of sugar given to us back at Camp Sunshine. When he presented them after the al-

137

most-noontime meal, I was amused and pleased to be the recipient of what had to be the world's most unusual birthday cake.

The noonday sun reached into the cleared patch in the jungle, warming the pavilions where several hundred men relaxed after eating their morning rice. This was the time we women generally went to the river to bathe and wash clothes. LuAnne was feeling better than she had for some time, but was still not strong enough to go to the river with us. I had bathed her just the day before outside the pavilion using water in the little Texas-Ware serving bowl we used to wash our hands in.

Today she seemed anxious to have me leave, and I knew by the excited glances she was giving her father that they shared a secret. I gathered up my little hand towel and the clothes I would change into, and headed for the gate with the other women.

Just outside the gate we stopped in front of the guard in his little bamboo and thatch guard-post and requested permission to go bathe. He nodded assent and we turned right toward the designated bathing spot when the guard stopped us.

"If you go toward the left, you could have more privacy," he suggested.

"Thank you, brother," I answered, trying to conceal my amazement, and we hurried off along the path to the left before he could change his mind. The path ran close to the river. We explored it happily and examined several sites before finally selecting a spot a short distance from the trail and protected from the view of anyone walking along it.

It was the first time in two months we experienced real privacy. It was an exhilarating feeling! We could actually take a bath with all our clothes off! We didn't have to try to change quickly behind a bush, watching lest any minute someone pop into view. I had learned to look the other way when I walked past a nude man standing in the river. They accorded us the same courtesy when they happened upon us in a state of partial undress. Never once had I heard any lewd or suggestive comment.

I sat in the river and luxuriated in the peace and beauty

around me. I hadn't realized how much I'd missed the privacy I was accustomed to. What a beautiful birthday gift God had given me, I thought, and thanked him for it.

We returned to camp with our wet clothes and hung them on the bamboo pole that served as our clothesline. John was still lying down, but LuAnne was waiting eagerly as I approached the pavilion.

"Happy Birthday, Mommy!" she said holding out a tiny package. It was wrapped in a quarter sheet of typed paper, a carbon copy of some of Dick's Mnong language material. I had to smile at that. Phillipses in lightening their heavy suitcase of books, linguistic journals, personal letters, and carbon and mimeographed copies of Mnong material, had kept the group supplied with toilet paper. Sometimes it proved quite interesting.

LuAnne watched excitedly as I read the card they had made and opened the little package. It contained a 40mm shell casing (about two inches in length and one and a half inches in diameter), shot from a Cobra Gunship.

"I wish I could have gotten you something really nice," John said apologetically, "but it was the only thing I could find. I thought maybe when we get out I could shine it up and you could use it for a paper weight, or put hair pins or paper clips in it."

"You know," he said, "I tried so hard to think of something I could give you for your birthday, but I couldn't think of anything. So I asked the Lord to show me something. And when I was out working clearing the area around the new fence the other day, I found this and figured God had given me your birthday present."

"It's a wonderful gift," I said, thinking not so much of the blackened shell casing as the love it represented. "I will always treasure it."

After the afternoon meal, Mrs. Phuong and Thuy were taken to see Mr. Spectacles at his headquarters. When she returned she told us she had been given permission to take the children and go to her parents in Saigon.

"I asked him if you and LuAnne could go with me," she said, "but he said no, your case was different and you would have to stay."

"I appreciate your asking," I told her. "When will you leave?"

"As soon as there is a vehicle going to Pleiku or Banmethuot," she answered. She offered to take out any notes or letters to friends in Vietnam. I wrote to one of the Bru lay-pastors to share with all our Bru friends, assuring them of our continued love and prayer.

The next day when we went to bathe there was a different guard at the gate from the day before. Lil was the first one out the gate.

"May we go up there to bathe?" she asked, indicating the path to the left.

"No," he answered.

"Yesterday we were allowed to go there," she persisted. But he refused to change his mind.

"I've decided," I said to Joan as we followed Lil to the general bath area, "that it's better never to ask permission if you're uncertain whether or not you can do something. When we ask permission for anything out of the routine no guard is willing to accept the risk of making a decision for which he could be blamed. But if we go ahead and do something, he is reluctant to forbid us to do it for the same reason. So it's better to just assume you can do something unless told otherwise."

"I think you're right," Joan agreed.

May 7 was the anniversary of the French defeat at Dien Bien Phu. The prisoners had a special lecture on the subject. Mr. Spectacles visited the camp and told us that the Australian government now had an embassy in Saigon. Peter requested to be able to contact it, but was again told to be patient. When Mr. Spectacles left, Peter pointedly refused to shake hands with him.

"I have nothing against him personally," he said to us, "but I refuse to shake his hand unless I can do it as a free man."

On the 11th, when the men were taken to another clearing for a political lecture, Mr. Spectacles told Jay that if we wanted LuAnne and I could go to another North Vietnamese army camp in a more healthy location.

Discussing the subject later with John, I said, "I don't think I could stand to be separated from you. We'd never be

140

sure we'd get back together again. Besides, it's bad enough not to know about our other kids. If I didn't know what was happening to you, it would be unbearable.

"I know," he agreed. "I wouldn't want you in another camp all by yourselves."

Norm's condition continued to worsen. The night of the 12th his fever was over 105, and he was incoherent. Lil had come down with a classic case of malaria, and LuAnne's fever was back up. Joan, Betty, Dick, and I had a special time of prayer. Joan bathed Norm with cool cloths, and wondered if he'd make it through to morning. By morning, though, all three seemed better.

On the 14th I awoke very depressed. Gordon would be eleven years old that day, and I wanted so badly to be with him. I wondered where he would spend the day. I had hoped so much we would be out by this time, but we weren't, and it seemed unlikely our situation would change any before Marge's 13th birthday in ten more days. But life as it was had to go on, so I wiped my tears on the blanket and crawled out of the net.

I was working at the fire when Mr. Spectacles came by and said he wanted to talk to me. "I am concerned about the health of your little girl," he said.

"So am I," I replied. "She is very weak and has lost a lot of weight."

"I would like to send her to an army hospital 35 kilometers from here. You could accompany her but your husband would have to stay. If the time comes to move you to another location, you would certainly go together."

"The final decision must be my husband's," I told him.

"Then go talk with him," he said, "and let me know your decision right away." With that he went into the pavilion and began to inquire about Norm.

I walked out of the camp, and down to the river where the men were working on a little bamboo booth where the women could change their clothing.

"Are you coming to inspect the project?" they called out gaily.

"Not this time," I said, trying to smile. Then I added, "John, I need to talk with you a minute."

He came over immediately, and we walked away from

141

the others as I related my conversation with Mr. Spectacles.

"He's gone in to talk with Norm and Joan, but he wants an answer immediately," I said.

We bowed our heads as we stood there and asked for wisdom to make the right decision. Not to go might mean to cut LuAnne off from whatever medical help was available. But to go. . . ? What would that mean for the future?

"I still feel I wouldn't want you and LuAnne to go by yourselves," John said. "But if Norm and Joan should go there, then I think you and LuAnne should go with them."

We walked back into the camp. Joan stepped out to meet me. "Norm and I have been ordered to go," she said, her eyes full of sympathy. "What did you and John decide?"

"If you're going, I guess LuAnne and I will go too," I said.

There was no time to think about the implications of the decision. We were to leave at once to walk the several kilometers to where a truck would pick us up. We quickly divided our belongings. John kept only what he needed, and sent everything else with me.

"You and LuAnne probably won't have to do much walking," he said, he said, "but I might."

Dick and Jay volunteered to help John carry the bags out, and we left immediately.

The walk out was easier than the walk in. It was daytime and the path was well trodden. But my heart was very heavy, because I knew I would miss John so much.

"LuAnne," John said, "do you remember the Psalm you learned in Banmethuot that says, 'The Lord is my shepherd, I shall not want?'"

"Yes," she said.

"You remember that Psalm while we're away from each other." John said to her. Then he gave me Psalm 138 to keep. "In the day when I cried thou answeredst me and strengthenedst me with strength in my soul."

"I've found Psalm 126 a real comfort lately," I said to him. "Right now we seem to be 'sowing in tears,' but the promise is that we will 'reap in joy.'"

As we walked into the supply base where I knew we would separate I was unable to restrain the tears any longer.

A tall thin soldier with a dignified bearing called out in English as I walked by, "Good morning, how are you?"

"Fine, thank you," I said, in an effort to be polite.

He came toward me eager for a chance to practice his English, but as he saw my tear-filled eyes he stopped, confused, and turned away.

The guard accompanying us led us to a small thatch hut where we were to wait for the truck. I thanked Jay and Dick for their help, kissed John goodbye and watched him walk away to go back to camp. LuAnne and I entered the hut, sat down on the bamboo bed inside, and with our arms around each other we sobbed.

SIX

The Hospital

Even in grief there was no privacy. In the hut a crowd of curious soldiers stood around the bed and pressed us with questions. They were particularly eager to know about Lu-Anne. "How old is she? Where was she born? Where is her father?"

I wiped my eyes and answered the questions. In addition to the soldiers there were two women in the house. The old woman had come from Saigon searching for her only son. The young woman with the baby was looking for her brother. They had, they said, been treated kindly by the camp officials but their search had been unsuccessful and they were also waiting for the truck to begin their trip home.

We ate with relish the food brought to us at noon from the soldiers' kitchen—rice with nicely seasoned squash soup, salt pork and piles of a green vegetable.

"Wow! I wish Daddy were here to eat with us," was LuAnne's comment. Then she added, "I wish all our guys were here," referring to the group back at camp.

"This will be the easiest trip we've had yet," I thought as we set out after lunch. Joan, LuAnne and I sat on the big brown suitcase in the back of a truck. Norm rode in the cab with two soldiers. The day was sunny. A few soldiers rode with us but the truck was not crowded. Mr. Spectacles rode in the cab of a truck preceding ours and had offered to take LuAnne with him but she started to cry and clung to me.

144

We were coming to learn, however, that no trip with the Liberation Army could be considered routine. Before we even left the camp area our truck slid off the road and we waited in the sun for an hour till the other truck came back to pull us out.

One of the soldiers gave LuAnne his key chain to play with. On the chain was a little can opener from a package of U.S. Army C-rations and a little gear mechanism. LuAnne was intrigued by the little gears that meshed together and made a ticking sound as she ran it up and down her pants leg.

"What is it?" I asked the soldier.

"Don't you know?" he said.

"No," I replied. "It looks as if it might have come from a clock."

"A clock?" he laughed. "It's the timing device from an American bomb."

A few hundred feet farther the motor gave out and we had to be towed the rest of the way. But the tow rope kept breaking, causing considerable friction between the drivers of the two trucks.

It was after dark before we pulled into what appeared to be a former district headquarters in the village of Thanh An. Norm was soaking wet with perspiration. He and LuAnne were both exhausted and thirsty. We hauled our stuff into the bare building where we were greeted with friendly courtesy by the officer in command. He brought a plate of bananas and LuAnne's eyes nearly popped out. He smiled at our expression of pleasure and gratitude.

"We do not have adequate accommodations here," he apologized, "but after tonight we will take you to another facility. "He indicated we should sleep on two cots in the adjoining room. We got out our tarps and nets and set them up. Some soldiers brought in an evening meal of rice, and we again answered scores of questions by soldiers curious to know who we were and where we had come from. We were just settling into the cots when a soldier bustled into the room.

"Get your things together and come," he said.

"Now?" we questioned in surprise.

"Yes, we're taking you directly to the hospital," he answered.

We took down the nets, gathered our things and followed him to a small confiscated South Vietnamese army truck. The truck drove out of the village and turned down a dirt road. I was puzzling over the reason for having a hospital in what appeared to be a desolate area when my thoughts were cut short. The truck lurched to a stop as one wheel fell through the rotten boards of a wooden bridge.

We could hear but not see the rushing water below. The bridge had no side railings.

"Please let us get out," Norm begged, as the driver made fruitless efforts to get out of the hole.

"You will have to walk the rest of the way," the soldiers decided.

"How far is it?" I asked, dreading the answer.

"Only about a kilometer," one of them said.

"Or maybe a little more," the other added.

When they saw I intended to leave the sewing machine and big brown suitcase in the truck, they protested, but it was obvious I couldn't carry them and they seemed unwilling to leave them. So each of them took one of the items.

"These poor guys must rue the day they took us," I said to Joan.

It was pitch black as we made our way up a hill. I had the impression of expanses of cleared area on both sides of the road. This was apparently not a jungle area. LuAnne walked without complaint between Joan and me, holding our hands. In front of us, though, Norm was having a struggle. He carried a bed roll of nets, mat and blankets, and his strength seemed to be giving out.

"Remember, Norm," Joan encouraged him, "we're doing this for Jesus." And he trudged on.

The guard turned off the road and approached a tiny cement block building. Through the open door we could see a desk with a tiny wick lamp.

"Go inside!" someone said loudly.

"Don't shout," Norm replied wearily, "we're going."

They motioned us to sit on a bench along the wall, and a loud argument ensued between the men who had brought us and the men in the building.

"What do you mean by bringing these people at this hour of the night and without papers?" a tall man with glasses demanded.

"We are only following orders," was the reply. "We were told to bring them, so we brought them."

The tall man walked over to Norm.

"What's the matter with you?" he demanded.

"I don't know," Norm said. Then grasping for the proper words in Vietnamese he added, "We were invited to come here but if we are not wanted we will go somewhere else."

It was an unfortunate choice of words. "We did not 'invite' you to come here," said the guard who accompanied us. "We *brought* you here, and here you will stay."

The tall man seemed at a loss to know what to do with us. Norm would have to go in one place, he decided, and the women in another. Norm requested to stay with Joan since they had only one net, but he shook his head. Joan gave Norm their net and he was led away. The tall man took Joan, LuAnne and me to the back side of another small cement building and into a room with nothing but a small wooden bed and a little bench in it.

"You and the child can sleep here," he said to me. "We will bring in two wooden desks and push them together for you to sleep on," he said to Joan, adding, "We haven't had time to get beds made and we do not have facilities for women and children."

Joan was worried lest the soldiers take offense at Norm's blunt manner of speaking. "Please excuse my husband," she said. "He is tired and ill, and we don't speak Vietnamese very fluently."

"That's all right," he replied walking out and leaving us to flop down on the beds. Mine was too short to stretch my legs out, but neither that nor the mosquitos buzzing around could keep me from sleeping.

We were awakened between 5 and 5:30 A.M. when the tall man walked into the room.

"Someone is going to market this morning," he said loudly, "do you need anything?"

"Oh yes!" I said, sitting up instantly. "Could someone buy us some bananas?" I was thankful I had brought money with me.

147

"Maybe they could get some soap, too," Joan suggested. The man agreed readily and hurried off.

"You know," I said to Joan, "maybe this man wasn't shouting at us last night. That seems to be his normal way of speaking."

We had all noticed a tendency on the part of the North Vietnamese to speak more loudly and stridently than the South Vietnamese. Even Peter who couldn't understand a word of Vietnamese had commented on this, but this man whom we later came to know as Dr. Son, and the hospital administrator whom we dubbed "Shouty" seemed to carry the trait to an extreme.

Norm came into the room and told us he was staying in another building just across the compound.

"I didn't sleep very well last night for wondering who was in the room with me," he said. "But this morning I met the other men. They're all South Vietnamese prisoners from another camp," he said, "and seem very friendly."

The hospital complex we could now see was a converted village headquarters compound of the previous government. Behind the compound and on both sides were houses we had been unable to see the night before. The building where Norm slept had obviously been a school, and the school desks served as hospital beds. Half the building had been destroyed by bombing or artillery. Other buildings on the compound were the small office building where we'd been taken initially, a clinic on the back side of which we had a room, and a living unit where staff and sick soldiers stayed. To these buildings had been added a thatch kitchen building and a wooden frame building used, we later observed, for re-education lectures and classes.

We asked about latrine facilities and were pointed to an area on the other side of an abandoned airstrip about 200 yards away. A waist high bamboo partition had been put around the hole. Joan, LuAnne and I shared this facility with the staff.

In the corner of the compound right outside our room was the deepest open well I had ever seen. The squeaky winch that took the buckets up and down as soldiers and villagers filled their water containers was the first sound we heard in the morning and the last at night. The well was also a social center at which village girls would linger to talk with the young northerners.

By midmorning the news of our arrival had spread through the village and it seemed that everyone in town had come to see us. The adults generally left after looking us over and asking a few questions. But the children seemed to have nothing more interesting to do than watch us. When we closed the door and window to wash ourselves and change our clothing, they continually pushed open the latchless door in spite of our efforts to hold it closed.

I was becoming irritated by the continuous staring. "Oh dear," I thought, "this is going to be worse than Camp Wilderness. There was no privacy there either, but at least we were all in it together. This is like being in a zoo!"

I was reminded of the attitude of Christ toward the crowds of people who constantly sought him out and pressed him for help. "Father," I prayed, "help me to stop being so concerned about my feelings and needs so that I can reach out in compassion even to these kids who are staring in the window."

Through the following days I could see how God was answering this prayer. To be sure the novelty of our presence wore off as the days passed, but even when I woke from an afternoon siesta to find several strange women standing beside my bed watching me, I experienced no feeling of annoyance. Instead I began to welcome the opportunities to talk to the villagers and to try to understand what they were experiencing.

All of them, we learned, had tried to flee to the coast when their home area changed hands but had been turned back before they reached the lowlands. In the confusion of the flight most of them lost what few possessions they had, and many returned to find homes and crops damaged or destroyed.

Dr. Son told us this had been the response of the people throughout the country toward their own "liberation."

"In Saigon," he said, "people were on top of buildings trying to get helicopters to take them out."

"Why were they so afraid?" I asked him.

"They had been told lies about us," he said sadly. "They thought we would kill them."

I remembered what had happened in Hue in 1968 when the Communist liberators had gone from door to door rounding up anyone who had any connection with the Saigon government. Among the thousands killed had been some close friends of ours. One was a French priest. Several others were German doctors who taught in the medical school. A Vietnamese friend whose husband was a minor village government worker told me her husband had been taken away at that time. "I know he was shot," she said, "but I don't know where he was buried." I had seen with my own eyes the location where several hundred bodies had been exhumed.

It seemed certain the liberators had changed tactics since that time. But how, I wondered, were the South Vietnamese people to know that? Like us, they had every reason to expect the worst.

The attitude of the villagers now seemed to be one of relief and gratitude that they were still alive and able to go on with the routine of living. They were concerned about their sons, husbands and brothers, many of whom were in re-education camps such as Camp Wilderness, but the courtesy the North Vietnamese soldiers demonstrated toward them made them cautiously hopeful.

Toward us they were unfailingly sympathetic and friendly. They were particularly understanding about our concern for our children. One woman who lived near the hospital did some shopping for us in Pleiku on two occasions and would accept nothing in return. We were so grateful to be able to get candles, sweetened condensed milk, peanuts, sanitary napkins, paper, rubber sandals. She even got some colored pens for LuAnne.

Our diet took an upswing during our stay at the hospital. Though it consisted of roughly the same ingredients, we received more salt pork and fish powder. We also received greens occasionally. And since rice tasted so much better with the milk, bananas and peanuts we purchased our rice intake also doubled.

150

Norm was put on an antibiotic treatment and seemed to be getting stronger every day. Dr. Son looked at the paper Lil had kept regarding LuAnne's symptoms and treatment and shook his head.

"It was very hit or miss," he commented.

"It certainly was," I agreed.

That first afternoon Dr. Son brought a pleasant, soft-spoken man to see LuAnne. "This is the head doctor," he explained. "He's more highly trained than I." The head doctor was not in residence here, we learned, but was responsible for all medical facilities in this area of the country.

After checking LuAnne carefully he told us, "Her tonsils are very enlarged. She will probably continue to have trouble with them. We will treat her as well as we can, but we are limited in what medicines we have available." How true this was we learned a few days later when the infection flared up again. A young medic brought five tetracycline tablets and told me that was all the hospital had.

After the first day we were told not to use the precious well water for bathing or washing our clothes.

"Where should we go?" we asked.

"To the river," was the reply.

"How do we get there?" I questioned.

"The best way is to go down the road till you come to it," he began.

"Oh yes," I replied, suddenly remembering the notorious bridge we'd fallen through in the dark. "We know the place."

Far from feeling aggrieved at having to walk so far to bathe, we could hardly believe our good fortune. Apparently we were to be allowed to walk unsupervised the mile or so to the river to bathe whenever we wanted to!

Norm was not strong enough to make the trip, but Joan, LuAnne and I felt like three kids let out of school as we headed for the river. A crowd of children followed us as we walked down the road between the airstrip and the village. Every little wood and thatch house was flying the new red and blue flag with the gold star. Most of them also displayed a political motto supporting the liberation of the country.

151

The most common was Ho Chi Minh's statement, "Nothing is more precious than independence and freedom."

"I'll buy that!" I said to Joan.

Young people under the supervision of the northerners were painting and hanging banners and posters across the road in honor of the coming celebration of Ho Chi Minh's birthday. "Long live the triumph of Marxist-Leninist thought," one of them read.

When we reached the end of the village and started down the hill, the children turned back. Alone we proceeded along the quiet country road, appreciating even this little taste of freedom, until we came to the rotting bridge. We walked a little way down the stream to a sheltered spot and chatted happily as we bathed and washed our clothes.

Most of the hospital staff was reserved and aloof, and the soldiers who worked in the kitchen were so grumpy we avoided them. But Dr. Son visited us often and we enjoyed his cheerful breezy manner.

He had gotten a bargain on bananas so he bought five large bunches for us. We were ecstatic and he was both pleased and amused.

When the head doctor stopped in that afternoon he expressed surprise at seeing so many bananas.

"They're going into business," Dr. Son said. "They're opening up a banana shop." Then turning to the ever-present visitors' gallery around the door and window he said, "What are you kids standing around here for? Did you come to buy bananas? If not, be on your way."

Dr. Son was the first soldier I met who was actually from the South. He had left his Saigon home in 1954 to go north and fight with the Liberation Army. He didn't know, he said, whether his mother was still alive or not, but he was hoping to find out soon. For years he lived in the jungles fighting with the guerilla troops before he requested and received training as a medic.

"I didn't marry," he told us, "because I always hoped I could return to Saigon to marry a girl from there." Apparently in 1968 he gave up that dream, because when he was sent to Hanoi for advanced training he had finally married a northern girl, and they had had one small child. He had seen the child, he said, only once.

The head doctor had also been away from home for most of his married life.

"But North Vietnamese wives are different from American ones," he told us. "They are faithful to their husbands even though they are gone for long periods."

The hospital compound seemed to be the nerve center for village life. Groups of young people gathered here to set out for work details, planting manioc or sweet potatoes. Sometimes the girls dropped in to visit us. The women stopped by after their long afternoon re-education sessions in the board building next to ours. All adults gathered at 4 A.M. on Ho Chi Minh's birthday to walk several miles to another village for the celebration.

In between times of entertaining visitors we kept busy cleaning and mopping our room, eating, reading, taking daily trips to the river and hemming bandages and surgical masks for the hospital staff.

Once when I walked over to the kitchen to fill our drinking water container, I paused to listen a moment as a group outside the administration building engaged in self-criticism. "I am guilty," an older man confessed, "of having worked for the American imperialists and having resisted the revolution." I walked on back to the room.

"I can't help wondering," I said to Joan, "what these people really think and feel underneath the rhetoric. When they're alone with us they speak longingly about the 'good old days' when the Americans were here. And when they're with the North Vietnamese they've learned to talk in glowing terms about liberation and revolution."

"They are probably mostly concerned with feeding their families and doing whatever they have to do to survive under whatever system is in charge," Joan said.

All over the area were reminders of the days of American military presence. Most obvious of these was the airstrip. Constructed from the finest materials and employing the latest engineering techniques, it looked as though it had been built to last a hundred years. But it lay completely idle,

153

shimmering in the noonday sun. Empty C-ration cans reminded us of foods that seemed to belong to a different world, such as ham slices and apricots.

LuAnne and I went out one afternoon to get fronds to make a broom, and stumbled onto an old military dump. Anything of possible value had long since been removed, but LuAnne was delighted with what we found. "Oh Mommy look!" she said, collecting some little plastic cups that were evidently part of the packaging for some sort of ammunition. "These look like cupcake holders." We picked up a plastic lid to use as a soap dish, and part of an ammunition box we could keep things in.

As we walked back with these treasures, I thought about the many Americans we had met in Vietnam. To the Bru they were all "your friends" simply because they were Americans. At times this notion presented problems. "Will you please tell your friends," a Bru village chief said to me shortly after the marines had set up a base in the Khe Sanh area, "to be more careful where they shoot their big guns. Some are exploding in our fields and villages, and we're getting tired of it." I could understand his concern. A mortar round had struck right next to our house a few days earlier.

We cringed inside when we once saw a GI in a truck ahead of us reach out and knock the hats off Vietnamese people riding bicycles along the road. Occasionally we were ashamed of the demanding and patronizing manner some of them displayed toward Vietnamese shopkeepers. One day a Special Forces captain said to me, "In my estimation this whole country is not worth the life of one American."

"I wish I'd had the presence of mind to remind him," I said to John later, "that in the sight of God every single person in this country is just as valuable as *any* American."

But these instances were not the norm. Far more often we noted a genuine concern for the Vietnamese people on the part of American soldiers. "Pe-ri" became a household word in Bru villages throughout the Khe Sanh area. It was the name of a genial bald-headed army medic, who held medical clinics in all the villages. He kept extending his tour in Vietnam until the army wouldn't let him stay any longer. The Bru also remembered "Brother Dan," the quiet, young

154

marine who learned their language and helped them in many ways.

Every American unit had some type of civic action project where the men got involved in building schools or playgrounds, or supplying orphanages and social action groups with clothing and supplies. One group purchased a large-print primer typewriter, and another a mimeograph machine to prepare reading material for new Bru readers. A Vietnamese Catholic nun, head of the largest private school and orphanage in the city of Danang, said to me one time, "When the Americans leave, it will be the schools and orphanages that will feel the greatest loss. They have done so much to help."

The amazement of the American GI's at seeing an American family up in the mountains of Vietnam was often humorous. Driving in our Land Rover to a rather remote area one day to check on some of our literacy teacher trainees, we met a convoy of American trucks coming out. Mouths dropped open as the soldiers looked at us. I laughed when I heard one of them say, "Must be a USO show."

Not infrequently soldiers from the base would stop by to visit or play with our children. They missed their own families and adopted ours. Margie's first big doll was a gift from a Special Forces captain who asked his wife to send it for Christmas.

One time my teacher-training session and John's translation time were interrupted by the arrival of a TV news team from one of the major American networks. The commanding officer of the Khe Sanh combat base later admitted to sending them. "It got them out of my hair," he said somewhat sheepishly. Then he added, "Anyway, I figured your work was more important than mine and deserved the publicity."

Only once were we asked to help in gathering military information. One of the military units had captured a tribal prisoner and couldn't communicate with him. An officer came to John to ask him to interpret. When John declined, he was understanding. "I figured that would be your answer," he said, "but I had to try."

During our time at the hospital I enjoyed getting to know

155

Norm and Joan more closely. Norm was outspoken and his lack of facility in Vietnamese didn't keep him from airing his grievances any time he got the ear of a passing North Vietnamese official. "Do you think it's right," he pressed, "that my children have to go back to Canada all alone?"

"Norm!" Joan would caution, trying to restrain him, "he doesn't have anything to do with it. Just keep still now."

They had been in Vietnam only four years, and unlike the rest of us had come when their two children, Pat and Doug, were entering their teen years. Norm told me how it happened.

"I was teaching school in Canada, enjoyed my work, had a lovely home, and was active in church work. But I gradually began to feel that God was asking me to go into full-time service."

"I did something," he continued, "that I never did before and haven't done since. I decided to put out a 'fleece.' I had to know if this was really God calling us, or if it was just an emotional impulse of mine."

Over the years since Norm had come to know Christ as a young man, he had been very burdened about his mother. Left a widow at the time of Norm's birth, she had at incredible personal sacrifice worked to support him and give him an education. She was fiercely proud of him, but bitterly antagonistic toward his Christian faith. She was also plagued by alcoholism.

"God," Norm prayed, "if my mother surrenders her life to you within one week, I will know that you are calling me to full-time Christian service."

"I figured that would be the end of it," he said. "I didn't really believe this would ever happen, but five days later she called me and said she had accepted Christ."

"It was a real miracle," Joan said. "You couldn't appreciate what that meant unless you had known Norm's mother. She made life miserable any time she was with us by constantly ridiculing the church and Christianity."

But completely unknown to Norm and Joan, she was seeking answers to her own deep personal needs, and had begun to read an old Swedish Bible she had. She became

156

deeply convicted and called a pastor she knew to come and pray with her. When she called Norm to tell him about the change in her life she had no idea she was also announcing a change in his.

Convinced of God's leading, Norm and Joan embarked on a course of seminary study and an assistant pastorship. Eventually they had volunteered for overseas service and accepted assignment to Vietnam.

Now they sometimes talked about what the future might hold for them and what they would do if they got out.

"I loved teaching, but I don't think I could ever go back to public school teaching again," Norm said, "after having promised God I'd give my life to full-time Christian service."

Norm and Joan's warm concern for each other made me miss John keenly. In the evening they sometimes walked together up and down the airfield, though camp officials put a stop to this when they learned of it.

"There are too many people around with guns," Shouty said, "and you might get shot by accident."

"I guess he's right," Joan admitted reluctantly. We often heard shooting in the distance and hospital personnel told us that raids were still being conducted against pockets of resistance in jungle areas.

We had seen nothing of Mr. Spectacles since the trip out of Camp Wilderness, but one day we were visited by the tall thin man I'd seen the day we left there. He again greeted us in English, but that was as far as his knowledge of the language extended, and he lapsed back into Vietnamese.

"You look happier than the last time I saw you," he said to me. "Are you being well taken care of here?"

"Yes," I said.

"And how is your daughter?" he asked.

"She is much stronger," I replied.

"Why were you crying that day?" he asked.

"The day you saw me was my son's eleventh birthday," I said. "I don't know where he is and I miss him terribly. On top of that our family was being split again. I was leaving my husband, and I didn't know where I was going or whether I would ever see him again."

"I go up to that camp quite often," he said, "because I have responsibilities there. I would be glad to take a letter for your husband or to bring one for you."

"Oh, would you?" I said eagerly. "I would be so grateful."

I asked him if he'd be willing to take a package of supplies for the group of foreigners, but he declined to do this.

"I don't think you need to send anything up to them," he said, "because they will soon be moved." This exciting bit of news was also confirmed by the head doctor.

"It is a very unhealthy location," he said, "and all the prisoners there are going to be brought out." He couldn't say, however, just when this might be.

"I understand the foreigners are to have a separate house," he said, "with private rooms for families."

Joan and I discussed it on the way to the river. "I'll believe it when I see it," she said. "The way most of these promises work out doesn't lead me to expect any improvement."

"I can hardly wait to see John again," I said. "I hope they move them soon."

"When you think of all the work that went into building that camp," Joan mused, "it all seems like such a waste. I wonder what those North Vietnamese soldiers are going to think when they're ordered to burn those houses down after having worked so hard to build them a few weeks earlier. Don't they sometimes question some of the seemingly senseless things they're told to do?"

"Of course they don't," I said. "If they're told to build houses, they build houses. And if they're told to burn them, they burn them. It may look senseless but they assume there must be a purpose. I don't think the idea that somebody higher up made a mistake would even occur to them. You know what they told us—the revolution doesn't make mistakes."

All of a sudden I was struck by the significance of what I'd just said, and I stopped walking. "Joan," I said, "that's exactly what we do too. We look at some of the incongruous things that happen to us, like our being here, for instance. We can't see any reason for it, but we feel sure there must be one because God doesn't make mistakes."

158

"These men operate on the same principle we do," I said, resuming the walk down the hill, "the principle of faith. I don't personally see how they can have such complete faith in a movement which is conceived and executed by other human beings, but it's obvious they have it. In fact the way they accept physical hardship, poverty and separation from family for the sake of the revolution puts a lot of us Christians to shame."

Whether through the kindness of the tall, thin man or someone else, I was overjoyed to receive a letter from John a few days later. I walked over toward the airfield and began to read the daily chronicle he'd been keeping since we left.

"Dear Kenna," he began, using a nickname his family had given me, "it's been one day and two hours since I left you guys and it seems like forever! It's so lonely here without you! It was difficult to say goodbye, but it really didn't hit me till we got back to camp, had lunch and then laid down for siesta. I had to get off by myself with the Lord. Took a short walk up by the fence at the bomb crater and just broke down and cried out to the Lord for help. I remembered your mentioning Psalm 126 as we were walking along. The Lord spoke to me and comforted my heart through it. Let's take this Psalm as God's promise to us until we are together again, and even back with our kids and loved ones. There certainly have been tears throughout this experience, and I longingly look forward to that joy that will be the fruit of those tears.

"Can't help but wonder how you guys are faring. How was the trip? How is LuAnne taking it all? How's Norm? So many unanswered questions—can but pray much for you and commit you to the Lord."

I took the letter back to share the newsy parts with Norm and Joan. We laughed at his account of how a man in our pavilion had caught a six foot long iguana lizard and turned it into soup for his eighty-some housemates. We were concerned about the outbreak of malaria and apparent lack of medicine. About Lil he wrote, "Dr. Ly says she should be on quinine for ten days, but the medic says three days is enough."

Our time at the hospital was a blessing in many ways, but

when Shouty came to us on the 29th of May and told us we would be taken to another camp that day, we were not sorry. "You don't need to be here any longer." Shouty said. "You're taking up space that is badly needed by others."

Since Dr. Son's sudden transfer a week earlier, the hospital staff had tolerated our presence with barely veiled annoyance. A few days earlier Shouty had come to the room angrily demanding that we take our clothes off their clothesline. Since we'd been hanging them there since our arrival, I asked him the reason for this. "It is not appropriate for men's and women's clothes to be hung on the same line," he said.

"Where should we hang them?" I asked.

"Anywhere else. Hang them on the barbed wire fence," was his suggestion.

Surprisingly enough one of the sullen kitchen workers, when he saw our predicament, offered to put up a line for our use.

We got our belongings together and waited for a vehicle to come get us. In addition to the things we had brought we also had the things bought for us in Pleiku and food items we had purchased for the rest of the group back at Camp Wilderness.

"Judging by the way the revolution generally operates they're apt to come and tell us we have to walk," I said jokingly to Joan.

At one o'clock Shouty appeared at the window with a gun-toting soldier. "You'd better get started," he said, "if you want to make it before dark."

"Did the vehicle come?" I asked, surprised that we hadn't heard any.

"Vehicle?" he said. "You're walking. You're only going a few kilometers to the other side of the valley."

"Why didn't you tell us we would be walking?" I asked. "We would have packed differently."

It took us several minutes to get some essentials from the big suitcase, and put some things in. We'd take the food · items, we decided, and leave clothing.

"You can't leave those things here," Shouty said. "You must take them."

"Maybe the guard and I could take the suitcase on a pole," Norm suggested.

"No, Norm," I said, and was glad when the guard declined. He would do nothing but accompany us. I knew Norm would have a hard enough time making the trip without the extra weight.

"There's no way we can carry all these things," I said. "We are going to leave the suitcase and the sewing machine."

Shouty looked dubious and said we would have to make out a receipt for those items. I agreed and wrote out a paper stating in English that I was leaving them. I signed my name and gave it to him.

"When are you coming back for these?" he asked.

That was too much! "How should I know when or if I'll come back?" I exploded. "I am a prisoner. I have nothing to say about what I do or where I go!" Then in a more moderate manner I added, "If I am allowed to return for these things and can get help in bringing them, I will come for them. That's all I can say. Thank you for the help you've given us. Goodbye, brother."

"Goodbye, sister," he replied.

We struck off on a footpath heading west. The guard was in a hurry, but uncertain of the way. Several times we had to retrace our steps when he chose a path leading nowhere. A woman working in her fields finally led him part of the way.

The small suitcase with the manuscripts was heavy, and so was the ammunition case and sandbag of canned milk. Once the guard let us stop briefly before urging us on.

"Why didn't they send a vehicle for us?" we asked him.

He looked at us scornfully. "Would the Americans send a vehicle for only four people?" he asked.

"Yes," Norm said, "they would send one for one person."

I looked at the guard and realized the vast difference between his experience and ours. In his experience if you needed to get somewhere you walked. It was as simple as that. He didn't even think in terms of vehicles.

We crossed a stream and made our way up the other side

161

of the valley. Curious villagers watched us as we approached a military post where northern soldiers were playing volleyball. The guard went into a thatch building and we flopped down on the ground outside. I wondered if perhaps John would be here but tried not to let myself hope.

"What are we supposed to do with them?" I heard someone inside ask.

"I don't know," was the answer. "I was only instructed to bring them here."

It was getting to be the story of our lives, I thought, with a wry smile. Nobody seemed to want us or know what to do with us.

SEVEN

Fat City

"Are there any other foreigners here?" I asked the soldier who was leading us into a large stockade. "We were told that a group from another camp was being brought here."

The stockade we entered was completely without occupants, but judging from the size of the long narrow shelters under construction, it was being built to accommodate several hundred prisoners. An adjoining stockade already bustled with life, and its occupants lined the fence to watch as we were taken into one of the shelters.

"The prisoners from that other camp have not yet arrived," the guard said. Then as an afterthought he added, "We have only one Filipino here."

"Ike!" we exclaimed happily. Then to the soldier we said, "Could we please see him? We know him and were with him in the other camp. He can give us news about the others."

"Tomorrow," the man replied. Seeing our disappointment he apparently reconsidered, because he disappeared and returned in a few minutes with a small, balding, dark-complected man we had never seen before.

Our faces must have registered our surprise because the man stood and watched us, puzzled and uncertain.

"We're glad to meet you," I said to him, "but we were expecting someone else. When they told us there was a Filipino here, we thought it was Ike Tolentino, who was with us at another camp."

163

At the mention of Ike's name, this man's face lit up. "Do you know Ike?" he asked. "He works for the same company I do. Was he captured too? Where is he? How is he?"

"He's with some other foreigners in a camp in the jungle, but we think they will be coming here."

Arellano Bugarin, or 'Bogh' as he told us to call him, had walked here a week before with several hundred Vietnamese prisoners from a large tea plantation near Pleiku where they had been held previously.

Bogh's heavily accented "Filipino English" was hard for us to understand, but as we shared the evening rice, fish powder and grease soup we exchanged experiences. He was a mechanical engineer and had been given a temporary duty assignment in Pleiku to work with the Vietnamese army. When President Thieu ordered the evacuation of Pleiku the week after Banmethuot fell, a South Vietnamese colonel promised Bogh a ride in a helicopter coming to take him out. The helicopter never came.

Exhausted from the walk over, we hung our nets in one end of the long empty shelter and went to bed early. When we awoke, we found Bogh had already built a fire and was boiling drinking water in a steel helmet he'd been given. He had skimmed the congealed lard from the uneaten grease soup and saved the uneaten rice.

"I make fried rice for you," he explained.

"That's a clever idea," we agreed, impressed.

"I learn to cook from the other prisoners," he told us. "I learn many things."

He was eager to accommodate to any procedures or ideas we might have, but seemed uncertain about what these might be. "You tell me, I do," he said.

His response to any suggestion was, "Sure, sure."

I hoped when Ike came, he would be more relaxed with us. At least then he'd have someone who spoke his language.

The officials at the camp were very friendly. They questioned us about our activities prior to capture, but didn't pressure or harass us in any way. In fact when a sentry guard forbade Bogh to put rice out to dry for "rice crunchies," one of the officers immediately came in and reversed the order.

"If only John were here," I thought. But by bedtime on the 31st there was no sign of the others. I crawled into the net to put LuAnne to sleep, and was so exhausted I didn't bother to get out again. Before Norm and Joan blew out the candle, I was asleep.

I was awakened by a commotion at the doorway and some familiar voices. I sat up inside the net just in time to see John walk in. His eyes spotted the stained white cotton net just about the time I crawled out, and we met in the narrow aisle in a tight embrace.

"I've missed you guys so much," he said. "It seemed like such a long time."

"It sure did," I agreed.

He looked in the net where LuAnne lay sleeping. She barely stirred as he kissed her.

Looking around then and greeting the others, I was shocked at their appearance. They were emaciated and gaunt looking, and collapsed onto the bamboo platforms. Until that moment, I hadn't realized what a blessing the two weeks spent at the hospital had been to the four of us.

"Everybody has had malaria except Paul and me," John said. "But Betty is in the worst shape now."

"Where is Betty?" I asked, alarmed.

"She's back at the truck," he said. "Several of the Vietnamese prisoners carried her to the truck when she collapsed on the trail before we left."

"Hey, somebody better come with me to get Aunt Betty," Paul called just then from the doorway. John and I headed out after him into the drizzling rain. Betty sat under the eaves of one of the guards' houses. She looked ravaged by the disease. Paul helped her to her feet, and with her arms around John and Paul she shuffled slowly over to the stockade. I picked up the rest of the baggage and followed.

Joan helped hang Betty's net and get her settled for the night. Ike was in the group and he and Bogh were soon chatting quietly in Tagalog. Most of the others had already turned in for the night when we moved LuAnne over and crawled under the net again. She woke then enough to know Daddy had come, but went right back to sleep.

John and I lay inside the net and talked for some time. He

165

told me conditions at Camp Wilderness had gone steadily downhill. The morale of the prisoners declined as malaria reached epidemic proportions.

"I stopped taking siestas," he said, "because that was the hardest time of the day for me. When I was busy I didn't miss you so much, but if I lay down to rest, it just seemed my mind would work overtime thinking of all the things that might happen to keep us apart. So I generally spent that time on a bench down by the fence reading the Bible and praying.

"I read the passage where Jesus said, 'Ask and you shall receive that your joy may be full,' and I decided to make a very specific request. I asked God to take us out of Camp Wilderness and bring us together by the end of the month, and to give us a speedy release. Last Sunday at Bible Study I shared with the other missionaries some of the things I had been studying, and they agreed to claim this with me.

"It was hard to believe God would answer our prayer to get out by the end of the month, especially when a visiting official promised Lil on the 30th that he would send us a supply of malaria medicine that would last for some time. The next day everything was proceeding according to routine until about four in the afternoon when they came to us and told us to bring our things out to the supply area because we were leaving! I've been praising the Lord all the way here, and I believe he's going to bring us back to our families soon."

The next morning John, LuAnne and I took the fire-blackened dried food can and set off for the river to get some water to boil. After we passed the guard post, LuAnne scampered happily ahead of us. Prisoners carrying containers of water up the steep hill to the camp kitchen greeted us as we passed them.

"Last week when I was down at the river bathing at Camp Wilderness," John said, "I picked out six little stones and brought them with me."

I looked at him questioningly and he went on, "I remembered how God told Joshua before he took them through the Jordan river that he should have someone from each tribe take a stone from the dry river bed and set them up as a

166

reminder to their children and their children's children of what God had done for them.

"When we get back together with the other kids," he continued, "I'm going to read that passage to them and give each member of the family one of these stones to keep as a reminder of what I believe God is going to do in bringing us together again."

Several encouraging things happened over the next few days. The day after the others arrived, a camp official told us he would allow one of us to walk to a small market six kilometers away to purchase items for the group, if we had money. We were delighted. Those worthless scraps of paper Jay had once suggested we "might as well use for toilet paper" could actually be used to improve our living situation! John was down with a bad headache, so Paul was the only one physically able to make the long walk and carry supplies back.

We had some misgivings as to how he'd make out when he set off. How could he bargain when he couldn't speak Vietnamese? None of us had any idea of what was available or how prices might have changed since liberation.

Paul returned a few hours later in good spirits and with a loaded knapsack. He had made out fine, he said, bargaining by using his fingers. And everyone was friendly and helpful. The guard who accompanied him was in no hurry and seemed glad for the opportunity to chat with some of the local girls. He even allowed Paul to stop for a glass of coffee at the local coffee shop, though he declined to join him.

Paul had bought garlics, onions and red peppers to spice up the rice. He also had raw peanuts, bananas, a tiny pineapple, a couple of notebooks to use for toilet paper, some cheap local cigarettes, candles and matches. We greeted each item with oohs and aahs as he took it from the knapsack.

The following day Mr. Spectacles paid us a visit. He had been away from the area, he said. He brought a second-hand Japanese-made camera he had purchased and asked Jay to teach him how to use it. He then asked Jay to take a picture of him with LuAnne.

"I'm glad to see her looking so well," he said. "I was

167

really worried about her that first time I saw her. I was afraid she wouldn't stand the trip."

"I have good news for you," he told us. "My superiors have decided to raise the food allowance for non-Asian prisoners from .6 to 1.2 piastres a day. You will still receive your meals from the camp kitchen, but you will receive extra rations. I don't know yet what they will be."

"What about the Filipinos?" Jay asked.

"This increase is only for non-Asians," he said, "because they are larger and are unaccustomed to a rice diet. It includes only Americans, Canadians, Australians and New Zealanders."

"New Zealanders?" Jay asked. But Mr. Spectacles changed the subject.

"We are preparing living quarters for you in the other compound," he said. "Would you prefer to have private rooms for the families?"

We looked at each other and shrugged. Not knowing what the options really were, we were reluctant to express an opinion. Somehow things never turned out as we envisioned. Finally Joan said, "Of course we would prefer private rooms, but we have become accustomed to living together over the last few months, and we would not want to be separated from each other."

"Of course not," he agreed, "but we will see that you have some privacy."

After Mr. Spectacles left we speculated about what New Zealanders might have been caught by the changeover.

"Maybe they were members of a medical team," was one suggestion.

"Or newspaper reporters," was another.

But Paul and Peter were convinced they were members of an all-girl band complete with instruments which would certainly join us any time! The mystery wasn't cleared up until our release months later when we learned one New Zealand medical doctor from a Catholic hospital in Kontum had been held for several months before being taken to Saigon and released.

The next day when we were told to move our belongings

into our new quarters we found prisoners from that compound still at work putting on the thatch walls and pounding forked branches into the ground to support the bamboo platform beds. One of them grinned at me.

"Isn't it beautiful?" he asked. "Just like the Hilton Hotel!"

"Of course," I agreed, looking up at the holes in the used-tin roof. "But when are you going to put in the electricity and air conditioning?"

"Later," he said.

We selected one of the four cubicles being added to one end. It was roughly six by eight feet in size, of which a four by six foot area was taken up by the split bamboo bed. It was separated by a six foot high partition of discarded tarpaulin and woven bamboo from Betty on one side and Norm and Joan on the other. Dick and Lil had the fourth cubicle and the five men were in the larger main section.

"I wish," I said to John, "now that we have our own room we could have a separate bed for LuAnne. She's such a restless sleeper and always seems to have her elbows in my back or her feet on top of me. Do you think we could ask them to put a shelf across the foot of our bed for her? We could put the small army net over her."

The prisoner workers smiled at the request and referred us to the North Vietnamese supervisor. He seemed to have difficulty understanding our suggestion but finally said, "You can use the leftover materials and make it any way you want."

The little shelf-bed we constructed proved to be an object of curiosity to the camp personnel. They pointed it out to visiting dignitaries and friends.

"Look," they would say, laughing, "the child doesn't sleep with her parents. She sleeps up there."

For us the new arrangement was ideal. LuAnne was close enough that we could touch her or whisper to her by simply sitting up. But her thrashing no longer kept me awake and I didn't have to worry about rolling over on her. The leftover thatch we put on the beds helped to soften them and keep out the cold drafts and all of us were sleeping more soundly.

But LuAnne was clearly not enthusiastic over the new set-up. "Can't I sleep with you?" she asked. "I'll lie very still."

One night as I prepared to tuck her in she burst out crying. I lifted her down and held her on my lap.

"What's the matter?" I asked.

"Mommy," she sobbed, "I wake up in the night and I can't see you and I wonder if you're still here. Sometimes I look to see if the suitcases are still here, because I think if the suitcases are here then you must be too." The suitcase containing the Bru New Testament manuscript was at her feet.

I was glad it was dark so she couldn't see my tears as I sought to reassure her. "Honey, Mommy and Daddy would never leave you. You are the most precious thing we have. We might leave everything we have. We might even leave the suitcases, but we wouldn't leave you."

"Not even if they came to get you in the night and I was sleeping?" she asked.

"No, LuAnne, we would wake you up and take you with us."

Reassured, she climbed up onto her shelf-bed and was asleep within minutes. But I sat there in the dark stunned by the realization of the deep burden my little girl had been carrying. The full impact of what it must mean to her to see the complete helplessness of her parents who had always before seemed so firmly in control of any situation now hit me. Every move we had made had been sudden and without warning. A command from the guards would set us scurrying to collect our things and we would be led away. No wonder she was uneasy about letting us out of her sight!

I slipped around to the main room to join the others around the fire for an hour or two, but I remained troubled. Later in our own bed, I told John about the conversation I had had with LuAnne.

"I don't care how uncomfortable it is," I said, tears flowing again, "if she continues to be afraid to sleep alone, I think we should bring her back in with us. I'm not in favor of a child sleeping with parents, but this isn't exactly a normal situation, and no child should have to carry a burden of fear like that."

Before we went to sleep we prayed together that God would deliver her from this fear and help us to point her to his love as her ultimate security. In the dark uncertainty that confronted us, we knew that was the only security any of us had.

Over succeeding days we rejoiced to see God answer that prayer. During the day LuAnne played happily around the area, visiting in Aunt Betty's room, watching Uncle Ike plant pepper bushes he found outside the fence, drawing pictures and letters in the dirt floor of the meeting hall next to our house, or squatting by the fire supervising our efforts to add variety to the prison kitchen fare.

The tiny room proved a tremendous blessing to both LuAnne and me. During the siesta hour she could sit on her bed, while John and I rested, and play with the paper dolls she had made, or her tiny yarn dolls. She could chatter to herself or even sing quietly without drawing disapproving looks. Here I could teach or discipline her out of sight, if not out of sound, of others. And here she could retreat and feel accepted when she was confused or hurt by reactions of the adult society around her.

Our friends from Camp Wilderness were brought into the stockade adjacent to the one where we were now living. We watched them line up in groups outside the fence near our house before requesting permission to go to the river. Their unmilitary antics and goof-ups in trying to count off left us in stitches. Over the fence we passed news and greetings.

Major Phuong reported that his wife and children had reached Saigon safely. She had sent him a food parcel and included a can of meat for us. Dr. Ly was very ill with malaria, and one or two had died from it. Pierre had no word about his family.

One man asked us to write out the words to the songs "Five Hundred Miles" and "I'm Leaving On A Jet Plane." I smiled at the selection, though I could identify with the sentiment. Our own theme song was, "Please release me, let me go, I don't like it any more . . ." though we did improvise a bit on "Don't need no barbed wire to remind me, I'm just a prisoner of war."

By the second week of June we began to receive supplemental issues of cans of Russian beef (dubbed "dog food" by Jay who was not tremendously impressed by its looks or flavor), powdered milk and sugar. It wasn't much, but compared to our situations in the previous camp this was Fat City.

On one occasion all prisoners received two packs of North Vietnamese cigarettes, a tube of toothpaste and several pieces of banana candy.

I turned over our cigarettes to Paul for the smokers in the group. They had in the past given cigarettes to other prisoners who had helped us—those who built our house, the kitchen workers, and others. But when LuAnne discovered I had given away "her cigarettes" she was indignant.

"I wanted to blow smoke bubbles like Uncle Jay does!" she said, referring to a demonstration Jay had given with a tiny bamboo tube and some soap water we had given LuAnne to play with.

The purpose of this camp was the political re-education of the men who had been officers in the South Vietnamese army. Group lectures were held in the morning in the large shelter near our house, and discussion sessions in the prisoners' quarters in the afternoon. The men were eager to get started on this program, hoping that completion of the course would result in their being able to return to their families.

We were not included in the re-education program and found ourselves left to our own devices for longer periods of time. We had no organization within our group. All decisions up until now had been made by "general consensus." It had gotten to be a joke when someone said, "general consensus is. . . ," because in our group of strong-minded individualists that generally meant the speaker had gotten one or two people to agree with him on a course of action.

"I really think," I said to John, "we need somebody who can make decisions. You know, like what to get at the market, how often to use the cans of meat, whether or not to have bananas today or save them till tomorrow, or how to divide the sugar ration. It's not that these are such difficult

172

decisions, but without somebody to make them it's confusion. Why couldn't we elect Paul, for example?"

"I think," John said, "you'd find he wouldn't want to do it. And probably the others would feel the same."

I knew he was right. Earlier suggestions about "organizing" group responsibilities had been firmly nixed by "general consensus." But the next day when we were going down to the river to bathe, I discussed the problem with the other women. If the men were not interested in doing anything, we decided, maybe we could.

"Joan," I said, "why don't you take the job to begin with and we'll all back you up. Then when you get tired of the job, one of us can take it."

Joan was dubious. "I'll try it," she finally said, "but if there's any flack from the men, I'll quit."

There was no objection from the men, and things went much more smoothly. Joan prepared market lists, but with camp personnel busy with political re-education it was becoming difficult to get permission to go to the market. She rationed out the supplies and decided what to use each day. Two weeks later when Lil was very ill and others, too, Joan's skill as a nurse was needed and she passed the job on to me. I continued to be "housemother" until we left for the North two months later.

Another time walking to the river we discussed the use of money. I compiled a list of how much each person had and gave it to Joan. Most had very little and some none at all. The money packet we had brought from Nha Trang (containing the equivalent of a little over $100 U.S.) represented the largest amount. Everyone agreed all money should be used for the whole group, but everyone's idea of how to spend it differed. I suggested that in addition to essential food purchases ordered by Joan, each individual should be given an allotment equivalent to a few cents a week to spend on whatever he chose. This could be used each week or accumulated for several weeks. The others agreed to the plan and before a market trip the "housemother" added these personal items to the list. The smokers generally ordered cigarettes. John and I preferred peanuts. LuAnne ordered candy.

Ike asked for a jar of hair pomade. Bogh rarely used his personal allotment, saying there was nothing he needed.

The rainy season had now begun in earnest. John contrived a series of bamboo troughs to catch the water from the leaks over our beds and carry it outside. Elsewhere we just walked around the drips. Inside the fence was a sea of mud, and the steep hill to the river was a disaster area.

The cold rains made us want to wear all the clothes we owned, but made it difficult to get them dry.

"Phew! You smell like a fire sale!" I said to John while climbing into bed one night.

"I know," he said, "I had to hold my shirt over the fire to get it dry."

One night it rained so hard the water overflowed the ditches we had dug around the house and swept across the dirt floor.

We fought not only against the water but also against assorted little beasts. Norm and Joan made a spectacular exit from their room one noon when a snake crawled along the wall above their bed seeking refuge from the rain. Every night we heard the patter of feet as the rats combed the house to see if we'd left any food they could get. They had no difficulty chewing through plastic or cloth to get sugar or peanuts.

John and I had been puzzled by a rhythmic rustling sound we heard in the nighttime. The puzzlement left us when our bed was invaded by a horde of termites. Their pincers clamped into the skin of my hand when I tried to brush them off and they chewed big holes in the net before we could get it up off the bed. We retreated to the bachelors' quarters for the rest of the night, and in the morning poured boiling water down the holes they had come up. The comfortable thatch on the bed was full of squashed dead termites and had to be thrown out.

The 12th of June was Philippine Independence Day. We opened the can of pork Mrs. Phuong had sent us, and had a special meal in honor of the occasion. Mr. Spectacles had come to camp the day before to lecture the other prisoners. He stopped by to tell Ike and Bogh that their government now had an embassy in Saigon. He was quite contemptuous, however, of the Philippine government.

174

"The Philippines is nothing but a colony of the United States," he told Ike.

Ike was incensed, but refrained from arguing while Mr. Spectacles was present. "Oh boy!" he said darkly after Mr. Spectacles had gone. That was as strong an oath as Ike would allow himself, at least in the presence of us women.

The rest of us were amused and not above teasing Ike a bit. "I don't know why we should celebrate Philippine Independence Day," someone said, "now that we know the Philippines is just a colony."

Every official who visited us had one piece of advice—"Keep healthy." We repeated the advice sarcastically to each other every time some fresh calamity befell. Bogh gashed his head on a rusty nail and a decayed tooth caused his face to swell with pain. Betty, Ike, Norm and Lil had a recurrence of malaria. LuAnne and I broke out with an itchy rash. Lil developed an infected carbuncle on her eye and others on her back.

The camp officials had put captured South Vietnamese doctors in charge of clinics in each of the camps. We found young Dr. Hai friendly and sympathetic. When he had medicine, he willingly gave it. Usually he had none. When LuAnne came down again with the same symptoms she had at Camp Wilderness, I went to the clinic. Dr. Hai listened as I described LuAnne's symptoms and said, "She should be given an antibiotic, but I have nothing here to give her. You might try talking to the camp authorities. I've tried it and gotten nothing."

After lunch I went into our room and lay down on the bed. LuAnne was sleeping on her shelf-bed. This was the third day she had eaten almost nothing. I felt discouraged. John came into the room and saw the tears in my eyes.

"What's the matter?" he asked, sitting down beside me.

"Oh, John," I said, "it's the same thing over and over. She gets so sick and there's nothing to give her. Whenever anyone does give her anything it's never enough to really knock the infection."

"I know," he said, "I've been thinking a lot about it. We don't really know what God's will is for LuAnne. We would like to see her healed and we know God is able to heal her with or without medicine. But if we have to face a long

175

imprisonment, or something really difficult for LuAnne to endure, it might be better for him to take her now. Let's commit her to him for whatever is best, because he does know."

John bowed his head and prayed. Then he crawled over to his side of the bed and lay down. My heart was at peace. We both had the calm assurance that God was in control.

A few minutes later I sat up aware of a movement at the doorway beside my head. A man stood there dressed in the usual prison garb. He held out his hand and gave me a small packet.

"Here," he said, "this is for the little girl."

I opened it and found a number of yellow tablets. I knew there were several prisoners working with the prison doctors, and I thought Dr. Hai must have received some new medicines and sent some over.

"Thank you," I said to the man. "How is she supposed to take it?"

"I don't know," he said. "You'll have to ask the doctor." With that he turned and left.

I thought it a bit odd that Dr. Hai had sent medicine without sending instructions for administering it, but after the siesta hour I hurried over to the clinic.

"Did you send the medicine over for my little girl?" I asked him.

His blank look gave me the answer even before he spoke. "No, I don't have anything to give her," he said.

I held out the packet for him to see. He recognized the medicine and said, "That's very good. It's just what she needs." And he told me what dosage to give her.

On the way back to our house I wondered who the man was and how he knew LuAnne was sick. I wished I had looked at him more carefully or thanked him more adequately. I could only thank God and ask him to reward this man who had shared something irreplaceable without considering his own possible need.

He was not the only prisoner to demonstrate concern. The first day we moved into the stockade a man gave me for LuAnne a vial of vitamin tablets his wife had sent him. When I protested taking something which he obviously needed, he told me, "It's all right. I still have some. Anyway, you and I have lived a good share of our lives. But she is young and has her whole life before her. We want her to make it through."

On the 23rd of June several of us were sitting in the house dethorning some weeds we had picked outside the fence so we could cook them for lunch. Ike had recognized them as edible. "In the Philippines," he said, "we feed them to the pigs."

Our first experiment with them had proved them tasty, but we hadn't been careful enough about the thorns! I felt a little like the loveable Tigger in *Winnie the Pooh*, who tried to eat thistles. This time we were more careful.

As we sat there working, a minor official hurried in to tell us to clean up the house. "You are going to be visited by a high official," he said.

We swept the dirt floor and put the sooty pans and cans out of sight. "He must be really important," someone said. "It's the first time they've ever given us advance warning."

"Wonder if he'd like to stay for lunch," I added, continuing to pick thorns off the weeds.

Numerous guards stood around the compound while the "Big Man" addressed the Vietnamese prisoners. When he finished, Mr. Spectacles brought him around to see us and introduced him as, "My superior from Hanoi." One of the South Vietnamese prisoners later told us he was a two-star general.

The man smiled and addressed us in a friendly manner. He explained that the investigation concerning us had been delayed because of the many more pressing matters confronting the new government.

"I assure you that you will eventually be allowed to return to your families," he said, "and when you do, I ask you to express our gratitude to the progressive people in your countries, who helped us achieve our goal of independence and freedom.

"In the meantime," he concluded, "be patient and keep yourselves healthy—especially the women, and most particularly, the child."

Mr. Spectacles asked Jay to translate the speech for those who did not understand Vietnamese. Then Joan said to Jay,

"Would you please tell him that we are doing everything we can to try to maintain our health, but it is absolutely impossible in this situation. Many of us are sick, and without proper food and medicines I am afraid that our health will continue to get worse."

"Yes, I realize the conditions are not ideal," he said, "but you must be patient."

When they left, several of us gave Mr. Spectacles short letters we had written to our families. He had told us to do this, but could promise nothing more than that he would give them to his superior. Unsealed and written in simple English, our letters stated merely that we were well and anxious to see our families, and that Vietnamese authorities were studying our case to make sure our activities were non-political in nature. Peter had added to his note that his beard was now four inches long.

"What did you put that in for?" Paul asked. "They'll probably figure that's a code message for something or other."

Paul decided one day we had been using the wrong techniques to try to better our living conditions. Turning to a supposedly hidden microphone in the rafters of the hut, he began reeling off a series of fulsome phrases in praise of the "glorious r-r-revolution." That afternoon to our absolute astonishment the guards gave us a piece of fresh beef!

"You see," Paul said smugly, "you just have to use the right psychology."

Evenings were the best part of the day. The gates were closed, the guards were all on the outside, and inside the fence everyone relaxed a bit. When the weather was clear the setting sun painted the sky vivid shades of pink, orange and violet before it slipped behind the Cambodian hills across the valley. Often we took LuAnne on an evening stroll around what she referred to as the "parameter," stopping briefly to visit with friends or watch the progress of an intricate game of Chinese chess. At one house LuAnne's special friends sometimes called her over to get a piece of brown sugar or a piece of candy one of them had received from his family. Once they gave her a box of crickets to play with, another time a tiny plastic toy they found on a work detail.

When the sky darkened we hurried home to hang the nets while we could still see and get LuAnne to bed. She liked to have John play the harmonica while she went to sleep. In the darkness it assured her that we were there.

Snatches of bantering conversation coming over the partition drew us around to the main room. It was still too early to go to bed and expect to sleep all night. Peter was rearranging the firewood under the five gallon container of bubbling and steaming water in the center of the room.

"Anybody seen my pipe?" Paul asked, fumbling around in the dark end of the room for the tiny bamboo pipe he had misplaced a hundred times since he'd made it.

"The water's finished," Peter announced, consulting his watch. John got up to help him lift the crossbar from which the can was suspended over the fire.

I put a handful of green tea leaves into two of the fire-blackened milk cans and filled them with the freshly boiled water. "Tea's on!" I called, and in a few minutes some of the others came in from their rooms, bowls in hand.

There was a relaxed, almost euphoric air about these evenings around the fire. Somehow we'd made it through another day. And barring some unexpected invasion by storm or termites we could now look forward to a few hours of escape from the unpleasant realities that claimed our attention during the day.

Even in sleep, however, we could not entirely escape because by now most of us were prisoners even in our dreams.

At Camp Sunshine Joan dreamed that her children, Pat and Doug, came to be with them, and she had felt glad and sorry all at the same time. John dreamed he'd been released and was sitting at a table loaded with food. But he couldn't eat any of it because everybody kept asking him questions so he had no time to eat.

"Now *that's* one I can believe might happen," I laughed.

In the quiet hours before falling asleep we sometimes just liked to think about what it might be like to be out again. Jay liked to imagine himself in Pennsylvania landing at the Harrisburg Airport and being met by all his family. Ike liked to imagine he was being released at Clark Air Force Base in the Philippines and told he could have anything he wanted from the PX or commissary. I liked to imagine us living in Houghton as a family. I could visualize myself playing tennis on the Houghton College courts overlooking the lovely Genessee Valley, taking art, voice and violin lessons and reading all the things I'd always wanted to read.

But before we entered the private world of our sleeping nets, we shared an hour or two around the fire. Sometimes we reminisced about family and friends, places we had been and things we had done. For several evenings we planned an itinerary for Peter if he got a chance to visit the United States. Sometimes we speculated about what was being done about us in the outside world.

Often we sang. The query, "Do you know this one?" followed by a few bars of a folk song, hit tune, hymn or spiritual usually found at least a few affirmative responses. Peter and Jay gave a pompous rendition of Gilbert and Sullivan's "We are peers of highest station." And Jay occasionally broke out with "God save our noble czar." But more typical were such selections as "Home On The Range" or "Waltzing Matilda." One evening Paul had the rest of us convulsed with laughter when he began singing in his best Nashville twang, "I've got tears in my ears from lying on my back in bed while I cry over you."

"That isn't really a song, is it?" one of us questioned. "You just now made that up."

"No," he protested. "I didn't make it up. It's a legitimate song. I heard it over the radio once, but I don't remember any of the rest of the words."

Sometimes we talked about politics or religion. "Tell me," Peter said to me one evening, "do Christians still believe that simplistic theory about creation?"

"What do you mean by 'simplistic?' " I asked cautiously.

"Oh, that God created the heavens and earth in seven days like it says in Genesis," he replied.

"Well," I said, "those who believe the Bible accept the Genesis account to be true, though there are many ideas as to its interpretation."

The discussion waxed hotter as others joined in. Finally Paul said, "It all comes down to whether or not you believe that however it actually came about, God was the one who

180

set things in motion, or whether they just happened by chance."

Jay walked in from visiting some of his Vietnamese friends just as the discussion was ending.

"Do you believe that Christianity is the only way a person can know God?" he asked. "What about all the Buddhists and Hindus and the people who've never even heard of Christianity? Is God going to reject them?"

"Jesus said he was the only way to God," I said. "He said, 'I am the way, the truth and the life. No man cometh to the Father but by me.'"

"I can't accept that," he said. "It seems so arrogant and unloving."

"That's not my opinion, Jay," I reminded him, "It's what Jesus said."

"Oh well," Paul joked, "we don't have to worry about it. "We're going to hell anyway. Right, Peter?"

Lying in bed that night I thought about the discussion. There were times when I thought God must have had a sense of humor when he threw our group together, but at other times I felt overwhelmed by my own inadequacy to represent Christ in this situation.

Why couldn't God have chosen someone more dynamic, more intellectual and more widely read? Someone who spoke Vietnamese fluently and related to the needs of the Vietnamese people all around us? Someone who more adequately demonstrated the Christian graces? I could think of any number of people in our own Wycliffe organization who would have been much better qualified than I. Not that I would wish any of them in this situation, I thought wryly. But from God's point of view, I thought he could have done a whole lot better in his selection.

I wished that somehow I could convey to the others that to me the fantastic good news of Christianity was not that there was *only* one way to God, but that there was in fact *any* way to a right relationship with him. Animism certainly didn't offer this, nor did the brand of Buddhism-Animism I had observed among the Vietnamese. The most these seemed to offer was an uneasy truce with the spirit world in this life and uncertainty about the life after death.

181

The plight of the people searching for God and not even knowing he had provided a way for them to know him had always concerned me. Their ultimate fate I was glad to trust to a loving and just God. I had recently read in the Gospel of Luke Jesus' statement that a man who does not know what his master requires and does things deserving punishment will receive more sympathetic treatment than one who knows and refuses to obey. But what about the ones who were looking for answers to questions about the meaning of their lives now?

I thought about Pa Tahn. Disgusted by the inadequacy of the spirit sacrifices to meet his personal needs, he had cried out to Yiang Sursĭ, the Creator of the universe, "I don't know anything about you, but if you can help me, please help me."

When he was sent to us by his chief to learn to read and write Bru, Pa Tahn read for the first time the Gospel of Mark in Bru. He eagerly accepted its message and was hungry for more. "Look at all of God's Word you have," he said reproachfully to us one day picking up one of our English Bibles, "and look at the tiny bit we have. We've *got* to get all of God's Word in our language."

How sad it would have been, I thought, if Pa Tahn had never heard that Yiang Sursĭ loved him and could help him. And how many hungry, seeking people like him there must be in other areas of the world.

On the 28th of June the camp authorities decided to move Lil to the hospital facility where the Johnsons, LuAnne and I had spent some time. Her eye was not healing. The carbuncles on her back were worse and she was very weak. The ambulance that came to get her consisted of six Vietnamese prisoners and a long pole. The men slung the Phillipses' tarp from the pole and Joan and Betty helped her in. Dick followed the Vietnamese men with a small bag of their things. He had not yet regained his strength from the battle with malaria. We were sorry to see them go, but relieved that something was finally being done for Lil.

We began to discuss ways we might celebrate the 4th of July. But as the day drew near enthusiasm waned. John's diary for July 2 records that Joan was sick in bed and Betty not well. Jay's malaria had returned and Bogh was in terrible pain from his toothache.

182

When the 4th of July proved to be cold and rainy, Paul commented, "That's not so unusual. It always used to rain every time we planned a 4th of July picnic!"

By supper time the weather had cleared enough so we could sit outside and eat the special fruit salad I had made from bananas, pineapple and a lemon.

"This evening," I said, "we'll have a party and fix noodle soup."

We decided to put LuAnne to bed as usual, but promised to save her some soup. John sat on our bed and played "My Country 'Tis of Thee," "God Bless America" and "America the Beautiful" on his harmonica while she went to sleep. Then we slipped out to join the others.

We were in high spirits as we launched into a rendition of "MacNamara's Band." Peter began beating out the time on one of the pots. Ike improvised drums with some bamboo tubes. And Paul went to get his comb and a piece of paper to use as an instrument.

"Quiet!" he called out from the other end of the building, and we broke off in surprise.

Then we heard it. The ominous rhythmic scrunching noise that meant we were being invaded by termites.

We groaned and fell into action. This time the hordes were coming up under Betty's and Peter's beds. We stirred up the fire and began heating cans of water. In the absence of insecticides, boiling water was the only weapon we had, and we plotted our defense with all the strategy of a military campaign. When we had reached a stand-off most of us drifted off to bed, but Peter and Paul did battle till after midnight.

"Wonder if any other 4th of July parties got cancelled today on account of termites," I said to John as we climbed wearily into bed. "Sometimes I have the feeling that the insects are taking over the world!"

EIGHT

The Potato Patch Camp

"Happy Birthday, Jay," I said handing him a small, with-ered-looking banana. It was the only one left from our last market trip.

"Thanks, Carolyn," he said unhappily, "but this is one birthday I'd just as soon forget."

"I know how you feel," I sympathized. "It hasn't been much of a day to celebrate, has it?"

It was the afternoon of July 6, but up till now we had been too busy to even remember it was Jay's birthday. Moving days with the "Liberation Army" were never pleasant. This move, while by far the easiest, was no exception.

I had been wakened that morning by the voice of a guard standing by the bed. He limped because of what seemed to be a sore foot. "Tell the others to get their things together and move them into the house being built for you outside the fence," he said.

I quickly got out of bed and went around to spread the news. We'd had rumors of a possible move, but as usual the actual order to move was sudden and without warning.

Before we'd had time to get our things together, Limpy was back with a work detail of South Vietnamese prisoners. He was very annoyed to find us still not ready to move. "I thought I told you to pack everything up," he said crossly.

"We're trying to," I said. "I didn't know there was any rush." The prisoner detail snickered openly and this irritated Limpy still further.

Turning to them, he snapped, "As soon as they get their things together, you take the beds apart and construct beds in the other house."

Then to me he said, "You get a broom and come sweep out the other house."

Leaving John to finish packing our things, I went around to get the twig broom and followed Limpy out of the compound.

"How did you hurt your foot?" I asked. But he didn't answer.

Outside the fence we approached an almost completed thatch building. The bright green of the thatch walls and roof advertised its newness. Thatch partitions divided it into a row of four rooms. Ducking under the low overhanging roof I looked into the rooms. They were a bit larger than our present cubicles but very dark, the only light in the building coming from the small doorways. "At least the roof looks rainproof," I thought peering up into the dark thatch.

A very young soldier wearing a royal blue sweater walked over as I started to sweep the pieces of thatch and bamboo from the dirt floor. "You're moving out with us now," he said with a smile. "How do you like the house?"

"It seems fine," I said, "but it has one room too few." He looked puzzled and I continued, "There are enough rooms for those of us here now, but when the man and woman who are in the hospital return, where will they stay?"

For just a moment his face registered dismay, and I knew this was something he hadn't considered. Then he said confidently, "We will take care of that when the time comes."

"Can you tell me who the camp commander is?" I asked him. "I would like to ask him what we are to do about food and water."

"I am the camp commander," he said, and smiled at my look of astonishment. He was so young I wondered if he was joking, but he went on to say, "For today you will continue to get food from the prison kitchen, but beginning tomorrow you will draw your own rations and do your own cooking. You will continue to bathe and wash clothes in the river, but you may draw water for drinking and cooking from the well over there." And he pointed in the direction of the soldiers' houses.

By now the others were bringing in armloads of our possessions. In addition to our belongings, we brought the table, benches and shelves we had constructed, the firewood we had gathered, and the pots, cans and utensils we had scrounged or borrowed. Peter and Paul were annoyed with Norm and John because they had left them to carry most of the firewood. John was putting up a bed for LuAnne and Norm was building a shelf in his room.

Jay was impatient with the rest of us because of our pack-rat instinct to take everything with us we might possibly to able to use. He was also feeling depressed at being separated from his Vietnamese companions with whom he had spent a major part of his time. His continuing battle with malaria left him weak and listless. After I gave him the banana, he flopped down on the sleeping platform in the men's section. His muddy feet in the rubber tire sandals given him before the walk to Camp Wilderness hung over the edge.

"Let's cook a special soup for supper," I said to Joan. "I've been saving a couple of cans of meat for Jay's birthday and we bought some rice noodles."

But before we could get a fire started under the tiny nearby shelter we were told to use as a kitchen, a downpour of water flooded the place, dousing the fire and soaking the firewood. We learned to our dismay that the roof was not leak-proof after all as streams of water trickled in on beds and belongings.

The young camp commander in the blue sweater returned after the rain stopped. He walked in and looked at Jay. "Take your shoes off," he said. "You'll get malaria lying there with your shoes on."

I smiled to myself. At Camp Wilderness the prisoners had been ordered to take some strange precautions to prevent malaria, but this was a new one.

Jay, however, was not amused. "I already have malaria," he said rather crossly and without moving, "so what difference does it make. This is the third time I've had it, and now we have to move out here away from our friends and into a house that leaks."

Blue Sweater appeared somewhat taken aback at the

response to his command, "We'll take care of the roof tomorrow," he said, and walked out.

Betty offered the dry space just inside her door as a temporary location for a fire, but it was after dark before we were able to get the soup together. The hot meal revived our spirits somewhat, but we were glad to turn in early that night.

The next day we speculated as to what the move meant. Did the fact that we were now outside the fence mean any change in our status? Would we be allowed any more freedom of movement? Or was the move merely to separate us from and limit our contact with the South Vietnamese prisoners?

"The best way to find out," Peter said, "is to try to go somewhere and see what happens."

The men who had gone to market had noted a small shop in one of the houses in the village adjacent to the camp. It was decided that Peter and I should try to walk there and see what was available. Perhaps we could even make arrangements with that lady to purchase some supplies for us from market.

The other members of the group busied themselves around camp as Peter and I set off with an air of nonchalance that we were far from feeling. We got as far as the main gate before we were hailed. We stopped and waited while the soldier hurried over, his face registering shock and alarm.

"Where are you going?" he asked.

"Greetings, brother," I said respectfully. "Perhaps you can help us. We would like to go into the village next to the camp and buy a few things we need. There is no one at the gate to ask and we are not certain if it is necessary to get permission to go such a short distance."

"Wait right here," he said and hurried off. A few minutes later he came back with a man who had a prominent gold tooth and a young gun-toting guard. We explained our actions to Gold Tooth adding, "If we are required to get permission, we would like to know how to do this."

"Just this once I will let you go with this guard," Gold Tooth replied, "but in the future you must ask me for permission in advance. I am the supervisor."

"Fine," I agreed. "Where do you live?"

"The guard will show you when you return," he said.

Peter and I returned to the group an hour or two later feeling the trip had been a huge success. We had gotten quite a few of the items on our list. The lady from whom we'd bought them was very willing to buy other things for us if we could tell her when we would come to get them. And best of all, it seemed we'd finally made contact with a man who had authority to give us permission to go in the future.

For the next week or so we busied ourselves with "home improvement" projects. We moved the little kitchen shelter over next to the house and dug a trench around the whole area to keep out flowing rain water. The Vietnamese prisoners added an additional communal room where we could eat and keep dry, and the arrangement and construction of benches, table, hearth and shelves for this "family room" was the subject of much debate. Peter sang lustily about the "Foggy Foggy Dew" as he fitted together pieces of wood and bamboo to an outdoor bench. John removed the barbs from pieces of barbed wire and then held the pieces of wood while Peter used the pliers from our big brown suitcase to brace and fasten them together with wire.

Each morning at six Joan or I received from the supply officer our day's ration of rice, salt, lard and fish powder. Occasionally he substituted salt pork for fish powder, and every ten days he gave a supplemental ration, generally of tinned meat, sugar and milk. Ike took charge of cooking the rice and we women racked our brains to come up with new ways to fix the other basic ingredients. We devised "dog meat hash," "glazed pork," and "fried fish cakes."

On all sides of the house were sweet potato plants. One of the soldiers had given us permission to pick and cook the leaves of these plants, thereby adding a tasty and nutritious item to our diet. But quite often we would no more than get started picking them before someone would come and make us stop.

The matter of who was in charge continued to baffle us. Gold Tooth seemed to enjoy giving us orders, but rarely bothered to see whether we followed them or not. One medic came by regularly to tell us the place was a disgrace and order us to sweep it. But nobody paid much attention to us.

One evening we were surprised when the Deputy from Camp Wilderness stopped by. We greeted him warmly and invited him in to visit.

"I've been assigned to another unit," he told us, "and was sent here on an errand."

We had chatted only a few minutes when another officer appeared in the doorway. Several weeks earlier we had been introduced to him by a junior political officer as Hong. "What are you doing here?" he asked the Deputy.

"Just visiting," he answered, looking uncomfortable.

"Will you please leave," Hong said sternly, and the Deputy made a quick exit.

We were somewhat stunned, and explained to Hong the man was a guard at a previous camp and his visit merely a social one. Hong entered the room and spoke to us courteously.

"I want you to understand that from now on the only person you need have any dealings with is myself. I am personally responsible for your care. No one else here has any authority to make decisions concerning you. I would like to ask you not to make requests of anyone else or discuss things with them."

"Please tell him," Paul said, "that we are glad to get this point cleared up and that we will be glad to cooperate in this."

"You might remind him, though," someone else said, "that we can't tell the other Liberation soldiers not to come here."

"I realize this," was Hong's reply, "and I will tell them they are not to be here except on business."

"We would like to know," Joan asked, "if we are allowed to pick and eat sweet potato leaves?"

"You may pick them," Hong replied, "if you take only the leaves."

"Another man told us we should ask him about going to market," I said.

"That is wrong," he said. "You should ask me."

Remembering the very young "camp commander" in the blue sweater, I asked Hong about him. Hong smiled when I described him. "He lives in my house and works with me," he said. "At the time you moved out here I was away on business."

After Hong left Peter quipped, "I can hardly wait till the next time Gold Tooth comes around to tell us what to do. Now we can tell him, 'You'd better get out of here or we'll tell Hong!'"

It wasn't to be that simple, however. We began to suspect we were caught in the middle of a power struggle among the camp officials. Hong's decisions were not always unchallenged. And when someone forbade us to do something he had given us permission to do, Hong's solution seemed to be to compromise. When the kitchen soldiers forbade us to use the well, he said we could continue to use it but should confine our trips to twice daily. When Gold Tooth forbade us to pick potato leaves, Hong told us we could continue to pick them but only in small quantities.

It soon became obvious, though, that even the guards who delighted in harassing us were careful not to do so too openly. This emboldened us to actions not always wise. One morning when the men came back from a trip to the well, Peter was shaking his head ruefully and chuckling.

"When we got over to the well," he said, "one of the kitchen workers told us we couldn't get any water. I, of course, couldn't understand what he said, but I flew into a rage and began shouting, "Tell that so-and-so that Hong told us we could get water here and we intend to get it!' When I finally stopped shouting, one of the other men said, 'Peter, he said the well is broken.' That slowed me down for a minute but then I went on, 'Well, why doesn't someone do something about it? Let me see what's the matter.' 'Peter,' someone said, 'they're already fixing it.' I must have looked a perfect idiot ranting and stomping around."

I knew the feeling. I had had an unfortunate encounter a few days before from which I hoped I had learned a lesson. It was during the siesta hour. John and I had gone to the well to fill the water can, and LuAnne followed us over. Right beside the well was a field of corn.

"Yesterday when Norm and I came over here, the soldiers were eating corn," John remarked.

"Boy, what I wouldn't give for an ear," I said. "I wonder what would happen if we took some? You know Mr. Spectacles said, "We'll all eat together, or we'll all go hungry together.""

Picking a couple of ears, I handed them to LuAnne to carry. Then shouldering one end of the bamboo pole from which the container of water was suspended, I set off. LuAnne followed us.

A soldier appeared in the doorway of a house we passed. "Where did you get that corn?" he shouted.

John gestured with his head in the direction of the well. "You can't take that corn!" the soldier shouted.

"Let's just keep going," I said to John, suiting my actions to the words. "Maybe he won't press the issue."

It was a mistake. The soldier followed us back to camp, shouting angrily. Sleepy and surprised faces popped out from all the doors as he approached the house.

"That corn belongs to the people," he said, "and you have no right to take the people's corn."

LuAnne stood there holding the corn, not understanding what the shouting was about. "Give it back to him," I said to her. "Give him the corn."

She walked over and handed him the ears, and he stalked off angrily.

Back in the room I was having second thoughts about the matter. I was not particularly remorseful at taking "the people's" corn. I had taken it believing it belonged to the soldiers responsible for our care, and I had made no effort to hide it. But by persisting in spite of the guard's shouting, I had exposed LuAnne to an unpleasant incident which might even have negative implications for the rest of the group. What if they decided to hold a "people's court" trial?

"God, how could I have been so stupid? And what do I do now to get out of this situation?" I prayed silently. I knew as I thought about it that the answer to the first question lay in my attitude toward the North Vietnamese soldiers. Like it or not, I was under the authority of these men, and I believed that except in matters which would violate my conscience I was obligated by obedience to God's Word to submit to that authority. But my attitude of late had been anything but submissive. As to the second question, I felt I should go to Hong and talk to him about the incident.

Peter and Paul were stirring up the fire to make tea when I walked into the family room after siesta hour. "I think I'm going to go to Hong and apologize," I said to them.

"If I were you, I would never apologize or admit to being wrong," Paul said. "It's like handing them a stick to beat you with."

"I don't think there's anything wrong with apologizing when you've done something wrong," Peter said, "but in this case I don't think it's been established that what you did was wrong. We were not forbidden to take that corn. I think you should first ask Hong who the corn belongs to and if we are allowed to pick it or not. Tell him this strange soldier followed you home shouting and took the corn from you. Tell him you didn't wish to do anything wrong, and remind him he told us only he had authority to make decisions concerning us."

Hong was not in his house when I went over. I told his housemates I would return later to talk with him. A few minutes later Gold Tooth came over.

"What did you want?" he asked me.

"I wanted to see Hong," I replied.

"What did you want to see him about?" he pressed.

"I prefer to wait and discuss it with Hong," I said. "Hong told us we should address all questions to him." His face darkened as he turned and left.

At supper time I saw Hong outside his house and went over. Following Peter's advice, I described the incident and asked for clarification. Hong had already heard about it. "I didn't know whether you picked it or whether it was the child," he said.

"It was not the child," I said. "I picked it and gave it to her to carry."

"I will explain the situation to you," he said patiently. "Anything to the right of the path belongs to the soldiers. I have already given you permission to use the sweet potato leaves. But the things on the other side belong to the local citizens, and we are responsible to see that nothing from those fields is taken. The corn we were eating was not from there, but was levied from the people for support of the soldiers."

I walked back to the house much relieved. "Thank you, God, for getting me out of a situation that could have been very bad," I prayed. "Forgive me for the stiff-necked attitude

192

that got me into the mess, and thank you for Hong's patience and courtesy."

In between hassles with the soldiers, life outside the fence settled into a routine. LuAnne struck up a close friendship with Bogh. When it wasn't raining, they sat on a bench Bogh had made a short distance from the house, and were lost in a pretend world. Sometimes LuAnne was a princess and Bogh was King II. (Though Daddy was never in the game, the title King I was reserved for him.) When Bogh threatened to quit unless he was promoted, she reluctantly allowed him to be King I, but only for a short time.

Bogh's rolled-up army jacket became "Bogh, Jr." and they spent long hours feeding and caring for him.

Sometimes LuAnne was a teacher and Bogh was the "baby-san." At other times the roles were reversed. She taught him a slightly garbled version of "My Country 'Tis of Thee," and he taught her "I Went To Your Wedding."

At great length they sang their rendition of the new Revolutionary National Anthem the Vietnamese prisoners were learning. The tune was generally faithful to the original, but the words after the first line or two were pure gibberish. When the constant repetition of this began to get under the skin of some in the group, I restricted LuAnne to singing it only twice a day. It was hard for her to break the habit, though, and often she would start to sing it and then break off with a guilty look.

One noon after lunch, I saw Bogh go from room to room checking on everyone's whereabouts. Satisfied that all were asleep, he went back to the bench and he and LuAnne began to sing their revolutionary song.

With Bogh LuAnne felt none of the tension she experienced with other adults. He was completely accepting and uncritical. He fit into whatever imaginary situation she devised and generally agreed with anything she said. She very early adopted the inflections and grammatical patterns of his speech, and with complete lack of self-consciousness she always conversed with him in the same heavily accented English he spoke.

Pronunciation was not the only thing she absorbed, however. Much of Bogh's English he had learned from

American GI's. He was completely unaware that some of the vocabulary they used was not considered acceptable in polite society. Paul was greatly amused to hear LuAnne come out with some of these crudities. "You are going to have to 're-educate' LuLu when you get back home," he said to me. "I can just imagine the reaction when she comes out with some of these in front of a Ladies' Missionary Circle."

I was not worried about this. This vocabulary was as compartmentalized as the accent. I was concerned, however, about something else. Bogh had bought a tiny mirror with a picture of a Vietnamese girl on the back that he convinced LuAnne was his wife. One day they were playing with the mirror, and Bogh compared his dark to LuAnne's fair skin. "I black," he said. "You white."

This, although exaggerated, was an obvious observation. But when on a later occasion I heard LuAnne say imperiously, "You no can sit here. You black," I was rather alarmed. Coming from a child who had lived all her life with dark-skinned people without any concern about skin color, it was a strange remark.

Later I questioned her about it. "Oh, Uncle Bogh says that in America black people can't sit down on the buses, and I was pretending we were in America."

I hastened to correct her misapprehension, adding, "Whether a person has dark or light skin makes no more difference than whether he has dark or light hair, or brown or blue eyes. All these are things parents pass on to their children and vary depending on what the parents look like. To treat someone differently because he has dark skin or light skin is not only silly, it is wrong." I hoped the message would get back to Uncle Bogh.

"Good grief!" I thought. "No wonder he's always seemed a bit wary of us. He must think we regard him as inferior on the basis of his race. He probably attributes Ike's easy rapport with us to his lighter skin. And how ironic that LuAnne should be taught racial discrimination by someone who perceived himself a victim of it."

On rainy days LuAnne spent more time in our room. I had forbidden her to be in the men's quarters without special permission, feeling that although they disclaimed the need for it they deserved some privacy. Whenever I was not busy with some group project, she begged me to play house with her. She never tired of this activity. She would be twelve-year-old Alice and I was her mother. Our big pillow was three-year-old Billy, and her little pillow was baby Gerry. She was never happier than when we were "shopping at the supermarket" or planning Christmas or birthday celebrations for Billy and Gerry. She had learned all the letters in the alphabet by now, and was glad to make out imaginary grocery lists.

I often wearied of the imaginary role. But though I suggested alternate activities, nothing had the appeal of playing house. "Maybe that imaginary life seems more normal and secure than the real one to her," I said to John. "Or maybe it's what all kids do and there just don't happen to be any other kids to pretend with."

I appreciated all the help I could get entertaining her. One afternoon she spent in rough and tumble play with Norm. He was Sleeping Beauty and she was the Shining Knight. "Did you post the guards, Shiny?" he would ask when he went to take a siesta.

"Yes, Sleepy," she would respond.

Peter remarked once, "LuAnne and Nate must have been very close to each other."

"Yes," I replied. "He's two years older than she, and they spent a lot of time together."

"I figured they must be close," he said, "because every time she recalls a happy experience, it always involves 'me and Nate.'"

A precise speaker of the English language, Peter disliked sloppiness or carelessness about its use. "I'm surprised," he said to me, "that being linguists you don't do more about correcting LuAnne's grammar."

"We're descriptive linguists, Peter, not prescriptive ones," I said lightly. "We don't tell people how to talk. We just describe how they do it." Then I added more seriously, "I guess I always figured if a child hears correct English spoken, she'll learn by imitation."

"Maybe," he conceded, "but I always felt that as a parent I had a responsibility to point out to my children when they made errors."

"You're probably right," I finally agreed.

When I was desperate for some new bedtime stories, it was Peter who came to my aid. "I've gone through every story in my repertoire," I complained after LuAnne had gone to sleep. "Anybody have any suggestions?"

"How about Bre'r Rabbit and the Tar Baby," Peter suggested.

"I've already told that one," I said. "I can sometimes get by with a repeat, but LuAnne's preference is a make believe story she hasn't heard."

"I used to like the Kipling 'Just So' stories when I was a kid," he said. "Do you know the one about 'How the Leopard Got His Spots?'"

"No, I don't know that one," I said. "How does it go?"

"It was down by the gray-green greasy Limpopo River all set about with fever trees," he began. We sat around the fire while Peter recounted several of his favorite tales, giving me story material for several more days.

"I'll sure be glad when we get out of here and I can go back to *reading* bedtime stories," I said to John.

I was impressed by the similarity of the revolutionary zeal of the North Vietnamese to Christian commitment. They gathered every night to sing their revolutionary songs and read Communist literature. Everything they did or said was related to their commitment to world revolution, and to this end they were industrious, morally almost puritanical, obedient and self-sacrificing. In these areas they put most church people I had known to shame.

Not all of them, to be sure. There was "Socks" who came rather furtively to do some black market business for himself. And the "Hai Phong Kid," who had an insatiable curiosity about the outside world and who readily admitted during one of his nighttime visits that he was in the Liberation Army only because he had to be. Some of the soldiers were preoccupied with getting some of the material goods they saw in abundance in the South. One of the soldiers told Jay a Northerner had "arrived" if he managed to get a watch, a radio and a bicycle, items too common in the South to be considered status symbols.

But by and large the people we met seemed convinced of the absolute rightness of their cause and committed to its ultimate domination. Was there anything about Christ's teaching about the Kingdom of God to recommend it over the revolution for which these men strove? Their stated aims of freedom, justice and equality were certainly admirable.

It was obvious to me that unlike the Kingdom Christ preached, this system was imposed by force. No pretense was made about its being the choice of the South Vietnamese people. When I commented to an interrogator that I had never heard the South Vietnamese express a desire to be "liberated," he explained to me this was because their minds had been so corrupted by capitalism they were not able to choose what was best for them.

In spite of expressed concern for the will of "the people," there seemed to be little value placed on individual persons. Sometimes we wondered jokingly just who "the people" were, and what one had to do to qualify as one of them. But then, I thought, apart from the Christian teaching of the value and permanence of the human soul, a person was of no more intrinsic worth than any other animal and was just as expendable.

But the greatest weakness of the revolution to me was its inability to change the human heart. The same striving for dominance would continue, and people would continue to suffer from the greed and prejudice of others just as they had under other systems. To expect that any political system would change a man's desire to promote his own interest seemed unrealistic. Only Christ had the power to make a man "a new creature." And despite self doubts and personal revulsion at many things that had been done in his name, I had observed this power at work in the lives of too many individuals to doubt its effectiveness.

I was deeply concerned about our Vietnamese fellow prisoners. For them the prospects of life under the new regime held little attraction. Cautious hopes that they would be released and could continue a normal life had changed to despair and almost desperation. They openly despised and ridiculed their captors. "They are so ignorant," one tribal prisoner told Paul. The prisoners sang forbidden Vietnamese popular music and made disparaging comments about the guards in English, which none of them understood. I was worried that their desperation might lead them to action

197

which would bring harsh reprisals. So far disciplinary action had been confined to being placed in stocks, kneeling or standing in the sun, or removal of privileges.

"They tell us several thousand South Vietnamese soldiers have not yet surrendered their weapons, and that a South Vietnamese general continues to lead resistance," one man told me. "I wish it were true," he said, "but I think it is only an excuse to keep us here."

All of them were concerned for their families as economic hardship began to be deeply felt. "My wife has spent all our savings and is now having to sell the furniture to get food," one reported. Another man said his wife had written him telling him if there were any way for him to join the resistance movement, he should do so and not worry about her. A demonstration by prisoners' families for their release was dispersed by gunfire, we were told.

Coming up from the river one day we met a friend from Camp Wilderness. He told us he had recovered from malaria, but seemed very depressed. "All of you foreigners will eventually get out of here," he told us. "Your governments or your organizations will do something to get you out, and you'll go back to freedom. But for us it's different. We'll be in prison the rest of our lives."

At times I felt like crying out like David in Psalm 73, "How doth God know? And is there knowledge in the most High? Behold these are the ungodly who prosper in the world . . . Verily I have cleansed my heart in vain."

Just as David found his sense of perspective restored by time spent in the presence of God, I found that time spent in the study of the Word of God and prayer brought answers to my questions. I realized that any person or movement which did not acknowledge God's sovereignty faced eventual destruction. David says, "As a dream when one awakest, so, O Lord, when thou awakest, thou shalt despise their image."

In considering God's sovereignty, I, like David was "pricked" by a sense of my own ignorance, and then overwhelmed by God's loving concern. "Nevertheless I am continually with thee," he says. "Thou hast holden me by my right hand. Thou shalt guide me with thy counsel, and afterward receive me to glory."

Apart from a belief in God's sovereignty I could see no

meaning to human existence or any hope for mankind. Ultimately, to believe or not to believe was an act of the will, and I chose to believe. If I was wrong, I felt I had nothing to lose, and if I was right, I had everything to gain.

"Whom have I in heaven but thee?" David asks. "And there is none upon earth that I desire beside thee. My flesh and my heart faileth: but God is the strength of my heart, and my portion for ever."

We were much concerned about Lil's condition. On July 11 we saw Dick briefly when he was brought over by a team of interrogators who had come to question all of us. After that we received occasional notes by way of other prisoners. The mass of carbuncles on Lil's back was surgically lanced leaving a hole in her back the size of a fist, but the infection continued to spread to other locations.

Jay continued to weaken, and on the 14th he was carried by the twelve-footed ambulance to the hospital. I was down that day with a painful tropical sore developing on my leg. Two days later it was no better so Joan and I went to the North Vietnamese medic to ask for medicine. We met Dr. Ly there and he paused to greet us. He had finally gotten over his malaria, he said, because his father had brought him an effective new Swiss drug from Nha Trang. We didn't dare linger because the medic was frowning. But as we turned to go Dr. Ly said, "Do you have a Bible you could give me?"

"We'll see if we can get one," we promised. Not till much later did I learn that Dr. Ly had talked with John during the difficult period when we were separated. "I need some encouragement," John had said to him. Then holding up the New Testament he was reading he added, "When I need encouragement, I always find it here."

We prayed that Dr. Ly and some of the others who understood English would find the same encouragement through the modern English translation Dick and Lil gave them when we moved away.

On the 21st we received notes from Jay and Dick. Jay reported he was much improved, bored to death and hoping to come back soon. Dick reported that Lil's medication had been increased and that they had been visited by several officials, all of whom seemed concerned that Lil's recovery be speeded. Their diet had drastically improved, and one official told Dick, "The solution to your case depends on the ability of your wife to undertake a long truck trip."

"Ha!" Peter said gleefully, "the only thing standing between me and freedom is a few carbuncles!"

As one day blended into another, however, and the nitty-gritty hassles continued, it was hard to be optimistic. All of us noted that our hair was beginning to fall out. Mine came out in gobs when I combed it. Bogh, who was already bald on top, was particularly concerned. We assumed it was caused by dietary deficiences. Market trips got fewer and then ceased altogether. Hong said he lacked authorization from his superiors to allow them. "There is very strict control now on movement between villages," he told me. "No one is allowed to go anywhere without papers."

Away from artificial lights, the night skies were brilliant and beautiful. One evening we counted 5 satellites and 17 meteorites in the hour or two before the clouds of mosquitos and chilly air caused us to seek refuge inside by the fire. We watched the changing phases of the moon as full moon approached, always hoping we wouldn't be there to see the next full moon.

At times the days passed in domestic contentment. The men chopped firewood, tended the fire and repaired things around the camp. We ate meals, had tea breaks, picked potato leaves, experimented with food delicacies such as rice-flour doughnuts and spent time at the river. For our wedding anniversary John carved me a wooden fork and spoon using the cheap kitchen knife we'd bought and pieces of broken glass.

"This simple life wouldn't be bad at all," I thought one day, "if we had our family, our freedom and some meaningful service to perform."

But all of us struggled with impatience and depression. "I'll find some way of getting even," Peter declared darkly, "even if I have to go to the International Court to do it!"

Paul spent hours to himself inside his net. I felt a particular compassion for Betty and the men without their wives. John and I could encourage each other. We didn't often have our "down days" at the same time.

John had been praying that we would be released by July

18. His diary entry for July 19 reads, "I am wondering what the Lord has in mind for us now that the 18th has passed and we are still here. He undoubtedly wants us to 'wait patiently for him' (Psalm 27:14). Psalm 42:11 from the Living Bible is a great encouragement, 'But O my soul, don't be discouraged. Don't be upset. Expect God to act! For I know that I shall again have plenty of reason to praise him for all that he will do. He is my help! He is my God.'"

On our wedding anniversary, July 28, we were surprised by a visit from the camp commander at the Rose Garden. In contrast to the previous time when he had us tied up as we left the Rose Garden, he was now very friendly.

"Your governments have expressed no interest in you," he told us. "But some of the peace movements have asked about you. I need your names and addresses so these groups can be informed as to who you are."

Other officials stopped by from time to time for no apparent reason except to look at us. Once when we were discussing her non-prisoner status, LuAnne commented, "I'm like the soldiers. I'm only here to watch the animals in the zoo." Then after thinking a moment, she added, "Maybe I'm in the zoo too. I guess I'm the smallest monkey in the zoo."

As August 1st, Nate's birthday, approached, I felt a rising sense of frustration. All three of our children had now turned a year older, and we had missed six months of their lives. Rebellion welled up within me at the pointlessness of my present life. "God, what are we doing here?" I asked. "We're accomplishing nothing and we are of no help to anyone."

I wondered if I should "storm the gates of heaven" and claim deliverance. But wouldn't my motives for this be largely selfish? As I lay and thought about it, a verse of Scripture came to my mind so suddenly and clearly that I felt it to be God's answer to my uncertainty. It was from the book of Hebrews which we had memorized in family devotions. "Ye have need of patience," it exhorted, "that after ye have done the will of God ye might receive the promise."

"God," I prayed in surrender, "you know I want to be out of here and back with my kids, but more than anything else I want to do your will." With the surrender came peace and the realization that God was just as concerned about working *in* me to make me more conformed to the image of his Son as he was in working *through* me to communicate his love to others.

Several times I had written letters to various of our Bru friends. I knew there was no possibility we would hear from them but I wanted them to know of our continued love, concern and prayers. Prisoners' wives had taken these letters to Protestant pastors in Pleiku and Banmethuot asking them to pass them on to our Bru friends. Now that we had been able to get paper, it occurred to me that we could use some of our time to copy off some of the New Testament epistles the Bru had no copies of.

On August 1st John began the tedious job of copying out I Thessalonians. For the next week and a half he worked steadily copying II Thessalonians, Titus, Philemon and James. "Isn't it funny," he commented, "that in the day and age of the computer, the Xerox machine, and the Friden Flexowriter we have to go back to copying by hand."

We proofread the material together and found places where his eyes had skipped a line when the same word occurred on a line below. "I've been reading in the Bible Dictionary about scribes who copied errors into ancient manuscripts of the Bible," he said. "The technical name for the kind of error I've just illustrated is *parablepsis*."

"I'm impressed," I replied.

We finished reading over the copies and I lay down on the bed for a siesta. John sat there composing a letter to one of the lay pastors to go with the copybook of Scripture. A tribal prisoner from Banmethuot had said his wife would take them for us and we wanted to get them to him as soon as possible.

I lay there and thought about our friends and wondered where they were and what their life would be like. Would they be moved back up north to their native areas? Would they be allowed to meet together? Would they be allowed to keep any of the mimeographed material we had left? The wife of one Raday prisoner said the church next to where we had lived was allowed to assemble once a week. Another wife reported that her Bible and hymnbook had been confiscated.

I felt a tremendous sadness that I would probably never

again see these very dear friends, or even know the problems they faced, or the joys they experienced. I would never know how God would deal with Nuan to resolve the bitterness he felt toward one of the other believers. I would never know whether Sauq's baby was a girl or boy, or even if it lived.

Tears made their way down both sides of my face. I was startled from my reverie.

"John," I said, "it's true!"

"What's true?" he asked.

"You *do* get tears in your ears when you lie on your back and cry!"

It was too much for John to take with a straight face. He burst out laughing at the ludicrous observation, and after a moment I joined him. We were both convulsed in laughter.

"What was so funny down at your end of the building this afternoon?" Norm asked as we gathered for tea.

"Yeah," Paul added, "sounded like you guys were having a good time."

"We made an important discovery," John said. "It is a fact that you do get tears in your ears when you lie on your back while crying!" And he went on to explain the reason for our mirth.

Jay returned from the hospital in good spirits and with news that Lil was much better. Notes from Dick and Lil told of continued progress. On August 13 Hong came over during siesta to summon Jay to his house. When we gathered for afternoon tea, Jay passed on his startling news.

"We are to be ready to leave very soon," Jay said. "Apparently we are going to be split up, Americans going first and non-Americans later. Tomorrow we Americans are to pick up our food rations for the rest of the month."

"That's all I know," he said as we began to bombard him with questions. "I don't know where we're going or when. He didn't tell me anything else."

Later in our room I said to John, "I think it's rather ominous that the group is being split into Americans and non-Americans."

"Well, we don't really know what it means," he cautioned.

"Let's face it, John," I said, "everyone else's government

has diplomatic relations with the Vietnam government. As long as we are all together I figure the chances are good for an early release. I think the separation can only mean one thing. They've decided to take the Americans to Hanoi and let the others go."

"I'm most concerned about LuAnne," I went on. "If only we could get her out so she could be with other children and start first grade, I wouldn't feel so bad about staying. I don't suppose they would tell us what they plan to do, but do you think it would be worth asking if we could send her with the Johnsons, if they are going to be released first?"

LuAnne came in and we broke off talking.

"Why don't you talk to Norm and Joan about it," John suggested. "LuAnne and I will go for a little walk."

Norm and Joan agreed without hesitation to take Lu-Anne with them, if the authorities indicated it would be best for her.

John and I walked over to see Hong. I explained the purpose of our visit, "Would you please convey to your superiors our concern about our daughter and our request to leave her with the Johnsons if this will lead to her earlier release."

"I think it would be better for you to keep her," he said hesitantly. "It's best for children to be with their parents."

"Of course it is," I agreed, embarrassed that I was unable to hold back my tears. "We don't want to be separated from her, but if it meant her freedom we would gladly let her go. The Johnsons live near her grandparents," I added, "and we hope her brothers and sister are there." Hong agreed to pass along our request.

We were eating our supper that evening when we looked over and saw two tired-looking figures walk in the gate. We hurried over to greet them. Dick had put on weight and looked good. Lil looked thin and pale, but had made it back under her own steam.

"The hospital administrator said he didn't like to discharge me as I wasn't completely recovered," she said, "but he had orders to do so."

Dick and Lil thought we were being taken to Hanoi. The

204

hospital administrator, while refusing to reveal their destination, had privately offered to exchange any South Vietnamese currency they had before he learned they had very little to exchange.

The next day Mr. Spectacles summoned the Americans to meet him in one of the soldiers' houses. He said he had received orders to send us to a place where we could be questioned by people of higher authority, and he hoped this would result in a satisfactory solution to our cases. We would leave the next morning.

"We consider the American people to be our good friends. Not the American government," he stressed, "but the American people."

"I think you have come to understand some of the hardships we suffered in fighting for our independence," he said. "Some of you even walked with me up the Ho Chi Minh trail."

He asked if we had any questions or complaints. Paul asked about the things taken from us at Camp Sunshine. "Those things were never turned over to me by the authorities in charge at the time," he said. "I don't know what happened to them."

"Just as a matter of curiosity," Jay asked, "why didn't LuAnne receive a supplementary ration? It would seem if anybody needed the milk, it was she."

"I didn't know she was not receiving it," he said. "I have been gone and perhaps no one wanted to make a decision about it."

Looking at LuAnne, he said to Jay, "She is very pretty. Is she prettier than most children?"

Jay shrugged, "She's pretty enough, I guess. But I think all children are cute."

The day passed in preparation. We wrote letters to send with the non-Americans, and they wrote letters to send with us. A soldier came to get a list of all the possessions we would take with us. We told him Johnsons had agreed to take the sewing machine since they had less baggage.

"Oh no," he protested, "you must take it. You won't have any more long walks."

205

That evening we had a special supper in John's honor. The following day was his birthday, but we knew there would be no opportunity to celebrate it.

In the gray dawn of the next morning we carried our things to the covered truck.

"Goodbye, little Princess," Ike said to LuAnne. He handed me a little wooden pendant he had carved for her. "Give this to her for me on her birthday," he said.

"Thank you for being so kind to LuAnne," I said to Bogh, my eyes filling with tears. "She's going to miss you."

I hugged Joan, too choked to say anything, shook hands with Peter and Norm and climbed up on the truck. Their goodbyes said, the others were getting on too. Some soldiers brought armloads of firewood to load on the truck, and just before we left a soldier climbed up and peered into the back, surveying the load.

"Do you have the sewing machine?" he asked, looking bewildered when we all burst out laughing.

"Yes," I assured him. "We have the sewing machine!"

NINE

Hanoi Hilton

I pressed my face up against a tiny crack in the canvas which completely covered the back of the truck. We were passing through the edge of the city of Hue, and my eyes hungrily took in every detail.

"There!" I said eagerly, "There's one of the houses we lived in!"

One of the two young guards riding on the back of the truck brought his head back inside the canvas and looked at me curiously.

"They used to live here in Hue," Jay explained, "in one of the houses we just passed."

A whole week had passed since we had said goodbye to our non-American friends. The first day took us through the edge of Pleiku city and from there down to the coast. Hungry for the sight of people living a normal everyday life, we watched eagerly through the open back of the truck as we passed through towns and villages. Only in one area as we neared the coast were there visible signs of recent heavy fighting.

As the truck pulled into the outskirts of Binh Dinh City our presence caused great interest. People stared and pointed to the back of the truck. We smiled and waved at them.

"The Americans are back!" one man shouted excitedly.

In a large abandoned housing complex built for families of South Vietnamese soldiers, and now used by transient

Liberation Army groups, we were ushered into two rooms, men in one, women in another. The rooms were bare except for several sheets of plywood placed on the cement floor to serve as beds. Each room opened out into an enclosed court-yard, where a tiny room with a bucket served as a latrine.

There to meet us was the team of interrogators who had questioned us a month earlier. That evening one of them, an English speaker, told us, "We will wait here until the other people join us before we resume the trip."

"Your people or our people?" Paul asked.

"Your people," he replied.

"Why didn't they come with us?" Paul asked, puzzled.

"There was a misinterpretation of the orders," he said.

I thought about the trauma of parting and my anxiety about the separation. "All this," I thought wryly, "because someone told Mr. Spectacles to send 'the Americans' down and he took them literally." Often they referred to our mixed group as "the Americans."

That evening we could scarcely believe our good fortune, when we were brought a tasty soup containing cabbage and tomatoes, and a side dish of egg to eat with our rice.

The young women soldiers who brought the food and a bucket of water regarded us curiously.

"You look just like Russians," one of them observed. "Where are you going?"

"We haven't been told," I replied, "but we think Hanoi."

"Oh," she said, "you'll like Hanoi. It's a beautiful place."

I wished I could share her enthusiasm. "Is it your home?" I asked.

"Yes," she replied.

We waited there for four days. It was oppressively hot. Water was scarce. For "security reasons" we were not al-lowed to leave the rooms, and at night the doors were locked and a guard posted outside them.

Only LuAnne was allowed out of the room. She watched a mechanic-driver work on a Russian jeep and collected the pieces he discarded. She sat in a hammock on the veranda with the officer in charge of the expedition and learned to sing one of Ho Chi Minh's favorite songs, "Our Unity Is Strength."

LuAnne was happy to have Aunty Lil back with the group. Lil's back was improving but still required twice daily dressing changes. LuAnne begged her for stories about a little fairy named Dewdrop, a character Lil had created to amuse her own children and whose adventures were now made to include LuAnne.

On Sunday we were taken individually for interviews by two English speaking members of the team. The man who questioned John was most interested in his motivation for coming to Vietnam. That afternoon he asked to borrow a Bible so he could look at it. The other man wanted to know what I felt when I was first captured.

"Did you expect to be killed?" he asked.

"I didn't know what to expect," I told him. "But I thought it quite likely that we would be killed."

"Was this because of what you had been told about us?" he asked.

"Probably, in part," I said, "but also because of what had happened to friends of ours."

"Do you still think you are going to be killed?" he asked.

"No," I said, "we have been told that we have nothing to fear if we were not engaged in political activity."

"You will certainly be released," he said, "but you must be patient."

"We have waited a very long time already," I said.

"After it is over it won't seem so long," he replied. "We waited a thousand years for our freedom." The thought was of scant comfort.

When a truck pulled in Tuesday evening bringing the Johnsons, Ike, Bogh and Peter, we were delighted to see them. But the feeling was hardly mutual. After we had gone camp officials told them that because their governments were more friendly than ours their cases were being handled differently. They would be taken to Saigon and released. When they pulled into this deserted compound and saw LuAnne standing in front of one of the buildings they realized with shocked surprise this was not true.

Neither was Mr. Spectacles' statement about our confiscated papers. Joan brought with her a paper that had been wrapped around some medicine given her by the camp medic. Paul recognized it as being from the folder of personal records taken from him at Camp Sunshine. He was livid. He was particularly disturbed about losing all Internal Revenue Service tax records.

"If I get the IRS on my back I'll never hear the end of it," he worried.

The day after the others arrived we resumed our trip north, this time in a completely enclosed truck. In our eagerness to see out we cajoled the two guards to lift the back flap, and we pulled at the edges of the canvas where the wind had loosened it. The view from the mountain pass between Danang and Hue was as exquisitely beautiful as I remembered it from the many times we had driven that road. Groups of young people worked along the road cutting down brush. Province boundaries had been changed. Traffic was very light. Communist slogans had replaced the old anti-Communist ones over the entrances to every house. Large pictures of Ho Chi Minh looked down from every public building, and signs everywhere proclaimed "Nothing is more precious than Independence and Freedom." Otherwise everything looked pretty much the same.

We stopped for the night at a large military installation just south of Hue. Formerly occupied by American and South Vietnamese soldiers, the camp had been taken over by the Liberation Forces. Like the one at Binh Dinh, it had been stripped of everything removable, including in this case doors and windows, and was partly reduced to rubble.

The next morning as we were about to resume our journey, we were severely reprimanded by the officer riding in the cab of our truck for our efforts to look out and for our failure to maintain strict silence when the truck was stopped. "I will not tolerate such actions," he said sternly. Only a protest by the two guards kept him from closing off the small ventilation hole in the canvas front.

But as we went through Hue I was determined to get a last look at this area so familiar to us. We had moved to Hue shortly after our marriage, and a tiny apartment there had been our first home while we studied the Vietnamese language. It was there we heard about a large group of people living in the mountains some 150 kilometers to the north-west. The Vietnamese called them Van Kieu. They called themselves Bru.

With another Wycliffe man John had made a trip up to visit the area. He talked with a Vietnamese pastor who had been sent as a missionary to the area by the Vietnamese Protestant Church, and with Vietnamese government officials in charge of the area. All of them were enthusiastic about our coming to live there. The Vietnamese pastor had tried to translate parts of the Bible for his own use but found it difficult. And he was hampered by not knowing how to write the strange sounds of the Bru language.

The Vietnamese district chief had had no end of trouble trying to bring education to the Bru villages for which he was responsible. He couldn't get Vietnamese teachers who were willing to stay in the area. They didn't want to live away from their own people, they feared the climate of the mountains and the "poisonous winds" which were said to be there, and they found the barriers of language and culture difficult to penetrate. "The mountain people are stupid and unable to learn," was their verdict. The district chief was willing to try anything, and our proposal to teach them to read and write their own language so that this could become a bridge to their learning the Vietnamese language was at least worth a try.

As we crossed the Perfume River and headed north out of Hue, I recalled the first time I had traveled that road. Married just five months and already expecting our first child, we had loaded all our belongings into a truck and were heading up to the mountains. With more enthusiasm than good sense perhaps, we were moving into an unknown area where with the exception of the few who spoke a little Vietnamese we couldn't even communicate with the people who lived there.

After stopping in at the district center to inform local officials of our arrival we went on to a Bru village several miles down the road toward the Laos border. The Vietnamese pastor was not home but a young man who worked for him went out to the village with us.

It was getting late in the day when we arrived at the village. The Vietnamese truck driver was in a hurry to unload the truck and get back to civilization, so the pastor's helper told us we could put our things temporarily in the small bamboo and thatch church building. The villagers came out en masse to help us carry the things down from the road, across the stream and up the hill to the village. Our arrival had all the elements of the circus coming to town.

John's inquiry about a place to live sent the village leaders into a discussion. Finally the chief indicated that one man was willing to sell us his house and move in with relatives until he could collect enough materials to build another.

"How much money does he want?" John asked.

"8,000 piastres," was the reply.

Following the pattern of barter used by the Vietnamese, John offered him 4,000. A perplexed look appeared on the face of the houseowner and another long discussion ensued.

"He says," the chief said finally, "if that is all you can afford to pay, he will let you have it for that amount."

It was our turn to be baffled. Wasn't he going to argue with us and try for a compromise? No, it seemed that the transaction was considered complete. Not till much later did we learn that price bargaining was not a part of Bru culture.

In the morning we watched as Khõi Nô moved his baskets of rice, gourds of rice alcohol, brass gongs and cooking pots out of the two room bamboo and thatch house built on poles about six feet above the ground. Then we moved in our metal drums of dishes and household utensils as well as the pieces of furniture we had brought with us. It was wise to check the location of a chair before sitting down, we learned, lest one end up suddenly on the floor as the legs went through a crack.

Those were golden days. Our neighbors laughed a great deal at our efforts to learn their language and their ways. But they were proud of us, and our presence seemed to give a certain status to their village. Our tape recorder which sang Bru courting songs and reproduced their musical instruments was an endless source of fascination.

We had come to serve but in those early days when there was little we could do to be of service, apart from running occasional errands for them with our Land Rover, the villagers ministered to us in countless ways.

Khõi Nô far from feeling resentment at having sold his

house for such an unreasonably low price became our close friend and neighbor. He swept the bare ground around our house when he swept around his own, screened our Bru visitors and fixed anything on the house that required repair.

Our neighbor on the other side made himself responsible for teaching us the language. Patiently he went over the tape recorded accounts of Bru funerals and weddings, explaining not only the words but the customs involved. He helped us translate the first verse of the Bible into Bru and proudly showed it to the constant stream of visitors that flowed through our house.

"Look at that," he would say, pointing to the hand-printed sheet of paper on our woven bamboo wall, "that's our language."

He and others began to come every night, asking us to teach them to read. No one in our village of approximately one hundred families had ever learned to read but the prospect was exciting to some of them.

As we learned to know their language and customs we were able to serve them with medical help, literacy and Bible teaching. We also helped them in their relations with the incomprehensible but steadily encroaching outside world. They were vocal in their thanks for all these avenues of service, but it was perhaps this last aspect that the majority of the Bru people considered our greatest area of help. We had lived with them, and they knew we loved them and understood them as few outsiders ever had. Yet as outsiders ourselves we were able to communicate effectively to outsiders on their behalf. Even when we were away from the area for long periods of time—at workshops, on group assignments or even on furlough—we sometimes received letters from Bru leaders asking us to communicate with Vietnamese or American officials about certain problems they were facing or misunderstandings that arose.

Thinking back on those early days I realized how little our neighbors understood our grandiose and future plans to help them in ways which to us were of such obvious importance. I recalled a conversation I overheard between a neighbor lady and a lady from another village. They were squatting on the ground in the shade under our house and

213

the other woman was asking our neighbor about the foreigners who lived in this house.

"What do they do?" she questioned.

"They are studying our language," the neighbor said.

"Yes, but what do they *do*? Do they make fields?" the woman persisted.

"No," was the reply.

"Do they buy and sell?"

"No."

"Then what *do* they do?"

By this time the woman was getting impatient and the neighbor was at a loss to know how to reply. Finally she said, "They don't do *anything*. They just study."

My thoughts jerked back to the present as the truck stopped. The guards were stopping in a small town south of the border with North Vietnam. Joan peeked through the opening in the canvas when they stepped out. Then she leaned over and whispered in my ear, "There are some little plastic dolls hanging in a shop right next to the truck."

"Tell Jay to ask the guard to get one for LuAnne when he comes back to the truck, will you?" I whispered back.

The officers in charge of us had collected all the money we had left saying if we needed to get something they would get it for us. I hoped for LuAnne's sake they would agree to purchase a doll.

I saw Joan, and then Jay, pass the request along. The guard disappeared again and returned with an inexpensive locally made thirteen inch molded plastic doll. "How frightfully ugly it is," I thought. It had vivid pink skin, curly orange painted hair, and bright blue painted eyes. "I wonder why the Vietnamese always try to make dolls look European rather than Asian?" I thought.

LuAnne, however, had no such misgivings. With a smile of pure pleasure she tenderly took the doll out of its plastic bag. "Isn't she pretty, Mommy?" she whispered. She decided to call her baby Susan.

So engrossed was she in Susan's care that she scarcely noted when we crossed the bridge over the Ben Hai river into North Vietnam. Our guards, however, were so openly relieved to be in the North that for the first time I realized with something of a shock the tension they must have felt being in the South. Everyone had been pleasant to them almost to the point of obsequiousness but it was unlikely they would have been unaware of the undercurrents of hostility and resentment.

"I'm getting a new understanding of what it must have been like in the South in America after the Civil War," I said to John.

That evening we pulled into a People's Army Camp near Dong Hoi. We sat quietly in the truck for over an hour until it was dark enough that our presence would not be noted. In spite of the precautions, however, curious eyes watched us through the cracks in the board walls of the dirt-floored room where we were fed and where we spent the night.

We were awakened early, had our morning soup and rice and were loaded on the truck by 7 A.M.

"This will be an easy day," the officer said to me as I climbed up over the tailgate. "We don't have far to go today."

"That's good!" I responded thankfully.

The truck pulled off the road in a deserted area around noon giving us a few minutes to stretch our legs, relieve ourselves and eat a bar of dried food. Then we continued north over the narrow, tree-lined asphalt road.

When the truck was in motion the guards kept the flap up and we watched the countryside with interest. The rice here grew in wide expanses of fields, unbroken by the barriers we were accustomed to seeing in the South dividing individual paddies. It was impossible to miss the indications of heavy bombing in the pock-marked fields, the by-passed bridges and severely damaged factories and railroad stations.

We noted few churches and pagodas, and the few that we saw were in varying stages of disrepair. Several large rivers were served by ferries and in each case our truck moved to the front of waiting lines. Other trucks going North carried items acquired in the South. One truckload of soldiers brought big plastic dolls. Another held an American jeep.

At 3 P.M. our truck had the misfortune to collide with

another vehicle and stopped abruptly. So far as we could tell no one was hurt, but our truck sustained radiator damage.

For three-and-a-half hours we sat quietly in the truck waiting for repairs. The afternoon sun beat down on the tarp making us perspire profusely. Our guards stood outside the truck preventing anyone from approaching but we heard one man say, "We know there are people inside that truck." An altercation with our officer about something resulted in one man being tied to a tree.

LuAnne sat beside me on the suitcase and we whispered and motioned to each other as we took Susan through one make-believe day after another. She seemed completely oblivious to the heat, the cramped position and the passage of time.

Repairs finished, the officer climbed into the cab. In the few minutes before the truck got into motion again, our two guards had a brisk business underway exchanging cigarettes for a chance to look at their cargo. We smiled and waved at the curious faces that popped up under the tarp and they smiled back. I seriously doubted whether it was worth a cigarette to see our dirty, sweaty and in some cases bearded countenances.

When it got too dark to see any longer, LuAnne put her head down on my knees and went to sleep. I passed the time singing hymns. No one could hear over the noisy motor of the truck and it helped keep me from feeling annoyance and self-pity.

It was 9 P.M. before we pulled into a stopping place. We'd been on the truck for fourteen hours with only one short break. "If that's an easy day," I thought, "I'd hate to go through a hard one!"

The little cement block building we were taken into was lit by one electric bulb. "Wow!" we exclaimed, walking inside the empty room. It was the first electricity we'd had in five-and-a-half months.

The moon was shining brightly as we washed away the dust and perspiration from the trip in a nearby irrigation ditch. It was cool and refreshing and in the darkness we weren't even aware of the fact that it was also muddy.

We were told that rice was being cooked for us but I

decided LuAnne and I wouldn't wait. I fixed her a drink of sweetened powdered milk, put a straw mat down on the cement floor and hung the net. As LuAnne crawled under the net, I got down on my knees beside her on the floor to hear her prayer.

"Thank you, God," she said, "that we had such a happy time today."

I didn't know whether to laugh or cry. I kissed her and then crawled in and stretched out beside her. From my point of view the day hadn't had much to recommend it. But LuAnne was completely happy. She'd had her doll and her mother's undivided attention in playing with her. Not once during the entire fourteen hours had she complained. For this I added my own prayer of thanks.

We resumed our travel the next morning in what we considered grand style—a small twenty passenger blue and white East German bus. Much to our disappointment, however, before we boarded it the windows were completely covered over with tarpaulin and newspapers and a tarp was stretched across the bus between us and the driver. The resulting enclosure was hot and stuffy, but the foam rubber padded seats represented the height of luxury.

LuAnne was allowed to sit in front of the divider and we urged her to do so. But when the bus stopped to take on another official she begged to come back with us.

The new officer pulled back the dividing curtain and looked at us. Then he spoke to us in fluent but slightly accented English. "You have had a long and difficult trip," he said, "and I understand conditions where you have been were not good. That is why you have been brought here. I think you will find conditions better and I hope we will get to know each other better in the days ahead."

"I'm not particularly interested in getting to know anybody better," I thought unhappily. "I just want out!" And when, a few hours later, we pulled off onto a dirt road and then into an isolated compound in a rural area I felt the chances of getting out soon were very slim.

"It doesn't look to me like the sort of place they'd take us, if they were planning to release us," I said to John as we waited for someone to tell us to get off the bus. Through a tiny three-cornered tear in the newspaper on my window I had seen a sign just before we turned onto the dirt road reading SƠN TÂY, but my knowledge of North Vietnamese geography didn't include this town.

We were taken into a room where chairs had been brought. There we drank small cups of green tea and were introduced to the camp commander. The officer who had accompanied us from Binh Dinh told us he would leave us and added sternly he hoped we would cooperate with the authorities here. The officer who had recently boarded the bus and seemed to be taking over from him said, "You will see another American here but we request that you not try to communicate with him. Perhaps later you will be allowed to talk to him but we do not have authorization for it at this time."

The camp commander, a man in his mid-forties, spoke in a quiet, almost shy manner and with a marked South Vietnamese accent. "I know you are tired from your trip and eager to rest," he said, "so I will not go into the camp regulations now. We will discuss them at a later meeting. Right now we will show you to your rooms."

A young assistant political officer, introduced to us as Mr. Khoi, took us to a long cement building. The room on the end was for the five "single" men, the next one for our family. I stepped up into the large twelve by twenty foot room and wondered how long it would be our home.

Pointing to a single bed with a kapok mattress, our guide said, "We don't have enough mattresses for everybody but we brought one for the little girl to use."

"Thank you," I said, "I'm sure she'll enjoy it."

Our larger bed consisted of wooden boards laid across sawhorses. Two small rough hewn tables and another board and sawhorse bench arrangement completed the furnishing of the room. A single electric bulb could be turned on by hooking two bare wires together.

The building was part of what had been at one time a conventional prison. Walls with unused guard towers surrounded the compound on three sides. The fourth wall separating us from the camp officials was largely broken down. The heavy wooden doors on some of the rooms still had sliding paneled peekholes, and all windows were barred. From the marks on the floor and ceiling we knew our room had at one time been divided into four tiny cells with entry rooms on each end.

We went to get our baggage. John carried "big brown," and called over his shoulder to me, "Wonder what kind of electricity they have here. Maybe you can use your sewing machine."

I looked to my left and saw a tall, thin young man watching us from across the courtyard. "He must be the other American," I thought.

"Hi!" I called to him. "We're not supposed to talk to you yet but it's good to see you."

He smiled and waved. I was intensely curious to know who he was and how he came to be here. Sometime later that day he met Paul on the way to the men's latrine and told him his name was Jim Lewis and that he had been captured in Phan Rang in April. Apart from that he made no attempt to communicate with us nor we with him.

The next day we gathered for our usual Sunday service. Norm led a study on Psalm 3. When we sang Jim came out of his room and walked as close as he dared. Knowing how much it meant to us to have each other's companionship we prayed for him. It was the only way we could reach out to him.

"If we are near Sơn Tây," Betty said, "then I think we are only 35 or 40 kilometers from Hanoi. Back in 1949 when Archie and I were living in Hanoi studying Vietnamese we were assigned to work in Sơn Tây. Archie made a trip to Sơn Tây to look things over but we never got to move there because the mission school in Dalat had an urgent need for houseparents and we went there instead."

The day before Betty had been the most depressed I had seen her. She had been assigned a small room to herself in a separate building and the fear of being locked in as we were at Binh Dinh was strong. Betty had seen our trip north as a means of making fuller inquiry about Archie, and when we were told there was an American man here she had felt a surge of wild hope that it was he. The let-down when she saw that it wasn't was acute. She was also suffering from a painful carbuncle on her buttocks and the long trip had been difficult.

The pace of the next few days was somewhat relaxed. We washed all our clothing which was filthy from the trip. We ate heartily the simple but tasty meals of rice mixed with noodles, soup with greens, squash and pork fat. Ike and Jay borrowed a guitar from the soldiers and we sang to it. We moved freely in and out of one another's rooms.

"Better enjoy ourselves while we can," Paul said, "before they decide to lay down the regulations."

But when the meeting with the camp commander finally took place six days after our arrival, the change was not severe. We were to observe the 5:30 A.M. rising and 9 P.M. retiring gongs. We were to sweep our rooms and the walkways around the camp daily and clean the latrines and wash rooms daily. Since the latrine was a cement chute opening into a field behind the wall, and the wash room had only a cement table and four large water tanks, this was not a difficult task. In addition we were told to be respectful toward all camp personnel. This caution seemed unnecessary since everyone we had met here thus far had been friendly and courteous.

On August 27th the man who had joined us on the bus gathered us all into the men's quarters for a meeting. He explained that we had been brought here at the request of the Provisional Ruling Government of South Vietnam because there were more adequate facilities for our care. He hoped arrangements for our release could be made by his government but it was very difficult and we must be patient.

"It is the policy of our government to show leniency," he assured us, "and we always do everything according to international law." I couldn't resist giving Peter a smile. He still had not been allowed to contact his embassy.

We had been given the usual set of questions to answer soon after our arrival but now, it seemed, more information was needed. We looked over the list.

"You political officers must all use the same book," Paul observed.

"Why?" the man wanted to know.

"Because this is the ninth time we've answered the same questions," Paul said.

"Is that so?" he answered, seemingly surprised. "Well, I can promise you this will be the last time you'll have to do it. I don't know what happened to the other papers. Those people in the South. . . ," and he shook his head meaningfully.

Peter objected to one question. "Why do you need to know what, if any, property I own in my home country?" he asked.

"Because," the man replied, "we are trying to determine who you are. You say you are an official of the Australian Broadcasting Commission but how do we know if that is true? Perhaps you are actually an agent of the CIA."

"I still don't see how telling you whether or not I own my own home in Australia will help you to determine whether or not I am who I say I am," Peter persisted.

"Your government would not consider asking Peter's wife to sell their home to pay for his release, would it?" Paul questioned.

"If there are any questions you do not wish to answer," the man said, "you may just leave them blank. Is there anything else you wish to ask?"

"I would like to know how we should address you," said Lil. "It is a bit awkward to know how to speak to you since we don't know your name."

He hesitated a moment, and then said, "You may call me Mr. Van."

Jay said, "I'm curious to know how long it took you to investigate LuAnne?"

Mr. Van was obviously not amused by the question. "She is here simply because her mother and father are under investigation," he replied.

"She could be sent back to America to be with her brothers and sister," Jay went on. "There are two international flights out of Hanoi every week, aren't there?"

Mr. Van's reaction to the question took us by surprise. "I do not have to tolerate questions like that," he said angrily, turning red in the face. "I have been sent here as a representative of my government and I have tried my best to make things pleasant for you. I will not permit you to demean my position."

We sat in stunned silence while Mr. Van struggled to regain control. "I would like for the women to look at the pieces of material I have brought," he continued, at last. "We will make two pairs of trousers and two shirts for each of you. I do not like to see you wearing the clothing you were given in the South. It is inappropriate for you."

Earlier Mr. Van had come to each of us to inquire about our health. He seemed particularly anxious to know how much weight we thought we had lost. John and I thought that was an encouraging sign. That afternoon a doctor examined all who were ill. He was particularly concerned about a hard mass in Lil's side. She could not even draw a deep breath because of it.

"It could be related to your recent illness," he said, "or it could be something more serious. We will have to conduct some tests to find out." Lil knew, as did we all, that he feared cancer.

Mr. Van left on the 28th of August telling us he would not return until after the holiday. Ever since our arrival in the North the Hanoi newspaper had contained almost nothing except plans for the upcoming celebration of the 30th anniversary of the declaration of Vietnam's independence by Chairman Ho Chi Minh. Of special interest this coming September 2 would be the opening to the public of Ho's mausoleum where his preserved body would lie in state. For days we had been reading accounts of the arrival of foreign dignitaries and seen pictures of them being greeted at the airport. There was even, we noted with interest, a delegation from our own country.

On September 1 Joan and I went over to the camp kitchen at the camp commander's request to help in the preparation of a special holiday meal. We picked feathers off ducks, washed green onions and grated green papaya. The staff was going all-out for this meal!

"Mr. Khoi," I said to the young political officer who was also working in the kitchen, "how many of us are there in this camp all together, counting guards, officers and prisoners?"

"Prisoners?" he retorted. "We don't have any prisoners here."

"Ah!" I said, catching Joan's eye, "What are *we* then? Guests?"

"Yes," he said, then added, "I guess all together there are about thirty here, counting guards, officers and *guests*."

"For guests we sure don't have much choice in the matter," I said to Joan.

Mr. Van returned that afternoon somewhat downcast. He gave no explanation as to why he had returned earlier than expected. "Probably his superiors told him to get back on the job," someone speculated.

He brought with him loudspeakers which he had installed in each room and some English reading material. Much of it was printed in Hanoi and concerned the progress of the Vietnamese revolutionary movement. But also included was a biography of Ernest Hemingway, Bernard Fall's *Last Reflections On A War*, and a copy of *Today's English Version* of the New Testament.

That evening Jay, Ike, Peter, John and I sat on our bed and played the makeshift game of Scrabble I had tried to reconstruct from memory. Since we had no dictionary to serve as an authority, the differences between Australian, Filipino and American English sometimes made "concensus" decisions hard to arrive at. Nevertheless interest ran high and the game became a nightly activity. Mr. Van wandered in and watched the game for a few minutes, then went next door to the Phillipses.

We quit promptly at 9 P.M., but as I took one last trip out back I saw that Mr. Van was still in the Phillips' room forcefully addressing them and the Johnsons.

"What was Mr. Van talking to you about last night?" I asked Joan in the morning.

She groaned. "First we got a discourse on the high quality of the medical profession here in North Vietnam. This was because Lil asked him if she needed surgery or hospitalization, couldn't she please go back to the U.S. where she could be near her children and her family. He told us that we should be trying to gain an understanding of their position, and Lil said, 'How are we supposed to get an understanding of the North Vietnamese people by sitting here in this camp?

Couldn't we at least get out and meet some of the people, perhaps visit some churches or museums?'

" 'The trouble with you Americans,' Mr. Van told her, 'is that you only think about yourselves. We try to give you everything you need. We give you better food than most of our own people have and you're still not satisfied. Have you ever considered what a burden you are to us? how much it costs to bring you here and to care for you? how many soldiers are tied up here to keep you, not to mention a senior political officer like myself?' "

"Aha!" I said to Joan. "There's the rub right there."

This was not the first time we had been told what a nuisance we were to them. To this we had always replied unsympathetically that all they had to do to get us off their hands was to let us go. But this outburst didn't seem in keeping with the more recent treatment we'd been receiving.

"Imagine how galling it must be to miss being on hand for the biggest national celebration ever held just to 'baby-sit' a bunch of foreigners. And it isn't as if we're important 'guests' either," I said. "I'm sure he feels his talents are being wasted here."

For the most part, however, Mr. Van did not demonstrate this attitude. When Betty talked to him about her quest for information about Archie, he was very sympathetic. "I tell you frankly and sincerely, Mrs. Mitchell," he said, "we are not holding your husband. If we were, I would know about it. I think he must have died in the jungles in the South."

"But wouldn't there be records somewhere to show this?" she questioned. "I know your people keep careful records."

"I don't know," he said, "but I will inquire."

He was puzzled by the attitude of skepticism with which we received some of his statements.

"Mr. Van," I told him, "we have been told so many things which later proved to be untrue that we don't know what to believe any more."

"You can believe me," he said, "I have never told a lie."

Several times Mr. Van came into our room and I had long talks with him. I was interested to know about housing, about food distribution, about any private enterprise. In the course of the discussions I learned much about him and his family.

His wife was a newspaper reporter and they had three children. His mother and sister lived with them. Like all other citizens they were eligible for state housing meted out according to number of dependents and government rank. But unlike most they owned their own home, a ten-room house in Hanoi. "No one is allowed to own land," he said, "but people can receive permission to buy or build houses if they have money."

"How do they get money?" I asked.

"By working outside the hours of their regular state jobs," he said. "My wife and I because of our knowledge of English have been able to earn extra money translating English books and papers into Vietnamese."

When we first arrived in the North I had asked why noodles were mixed with the rice, and was told it was done to make it more tasty for us. Now I learned that a mandatory ratio of noodles to rice was determined by the government depending on how much rice was available. Never had there been enough to allow the people to eat plain rice, though the percentage of noodles had decreased in recent months. Rice and other commodities such as soap, toothpaste and cigarettes were purchased at controlled prices with coupons issued by the government. Buying amounts beyond one's prescribed quota was costly and selling or trading unused coupons was frowned upon. Fresh fruit and vegetables could be grown and sold privately on a small scale. Other home industries were also permitted outside of working hours. Barber shop, tailor shop and watch repair concessions usually went to wounded veterans.

The son of highly educated parents, Mr. Van was eleven years old when Chairman Ho declared Vietnam to be independent from France. He was old enough to remember the terrible famine which gripped the country several years earlier. Because his family, as teachers, had had a comfortable income they were able to subsist but he never got over the horror of seeing so many of his countrymen die of starvation.

One incident he related about his childhood gave me a

keener insight into his feelings about us. He had gone for a while to a school where French and Vietnamese boys studied together.

"One day as I came out of school," he said, "a French boy splattered ink on the front of my white school shirt. Then he accused me of having wasted his ink. I pointed out that he had ruined my only good shirt but that only made him madder. He slapped me and I hit him back. I was taken to the office and punished severely for hitting a French boy. He was not even reprimanded. My father withdrew me from the school."

I hurt for him as he told me the story and I knew the experience had left a scar. I could understand his lashing out when he felt we were pushing him during that early meeting. I knew why he looked uncertain in the presence of Norm's buffoonery and Paul's sharp wit, wanting to laugh with us but afraid that in some way we were laughing at him.

His contact with American POWs had probably not helped to build self-confidence, I mused. From what I had read, in order to maintain their own self-esteem under intense pressure those men had not lost many opportunities to make their captors look inept or foolish, filling their "confessions" with double entendres and fictional references.

I had noted earlier the curious combination of pride mixed with defensiveness and fear of disparagement on the part of other North Vietnamese. At Camp Wilderness I had made a laughing remark in conversation that contained the words "we see." Almost instantly a guard walked over and questioned me, "What did you say?"

Startled, I repeated my innocuous statement, this time in Vietnamese.

"Didn't you say something about the Communists?" he asked.

"No," I answered.

Still unconvinced, he pressed, "Don't Americans call Communists V.C.?"

"Oh!" I said, suddenly comprehending. "That's different." But even as I tried to explain the difference I knew that to him V and W both sounded the same and he probably still thought we were laughing at the Vietcong.

226

"Oh dear!" I said to John after my talk with Mr. Van. "I'm just realizing how careful we need to be in what we say around Mr. Van. He speaks English so well that we tend to expect him to react like a Westerner to jokes or putdowns. But he doesn't. He is expecting us as Westerners to look down on him and his country and he'll interpret everything we say on that basis."

More than ever since our arrival in North Vietnam I had come to feel that if we were to have any effective ministry as Americans in "third-world" countries we would have to demonstrate our willingness to be servants. Jesus set the example for this when he washed the feet of those who rightly regarded him as their teacher, and Paul in II Corinthians 4:5 said, "We preach Christ Jesus the Lord and ourselves your servants for Jesus' sake."

"We know we have many needs in our country," Mr. Van told me. "We need help and we are willing to accept help from anyone as long as it is not patronizing and does not impose on our freedom to manage our own affairs."

One of the policies of the Summer Institute of Linguistics organization which had appealed to me most strongly before I became a member was its emphasis on service to everyone who requested it. I still regarded this as an important policy. But I began to see how hard it was to step outside of a role which history had cast. People in the ex-colonial areas had been taught to consider Westerners as superior. Some of them still did. Others recognizing the fallacy of this teaching asserted their own equality but struggled resentfully with feelings of inferiority. How could we convince people like this that we genuinely wanted to be their servants?

I felt I had a lot to learn in this regard. As I talked with Mr. Van and read both from the Bible and from the material we were given to read I began to realize how much my opinions and reactions reflected my own cultural and socio-economic background rather than the teachings of the gospel of Christ. As an individual I would always be influenced by the culture and society in which I had been raised. Yet as an ambassador for Christ I had a mission which transcended political, cultural and socio-economic boundaries. I could see how much harm had been done by missionaries who had combined their own cultural and social values into one package with the gospel of Christ. If we were to represent him adequately to cultures and societies other than our own, we would have to learn to separate those two areas.

We could not be apologists for any system of human government. Our concern, like that of Christ, had to be for the needs of individual human beings and teaching the Word of God which Christ had pronounced to be truth.

"How easy it would be," I thought, "if we could leave all extraneous values back in the homeland and export only the universal truth of our message."

But God chose to send us as individuals with all the inconsistencies and failings that make up our total personalities. And each new cultural and social situation we face continues to require critical examination of ideas we previously took for granted, under the penetrating light of God's Word.

After the Independence Day celebration visitors to the camp increased. Some of them came as interrogators. We learned that an inevitable sign someone was going to be questioned was the sight of one of the guards carrying a white table cloth, a thermos of water and a tiny tea set to one of the empty rooms. These props accompanied every session. Jay was one of the first to be questioned.

"How did it go, Jay?" I asked him.

"It was strange," he said. "They weren't even interested in the years I taught English and the time I worked for Pan Am. But they were really upset about my photographing the Cham manuscripts. Seemed to think I was exploiting them."

"Even though you voluntarily offered them all the exposed film you left in the South?" I questioned, referring to a letter he had written to a scientific agency in Hanoi several months before. "Didn't that convince them you were seriously concerned about their preservation?"

Jay just shrugged.

Periodically officials came out not to question but to visit. Sunday was often "visiting day at the zoo."

"I don't think I'll ever be able to go to a zoo again without feeling sympathy for the animals," John said.

The visitors were usually taken from room to room by

camp officials. In each room they would exchange a few pleasantries before moving on to the next. One man brought with him his young son, a polite child who folded his arms and bowed politely when instructed by his father to greet us. LuAnne to my chagrin ducked behind me and could not be persuaded to say a word.

To this man I expressed my concern for her. "One week from today she will be six years old," I told him.

"Is that so!" he exclaimed. "In that case she must have a party." Turning to Mr. Van he instructed, "See that she is given a party on her birthday." Mr. Van nodded his agreement.

"In America the other children her age have already started school," I said, more concerned at that moment with the progress of LuAnne's life than the celebration of her birth. "I am concerned that if she is not able to start school very soon she will miss a whole year."

He dismissed the matter lightly. "You can teach her," he said and turned to go to the next room.

Later I discussed the matter with Mr. Van. "Neither my husband nor I are familiar with the first grade curriculum. We don't know what she is supposed to learn and we have no books to use to teach her."

He gave the answer we had come to expect each time we were instructed to do the impossible. "Try!"

"Well," said John philosophically when we discussed the matter privately, "There really isn't anything else we can do. We'll just have to do the best we can."

We decided to delay the program until after her birthday.

LuAnne had adjusted beautifully to the new location. Within the security of the high walls she ran around happily exploring her new world. She ate very little but except for occasional bouts of diarrhea seemed in good health. Uncle Bogh continued to be her favorite companion, though she enjoyed visiting Aunt Betty's room for a game of "I Spy" or stopping in for tea with Aunty Lil.

One young guard quickly made friends with her and often they could be seen squatting together in the courtyard, he teaching her to write letters and numbers in the dirt with a stick. In conversation with him one day I learned that he knew a few words of the Bru language. He had been living in the jungles around Khe Sanh during some of the same years we had been living in that area. Strange to think he had been one of the "jungle ones" our neighbors had feared. He could even have been one of the ones who came into the village one day and dumped all the things out of our house onto the ground while we were gone.

One day while I was in an interrogation session I was startled by a series of shrieks which I recognized as coming from LuAnne. I was restrained from rushing out when the shrieks were followed by delighted laughter. I knew John was in the room and could handle whatever had happened but I was curious about what could have caused such excitement.

When I left the interrogation room LuAnne met me. "Mommy, Mommy!" she said. "I caught a fish! Come and see! I caught a fish!"

She led me by the hand to one of the outdoor water storage tanks. Bogh was sitting on the edge of it. He smiled as LuAnne showed me the four inch fish swimming around in a tin can, and the line he had made from a piece of thread and a bent pin. He had even baited the hook with part of a grasshopper but LuAnne said proudly, "I caught it all by myself."

Later that day her Dad asked her what they had done with the fish.

"We put him back in so he could be with his brothers and sisters," she said, "and so we could catch him again."

At dusk LuAnne and I usually went to the ladies washroom for a bedtime shower. I soaped her up with the strong brown soap we were given and listened to her shivery squeals as I poured cans of cold water over her to rinse her. As I repeated the process for myself LuAnne put on the sleeveless cotton shift I had made for her by hand from some material given us by camp authorities. We'd have to wait to know whether the sewing machine was still functional after its jungle experience. The electricity here was the wrong voltage. I donned the larger version I had made for myself, thinking what a luxury it was, after six months of sleeping in my clothes, to be able to change into something loose fitting.
230

"Here come the twins," LuAnne sang out proudly as we walked past the Phillipses' door on the way back to our room.

"That child has come a long way since the early days of our capture," I marvelled to John later. "She seems so much more mature and confident now."

"I've thought the same thing," he replied. "I know the Lord has been answering many prayers that have been offered for her."

Mr. Van was determined that LuAnne should have a birthday party on September 16 "just like she would have at home." He questioned me at length about American customs concerning birthday celebrations and began to ponder how he could come up with certain difficult items such as cake, candles and presents.

Two days before LuAnne's birthday he came back from a trip to Hanoi bringing with him his three year old daughter Ly. We first saw her when the camp commander brought her into our room.

"She's darling!" I said, admiring her shy black eyes, her glossy black bobbed hair and her chubby arms and legs. "Is she Mr. Van's little girl?"

"No," the commander said. "She's Brother Dung's little girl."

I thought nothing more of the matter until a short time later Mr. Van walked into the room carrying the same child.

"This is my little daughter, Ly," he told us proudly. Suddenly I understood why none of the Vietnamese seemed to know who we were talking about when we referred to Mr. Van. That particular alias for Brother Dung must be solely for our use, I decided.

Mr. Van was pleased that he had been able to purchase cake for the party. He took me up to the office next to his quarters to show me the squares of white cake with pink frosting purchased, he said, "From the hotel in Hanoi which caters to foreigners."

He had also brought her some things with which she could "play house"—handmade and hand-painted miniature household items such as a thermos, a washtub, a teakettle and a set of scales made out of tin. There was also a tin rabbit that beat a drum when pulled along by a string, some tiny molded plastic chairs and table and two tiny plastic glasses.

"I'm certain LuAnne will be delighted with them," I told him.

Candles, however, had proven beyond his power to procure. I was surprised at this since in the South they were universally available and at a negligible cost.

The day before LuAnne's birthday I found myself more depressed than I had been for some time. I had been bothered since before we came North with frequent diarrhea and stomach pain. That morning the camp medic had given me medicine for what he thought might be amoebic dysentery as well as shots of strychnine and Vitamin B to improve my appetite.

I was lying on the bed because the pain in my stomach was less acute when I was in the prone position. John was sitting on the other edge of the bed reading and LuAnne was out playing.

"John," I said, my mind drifting to my conversation with Mr. Van the day before, "don't we have a candle we brought with us from the South that we could cut into six pieces?"

"We do have one candle," he said, "but I think we should save it for emergency use. It doesn't really matter if LuAnne has candles on her cake or not."

"Yeah," I agreed. With LuAnne's birthday coming up I was feeling the absence of the other three children acutely. Birthdays had always been such happy family times. John looked over just as I reached up to wipe away a tear.

"If it means that much to you to have candles for Lu-Anne's birthday," he said, his face registering surprise and a touch of anxiety, "by all means use the one we have."

"Oh, John," I said, the tears now falling in earnest, "I don't care about the stupid candles. I miss my kids!" I sobbed quietly while John reached over to comfort me.

"I know how it is," he sympathized, "sometimes it just seems impossible to wait any longer. But the time will come. Remember our verse says we will 'doubtless come again with rejoicing.'"

LuAnne's birthday was a beautiful, sunny day and she

could scarcely contain her excitement over all the delicious secrets she knew were in store for her that day. Her party was planned for the afternoon but Mr. Van invited her to ride along on a trip to the military hospital that morning. Lil's condition had been diagnosed not to be cancer but further tests needed to be conducted and Joan was under treatment for a severe infection. LuAnne declined the invitation until Mr. Van decided that I should also go to have the doctor check my stomach problems. Then she was eager to go.

It seemed strange to be mingling with people who were not prisoners as we made our way into the waiting room. LuAnne clung to my hand and skipped excitedly along beside me. She stayed with Joan while I was taken for an examination by a woman doctor who prescribed several kinds of medicine. These were supplied by the hospital. It was obvious from the curious stares we received that the presence of Western women and children was not common here. I wondered what would happen if they started to ask us questions.

I smiled to myself remembering Jay's experience when he was brought here to see a dentist a week or two earlier. He had been taken off-guard when a man asked him in a friendly manner, "What work do you do, Comrade?"

Not knowing how to answer, Jay referred him to the soldier accompanying him. Jay was amused to hear the soldier tell him seriously, "It's top secret."

Definitely impressed, the man had asked no further questions.

Eventually the inevitable happened. Joan and I were through but Lil who had been taken to another building was delayed. The medic accompanying us had stepped outside to buy some sticky fried confections for LuAnne when the man seated next to me began to question me.

The conversation went smoothly while he inquired about LuAnne. I told him we were staying in a camp near here.

"What work does your husband do?" he asked.

"Just at present we're not doing any work," I said. "We're waiting to return to our home country."

"What work did you do?" he asked.

"We worked with the ethnic minority groups in the South," I said as noncommitally as I could. I could tell he was turning this over in his mind.

Then he asked the question I was dreading, "Where is your home country?"

"America," I answered, and waited for some reaction.

None came. I could almost hear the wheels going around as he digested that information. But he asked no more questions. A little later he politely took his leave.

A little boy in the waiting room had been watching LuAnne with fascination. When Joan and the medic took her out to wash her sticky hands the child was upset.

"Where is the doll, Mommy?" he kept saying. "Where did the doll go?"

His mother smiled at me rather apologetically. "Last week," she explained, "he saw one of those big dolls the soldiers brought back from the South. Then when we walked in here today and he saw your little girl he must have thought she looked the same. He said to me, 'I want a doll like that one, Mommy! Please buy me a doll like that.'"

"There's the doll!" the little boy interrupted happily as LuAnne walked back in.

We arrived back at camp late for lunch. After a brief rest Joan and I went up to the office building to help set up for the party. Betty was very ill with a recurrence of malaria and would not be able to come. I asked Mr. Van if he would allow the other American to come. "I don't think much information could be exchanged at a birthday party," I said, "and he must be very lonesome."

After thinking it over carefully Mr. Van decided that he could come. "This is your party," he said, "and I want you to take charge of it. Just pretend this is your home and you have invited us here."

I looked around at the bare cement walls and dusty cement floor and thought about the proposed party. "There is no way I can stretch my imagination that far," I thought to myself.

Nevertheless as Joan and I swept the room, arranged the chairs and benches around the room and picked a bouquet of flowers from a bush outside the office I was determined that the party should be a success almost as much for Mr. Van's sake as LuAnne's. He had gone to considerable trouble to please us. I asked Mr. Van if all the camp staff could be invited but he said since there were so many, he and Mr. Khoi would represent the political staff and the camp commander and the medic would represent the military staff.

Hurrying back to the rooms to invite everyone to come and remind them to bring their own cups I stopped in amazement. Peter, Paul and Ike were decked out in the dressiest outfits they had brought along. Bogh had borrowed an outfit from Ike, and all of them looked like well-dressed tourists.

"Wow!" I said, suddenly aware of my faded blue pants and loose-fitting top. "I must be in the wrong place. You guys look smashing."

"John!" I whispered in panic as everyone filed in, "Shouldn't we make a speech of some sort thanking Mr. Van and the officials who provided the party? Every Vietnamese dinner or party I've ever been to someone has made a speech and Mr. Van has turned the affair over to us."

"Not me," he said. "I'm no good at making speeches in English and I'm not about to try it in Vietnamese. If you want a speech you'll have to make it yourself."

Rather awkwardly I welcomed everyone to the party and thanked them for coming. I asked Mr. Van to convey our appreciation to everyone who had helped make it possible, and said that we and LuAnne would always remember this kindness. Then we passed out the cake, sweetened black coffee, bananas and banana candy provided for the occasion. "Mr. X," as we called Jim, sat quietly next to Mr. Khoi but seemed happy to be included.

LuAnne was delighted with her gifts. In addition to the gifts from Mr. Van she received the wooden pendant from Ike, a tiny brass fish Peter had shaped from a shell casing, a picture of Dewdrop from Lil and Dick and a partly filled bottle of cologne from Sleeping Beauty and Aunt Joan. I had made her a wardrobe of clothes for her doll Susan, using pieces of some of our worn-out clothing and bits of leftover

TEN

Trips To Hanoi

Our spirits were high as we boarded the bus at 6 A.M. the morning of October 3. No newspapers covered the windows of the special bus which had been brought into the camp the night before. This time we were to be allowed an unrestricted view of the North Vietnamese countryside and we were told we would visit some places of cultural interest in the city of Hanoi. Happily unaware of the week that lay ahead of us we felt almost like tourists setting out for a day of sightseeing.

LuAnne's schooling was progressing quite well, I thought. We had begun formal studies two days after her birthday and since she was already convinced that reaching the magical age of six and going to school were somehow interrelated she tackled the work we gave her with determination.

I worked on reading, writing and spelling with her for an hour in the morning using hand printed stories and flash cards which I had prepared in advance.

When she wrote all her first week's spelling words correctly I gave her as a prize a tiny nightgown for her yarn doll to match hers and Susan's. She was so pleased she began working toward a prize each week and I had to rack my brains to keep thinking up prizes.

In the afternoon John taught her arithmetic. Using stones and pieces of sticks he taught her the principles of adding and subtracting and using flash cards taught her the number combinations up to ten. She learned to "borrow" and "carry" numbers, but when I heard John giving her problems involving

237

the addition of long columns of several-digit numbers I said hesitantly, "John, I don't think they teach that in first grade."

"Really?" he said. "I just figured that was the next step."

"She may not be getting a very conventional start," I thought as we pulled out that morning, "but how many American children have ever taken a field trip to Hanoi!"

Other things contributed to our sense of well-being that day. One was the fact that everyone of our group was along. Betty had recovered from her malaria attack and Lil's condition had improved. Jay and I continued to be bothered with stomach pain and Jay was able to eat very little but both of us were able to make the trip.

The preceding week Paul had angered Mr. Van by some sarcastic remark. Mr. Van had retaliated by moving him to a room by himself and forbidding him to speak to any of the rest of us. That afternoon he had explained the action to John and me.

"Even if Mr. Paul has no respect for me as a person," he said, "still he must be made to show respect for my position as a representative of my government."

"I don't think Paul meant to be disrespectful to you or your government, Mr. Van," I said. "That's just the way he talks. Also he is feeling depressed because his son just had his first birthday and he has missed over half of his boy's life."

In an unprecedented move Mr. Van later actually admitted to Paul that he felt he had overreacted. He also removed the ban on communication with us.

Another reason for encouragement for us personally was that some steps seemed to have been taken to effect our release. A couple of weeks earlier the non-Americans had been instucted to write letters to the prime minister of the new Provisional Ruling Government of South Vietnam to request repatriation. They had been allowed to record messages for their families which they were told would be broadcast over shortwave radio. Mr. Van told us that quite possibly we would not all be released at the same time and I again asked permission to send LuAnne out with the first ones released.

About a week later he called John and me into the office to tell us he had made a special recommendation that our family be among the first to be released because of problems connected with LuAnne's care. His superiors had instructed him, he said, to have us write a letter requesting release.

With Mr. Van's help we had carefully formulated a letter to Prime Minister Huynh Tan Phat. But two days later the letter was sent back with a sharp protest.

"They say," explained Mr. Van, "it sounds as though they had taken prisoner a five-and-a-half-year-old child and held her for seven months."

It was obviously a very sensitive issue. Presumably we were asking for special consideration because of LuAnne's presence, yet to mention her in the letter too prominently sounded accusatory. Eventually we relegated her mention to the end of a middle paragraph and the letter was resent. Mr. Van told us he delivered the letter personally to the PRG office in Hanoi and talked with them about our case.

While he was in Hanoi he had purchased a General Electric steam iron which he brought in to show me.

"Is it a good product?" he wanted to know. "And can you show me how to use it?" He told us the price of radios in Hanoi had dropped by half in the last two months. This he gave as an example of increased production. To us it was an indication that material "goodies" from the South were beginning to flow North.

Few signs of this were evident, however, as we entered the outskirts of Hanoi. The houses and shops reflected the simplicity and austerity we had come to expect of life in the North. Traffic except for the few buses and the streetcars in the downtown area consisted primarily of bicycles. Most of the cement construction buildings appeared to date back to the era of French colonization.

One notable exception to this was the large building where our bus stopped first.

"This exhibition center was just opened for the 30th anniversary celebration of independence," we were told. Huge cement letters atop the building carried the famous quotation about independence and freedom. We were taken into a VIP reception room where we met the director of the center and sipped tea. The center had two main levels. On the lower level we saw photos and displays depicting the struggle for independence and unification. Betty carefully scanned one large display of photos of American POWs but failed to see any sign of Archie. The *pièce de résistance* on this level was an audio-visual display of the final Ho Chi Minh campaign. We watched arrows on the map light up as the initial battle for Banmethuot was described and followed the progress of the campaign through successive stages to the eventual "liberation" of the entire country. The battle for Saigon was graphically re-enacted on a scale model reproduction of the city and its environs. It was complete with tiny moving columns of tanks which belched smoke, simulated explosions of artillery, and airplanes which flew overhead on fine wires.

Then we were taken upstairs to view displays depicting 30 years of progress in such areas as education, manufacturing and handicrafts. I wished for more time to look at these displays but we had to hurry to the next area outside the building where a large lot was covered with samples of Russian and American military hardware. Here we saw the private helicopter given to Chairman Ho by the Russian government, the South Vietnamese plane which bombed the Saigon palace before defecting to the North and the guns credited with shooting down the most American planes.

Back on the bus again we were taken to a small private home where the camp cook had gone ahead to prepare lunch. A few days earlier Mr. Van had told us his superiors were not satisfied with the rate of improvement in our health and had decided to increase our food allowance. Our meal that noon reflected this. We had bean soup with rather heavy French-type bread and thin slices of boiled pork. While we waited for lunch one of the guards went out and bought some popsicles which we gratefully devoured.

Bottles of North Vietnamese beer were served with the meal. Mr. Van was somewhat disappointed when a number of us declined the beer but the beer drinkers in the group were delighted. They would be glad to take care of our portion they assured him.

After lunch we were taken on a tour of the National Museum of Natural History. I was tremendously impressed by the vast span of history covered by the exhibits, as I had been earlier on visits to museums in Korea and Taiwan. The very oldest artifacts of Western civilization seem about as recent as

240

yesterday's newspaper when compared with some of the items that were on display here.

Of interest to us as linguists was a display featuring Father Alexander de Rhodes, the missionary priest generally credited with developing the excellent writing system still in use for the Vietnamese language. Here, however, he was portrayed as the villain who paved the way for French colonial rule.

"Our people have come to hate missionaries," Mr. Van explained, "because although they claim to preach religion they always work to bring foreign domination."

We arrived back at the camp late that afternoon tired but pleased with the day's activities. Our first indication that all was not well came that evening.

"Is your room just like you left it this morning?" Betty asked, coming into our room, "or have things been moved around?"

"I don't know, Betty," I said looking around the room. "I guess I wouldn't know. I didn't pay much attention to how we left it."

"Well, my room has definitely been searched and so has the Johnsons'," she said. "I know I left the flashlight I borrowed from you on my table and when I came back I found it in my suitcase with the lens cracked. The papers in my Bible were rearranged and even my bedding was messed up."

"Do you suppose that was why they took us on that trip today?" I said. "To get us out so they could go through our stuff?" Nevertheless I was not particularly worried. We had nothing to hide.

Norm, however, took the matter up with Mr. Van. "It's not that we object to your going through our belongings," he said. "They've already been inspected two or three times. But if someone wanted to go through our things why didn't he say so?"

Mr. Van denied that any inspection had been carried out. "Maybe one of the guards walked in and picked something up to look at it," he said.

The day after the trip was Saturday. Mr. Van went home for the weekend, returning Sunday night with a movie and sound truck. We were shown a documentary film about the liberation of Saigon and a colorful travelog of North Vietnam.

241

Early Monday morning coming back from the latrine I saw Paul standing by the window of his room putting his things into his bag. Mr. Van stood beside him watching.

"Paul," I said, "what are you doing? Where are you going?"

"I don't know," he said grimly, "I'm being taken somewhere to 'work.'"

"How long will he be gone?" I asked Mr. Van in alarm.

"Probably a few days," he said. "I received orders from my superiors to send him to another location."

"Is there anything we have you'd like to take with you?" I asked.

"I don't think so, Carolyn," he replied. "Thanks anyway."

"We'll be praying for you, Paul," I assured him.

Mr. Van led him to a waiting jeep. Mr. Khoi would accompany him. By this time the others in our group, aware of what was happening, had gathered near the jeep to say goodbye. We were saddened and deeply concerned. All along Paul had feared he would be separated from the rest of us and what this might mean in terms of his treatment we didn't know. We also feared that Paul's isolation might be just the first step. We felt no assurance that the same thing wouldn't happen to the rest of us.

We hadn't much time to speculate about the meaning of events, however. White tablecloths and tea sets going to four separate locations ushered in a period of "work" such as we had not known before.

Interrogation sessions up until now had been rather low-keyed. One man asked what my understanding was about American involvement in the Vietnam war.

"My only knowledge about that comes from what I have read," I answered. "And I know it differs from your understanding."

"Nevertheless, I am interested in hearing your view," he persisted.

"According to what I have read," I told him, "the United States became involved in Vietnam because the South Vietnamese government asked the U.S. to help them resist armed aggression from the North."

The man smiled slightly and shook his head. He explained to me again that the U.S. was in the war because it needed

South Vietnam for military bases and as an outlet for its manu-factured goods. The former South Vietnamese government was not a legitimate government, he said, but merely a puppet government of the American imperialists. Now under a true people's government the South would make great progress. When he finished his lengthy explanation, he again asked my opinion.

"Sir," I said, "I understand what you have told me but as far as my own opinion goes I must simply say I do not yet know. In the past I was told that a Communist government would be bad and would result in the loss of freedom for the people of South Vietnam. Now you tell me that the previous regime was bad and that Communism will bring freedom and economic and educational advancement to the South. How do I know which is right?

"If I come back to the South in a few years and find that the people are better fed and better educated and that they have freedom to assemble, freedom of movement and freedom of religion," I said, "then I will gladly admit that what you are telling me is right and that what I have been told in the past is completely false. I sincerely hope," I went on, "that what you say is true but some things I was told in the South have made me concerned."

"What are these?" he asked.

I told him about the tribal women who reported her Bible and hymnal had been taken away from her and about the Liberation Army soldier who told me no one was allowed to go from one village to the next without papers of permission. "This doesn't sound like freedom," I said.

"That is only a temporary condition because of the security situation in the South," he said.

On another occasion a man we referred to as the "America Watcher" asked John if he had read the Pentagon Papers. John confessed that he had not.

"I have read them," he said, "all forty-seven volumes of them. But I want to know more than that. I want to know what was behind those papers. I want to know what was in the minds of the officials involved."

"I'm afraid I can't help you much with that," John said, "but I would be glad to hear your views on the subject."

The America Watcher had quizzed me a few days later on the international structure of our organization. It was the only session I had which was conducted in English.

"What is the difference between the 'Summer Institute of Linguistics' and the 'Wycliffe Bible Translators?' " he wanted to know.

I explained to him that, although the membership of both organizations was largely the same, because the scientific and religious programs were of such different natures it was decided to incorporate these programs under separate organizations.

"That's ridiculous!" was his response. "There's nothing to prevent one organization from having two separate programs, is there? You should make it one."

I smiled and told him I doubted whether I could do much to influence that decision and he agreed rather good-naturedly.

Often the sessions were designed to point out our "crime," though no two interrogators seemed to agree on this. One man told John and me in our only joint session that we were guilty of helping the Thieu government, since by helping the people we had made that government's task easier.

"If the Thieu government hadn't felt you were helping them you wouldn't have been allowed in the country," he said. And we had to agree that he had a point.

Dick Phillips came back from a session with "Blue Shirt," the religious specialist, smiling broadly.

"I've finally found out my crime," he said.

"What is it, Dick?" John and I questioned.

"The man told me I was too good," he answered. "He said I was guilty of confusing the Vietnamese people by making them think that all Americans were good. I told him I was certain the South Vietnamese people had seen enough Americans to be able to judge for themselves that some were bad and some were good, but he didn't seem convinced."

My own session with Blue Shirt had left me somewhat shaken. He asked me about our translation work, about how many Christian believers there were among the Bru and in what villages they lived, about the methods and results of our various programs.

"You believe in God," he said, "because from the time you

were a child your parents took you to church and taught you about God. You don't really *know* there's a God. Maybe there is and maybe there isn't. But you *believe*."

"Yes," I replied, thinking of my past struggles in the area of faith. "I believe."

"Then you came to Vietnam," he went on, "and you taught the Bru people about God. They don't know whether what you have taught them is true or not. Maybe it is and maybe it isn't. But some of them have believed. They don't sacrifice to the spirits anymore. They follow the Christian way now."

"That's right," I agreed, wondering what he was leading to.

"These people will not forget you," he said firmly. "No, they won't. They'll remember you."

"We will certainly remember them," I said, starting to choke up. "Many of them are like our own family to us."

"Oh, they'll remember you," he said. "Every time they see their language in writing they'll remember you because you were the ones who put their language into written form. And every time they read a piece of Bru Scripture they will remember you because you were the ones who translated it into their language."

By now I was thoroughly confused. It sounded as though he were trying to compliment or console me, especially since in Vietnamese the word to "remember" someone else means to "miss" someone. "Is he trying to comfort me because he knows how badly I feel about leaving my Bru friends?" I wondered.

But as he continued it suddenly dawned on me that he was pointing out my crime!

"Not only will these people remember you," he said, "but they will tell their children about you and their children will tell their children. It will be many years before the effects of what you have done will be able to be undone.

"These people have only now begun to learn about the revolution," he continued, "but they will learn. And they will discover that the revolution is the solution to their needs."

He dismissed me and I returned to the room emotionally unstrung and greatly troubled. Still trying to sort out in my mind the implications of the interview I related parts of it to John and Jay who were standing in the doorway.

John's reaction surprised me. "Praise the Lord!" he said. "That's a pretty good testimonial to the effectiveness of our work."

The sessions which began that Monday morning after the Hanoi trip were more intensive than any we had had so far. LuAnne's lessons were neglected as John and I spent morning and afternoon in interrogation sessions.

The man who questioned me that day was middle-aged and had a narrow face with prominent teeth. He was pleasant and expressed concern about my continuing stomach problems. As we sipped the tiny cups of bitter tea at the beginning of the session he told me this particular kind of tea often had a healing effect on stomach disorders.

"Now I want you to tell me just why you came to Vietnam in the first place," he said. "What was your motivation for coming here?"

I wondered how I could get across what had motivated me to come to Vietnam to this man whose only frame of reference was political and social. Should I point out the obvious social benefits of our program to the minority people through literacy and bilingual education? But that was not my primary motivation for coming to Vietnam.

"Sir," I began, "I believe that when someone has something of great value and great importance, that person has a responsibility before God to share it with others who do not have it. I believe the Bible is a message from God and because I believe this the Bible is very precious to me.

"When I learned," I went on, "that in South Vietnam there were more than thirty language groups that did not have this message in their language I wanted to share with them this message which I valued so highly. That is why I came to Vietnam."

"Whether one says he has a responsibility to God or merely to his own conscience," the man replied, "certainly it is good to share with others things of value."

We moved on to other areas. He asked about my early life and educational preparation. He inquired about the various aspects of our work, all the places we had lived in Vietnam and all the people we had known in each place, both nationals and expatriates.

246

Sometimes I struggled to get the proper Vietnamese word to express what I was trying to convey. He listened patiently, suggesting a word from time to time. John and I felt there was nothing concerning our activities to which we would hesitate to respond. We told them we had worked in cooperation with the Department of Education of the former government, the Universities of Saigon and Hue and many religious organizations.

"We worked with anyone who was concerned about helping the mountain people," I told him.

"Why didn't you work in any of the liberated areas?" he asked.

"No one ever invited us to go there," I said.

At the close of that day's session the man handed me a sheaf of lined gray paper.

"I want you to go back to your room and write down everything you have told me today," he said. "Write down your personal history and the names of everyone you associated with during the time you were in Vietnam. Tell how you knew them and where they lived."

I was dumbfounded at the request.

"How can I possibly do that?" I protested. "We've been talking all day! I can't even remember all I've told you, much less write it all down."

I might as well have saved my breath. I should have known what the answer would be. "Try!"

I went back to the room feeling aggrieved. I was tired from the all-day session. I was depressed because Paul had been taken away. And to make matters worse we'd had photographs taken that afternoon. We were told to face the camera, unsmiling, with hair pulled back behind the ears. The feeling that these "mug shots" were like the kind taken of the most wanted criminals and hung in post offices in America was heightened when a complete set of our fingerprints was taken and all our distinguishing physical peculiarities were carefully noted on a form.

When John came back from his session I was still feeling grumpy and annoyed. "If he wanted all this on paper why couldn't he have made notes when I was telling him in the first place," I fumed.

247

"Don't get upset about it," John cautioned. "Time is something we have plenty of here. Just put down what you remember and turn it in. If he wants more he'll ask for it."

Jay wandered in just then. He'd been asked for the names of his students and had written out eight pages of names and villages in his tiny script.

"How in the world could you remember all those?" I asked.

"I lived with those kids and knew them well," he shrugged. "I just mentally went down the rows of every classroom for the three years I was teaching. I don't think I missed many."

That evening the audio-visual truck showed another film. It was an East German movie about racial oppression in the 19th century United States. When it began to get violent I took LuAnne back to the room and played dolls with her till bedtime.

"All in all," John said as we crawled into bed that evening, "it's been a very depressing day." But it was to get worse.

The next morning John, Jay and Betty were taken to the hospital. John was to leave his partial plate at the dental clinic for repairs, Jay was still unable to eat and Betty's glasses were broken. Mr. Van called the rest of us into the fellows' quarters.

"It has been brought to our attention that some of you have valuable items in your rooms such as watches and jewelry. While the risk of these things being stolen here is very small still we think we should take them and keep them for you. One of our officers will inspect your things and we will write out a receipt for whatever is taken."

When I went back to the room I was surprised to see a soldier standing just inside the door. I sat down on the bed and waited. In a little while Mr. Van came in with a young soldier to act as scribe.

He began to set aside certain things to take making sure the serial number of my engagement watch was carefully recorded, and entering the exact number of pearls on my string.

I was surprised when he set aside the folders of Bru New Testament manuscripts. "You don't need to take those," I said. "Nobody would want to take them."

"No," he said, "but that's the second part of the inspection I

248

mentioned. We're to take all printed and written material except what we have given you."

"But we are still working on these," I objected, "and we need to use them."

"If you want to use them," he said, "you may request them. Don't worry, you'll get all these things back. We only want to inspect them."

After he had systematically gone through everything Mr. Van read over the list of things to be taken. He berated the young soldier for a number of spelling mistakes. "What grade did you study to?" he asked. "Copy the list over in duplicate and without mistakes."

After he left the room I gave the young soldier a piece of carbon paper to use so he would only have to recopy once. Just before he and I both signed the two copies, John walked in.

"What's going on?" he wanted to know.

I told him sadly. LuAnne's papers and lessons were not taken but the letter John had been writing to our other children over the past four or five months was gone. His diary he had taken with him to read while waiting at the hospital so it remained. We learned that Dick and Lil had lost all their Mnong manuscripts as well as the corrected version of the doctoral dissertation Dick had prepared to submit to Cornell University. Norm and Joan had nothing to lose except the journals they had been keeping since Camp Sunshine days.

"Remember when Happy suggested that we keep diaries so we could show them to our children?" Norm recalled. "I wonder if he had this in mind when he suggested it?"

That night for the second time in my life I was awake the entire night. The first time was during college when I drank coffee and paced the floor to keep awake to study for an American History exam. This time it was my own turbulent thoughts which kept me from sleeping.

What did all the recent developments mean? In the courtyard a loudspeaker had been set up and all day long we heard radio Hanoi played at top volume. We didn't know whether it had been added because we usually kept the speakers in our rooms turned down or whether it was for the soldiers' benefit.

"Now I know why the North Vietnamese soldiers talk so loud," I shouted to John one day over the blaring loudspeaker. "If they have these in every camp and village (and we could sometimes hear one from a nearby labor camp), the people must all have damaged auditory nerves."

Most of the time none of us except Jay could understand much that was said except during the fifteen minute English news broadcast. This was enough, though, to let us know the sense of outrage the Vietnamese felt when the U.S. vetoed the entrance of the two Vietnams into the United Nations. I wondered if the change in our treatment reflected the current political situation. If so, we were in real trouble.

As I thought about the confiscation of our manuscripts I realized that Mr. Van's studied nonchalance was a strong indication this was the whole purpose of the inspection. Had we been too careful about them, I wondered? If we had let LuAnne write on them and draw pictures all over them we'd probably still have them. Perhaps our very concern about them would make the Vietnamese suspicious. But how could we have known this? If as Blue Shirt indicated they were concerned about wiping out the effects of our work they would see this as a golden opportunity. I would, I decided, look for an opportunity to let Mr. Van know that there were other copies of the manuscripts outside of the country.

I got up the next morning feeling mentally, physically and emotionally drained. I dreaded another day filled with uncertainty and interrogation. Mr. Van had returned our Bible the evening before and I recalled Joan's mentioning recently that she had been helped by reading the Epistle of First Peter. As I began to read, the whole book seemed alive with new meaning and assurance that morning. Two verses in chapter 3 seemed especially pertinent to my need:

"Usually no one will hurt you for wanting to do good. But even if they should you are to be envied, for God will reward you for it. Quietly trust yourself to Christ your Lord and if anybody asks why you believe as you do, be ready to tell him, and do it in a gentle and respectful way."

"Thank you, Father," I prayed silently. "I really needed that today. Help me to view these sessions as opportunities to show what you mean to me. And help me to do it in a gentle and respectful way."

I noticed then that the two verses were underlined in red and that John had written "8 Oct 1975" beside them.

"John," I questioned, "were you reading in I Peter this morning?"

"Yes," he answered.

"It looks as though God gave you the same two verses he gave me," I said. I walked next door to share the verses with Lil.

"I'd like to copy those down," Lil said. "Thank you for sharing them. Today is our wedding anniversary and this has given me something special to remember the day by."

Dick and Lil went into long sessions with the men who had questioned John and me the day before. Everyone who was not in session was busy writing. John's "life story" was really an account of God's working in his life. "He asked for it," John said, "so I'm giving it to him!"

Mr. Van walked into the room while I was teaching Lu-Anne. "Mr. Van," I said, "we are very anxious to get back the papers that were taken from us because the handwritten corrections in them represent months of hard work on our part and the part of others. They are not, however, complete. If your government is interested in having these materials for linguists or others studying tribal languages, we would be happy to see that they receive a complete set of these and all other portions we have translated from copies which are on file in our home office."

"I don't think they'd be interested in them," he said.

It was another low day on the interrogation front. Betty returned to her room in tears. Her interrogator using Mr. Van for an interpreter had accused her of withholding information when she could not give him the names of everyone who had served on the C&MA field council since 1954.

"How do you ever expect to get out of here if you won't cooperate?" he asked her.

When Betty asked him if he remembered details of things that happened that long ago, he answered angrily, "I am asking the questions. You are not allowed to question me!"

Lil found it difficult to talk about her children when she missed them so intensely, and Dick's interrogator had made a statement which alarmed us all. He indicated that Dick would not be released unless he wrote a statement condemning U.S. foreign policy toward Vietnam.

John and I felt quite strongly that we should resist making political statements of any kind. While we felt under no obligation to defend American government policies, we were likewise unwilling to enter the arena to publicly condemn them.

"Wycliffe has workers in countries with almost every conceivable type of government," John said, "and if we were to make political statements of any kind it would certainly damage our standing in some of these."

"We refused to make public statements about political issues connected with Vietnam even in our own country," I said. "Why should we make them here?"

At the same time we had no illusions about our ability to withstand pressure to make these or any other kinds of statements they might decide to make us sign. We might then be expected to sign confessions to our "crimes." The thought of forced statements of any kind opened up a "Pandora's Box" of prospects we were reluctant to face. Having LuAnne with us put us in a particularly vulnerable position. John and I faced seriously what our non-cooperation might mean to her, and the possibilities frightened us.

"John," I said, "we can only claim God's promise that we won't be asked to undergo any test that we will not be able by his strength to endure."

As I lay down for a siesta that noon I felt overwhelmed by feelings of helplessness and uncertainty about the immediate future. "God," I prayed desperately, "I know people are praying for us. Please help them not to give up because we surely need their prayers now."

In the washroom that afternoon I discussed the situation with Joan.

"Norm and I talked it over and decided we won't sign anything we don't feel is true, even if it means we get separated or we never get back home," she said. "But I can see that your situation is more difficult since you have LuAnne to consider. We'll pray that you'll know what to do."

Joan told me that Mr. Van had somehow learned about Dick and Lil's anniversary and asked her for suggestions about a surprise party for them that evening.

"Oh, Joan, I don't think anybody is in the mood for a party," I said. And then looking over to where they sat writing at their

252

table by the window, I added, "Least of all, Dick and Lil. Couldn't you talk him out of it?"

"I tried," she replied. "I told him anniversaries were usually celebrated only by the people directly involved and that they usually went out to dinner together or something. But he insists on a party.

"Jay's been complaining that we never sing together anymore," she said. "Maybe we could just get together and sing for a while."

LuAnne was delighted at the prospect of a surprise party and went to work on an anniversary card. She helped Joan and me set up the room by the office and waited impatiently for the time of the party. When the others were gathered we suggested that Mr. Van call Dick and Lil to come over for clarification of something they had written on their interrogation papers.

The surprise was complete. Mr. Van had provided coffee and bananas for refreshments and as we sipped and sang, cheerfully determined to make it a happy occasion for Dick and Lil, most of us found our spirits lifted.

Mr. Van suggested we sing "Love's Sweet Song." It was one of the few English songs he knew. After the first few bars Peter got up and walked out. When he returned he seemed unusually quiet.

"That was Peg's and my song," he told us later. Hearing it sung made him painfully conscious of their separation.

The next day I spent the entire day in bed with diarrhea and stomach pain. Mr. Van came in to express his concern. "What do you think is causing this?" he asked.

"I don't know," I told him. "But if I had to guess I'd say intestinal parasites. I know LuAnne and some of the others have had these and I wouldn't be surprised if we all did. If I were in Banmethuot I'd probably take a worm treatment. Worm medicine was inexpensive and readily available in the South and it would at least eliminate one possibility."

"I'll see if we can get some," he said.

John taught LuAnne both morning and afternoon sessions when he was not being interrogated. Knowing the hard time Dick had had the day before I prayed that God would help him in the interview.

When he came back John reported that he had felt unusual

253

freedom in speaking. The interrogator referred to papers John had written concerning his life history. "I'm not questioning your high purpose in coming to Vietnam," he told John. "I understand that. But I want to know more about your organization and your work."

He was particularly anxious to know the name of the individual who had sent John to Vietnam and had difficulty understanding the volunteer nature of our work. John was instructed to make a list of all the members of our organization in Vietnam, their nationalities, their job descriptions, where they lived, what language they studied and what they had produced.

"I told him," John said, "I didn't know what all the other teams had produced. For that kind of information they should have gotten the director!"

"Why didn't you suggest they simply write our office and ask for it?" I asked. "I'm sure our organization would be glad to supply it and it would be a lot more accurate than what we can give."

"I did," he replied, "but the man said . . ."

"I know, I know," I interrupted. "Try!"

We did not know it but even at that time members of our organization continued to send copies of linguistic articles and dictionaries prepared by members of the group to various places, as they tried every way to gain information about us.

"Did the interrogator say anything about having to make a political statement?" I asked anxiously.

"No, he didn't," John said. "He asked me about my feelings concerning our treatment and I told him that so far these were fairly positive but that if we were held for a long time or forced to sign statements which we could not conscientiously sign my feelings would definitely change."

Mr. Khoi came back to camp from time to time. He told us Paul was in another camp not far from ours and assured us he was fine. One afternoon I heard Mr. Khoi talking to Betty in her room. The voices went on for some time but I caught just a snatch of the conversation when I went to get a drink of water from the metal container outside the men's quarters.

"When you stand before God," Betty was saying, "don't you tell him you didn't know about him or that he loved you because I'm telling you right now."

254

Peter came into our room chuckling. "Now that's what I call funny," he said to us, "two fanatics each trying to convince the other that his own view is right."

I smiled. A few months earlier the term "fanatic" would have prompted me to defensiveness. Now I had come to grips with my beliefs and accepted the charge easily. "He's right," I thought to myself, "we are fanatics."

I felt under no compulsion, however, to try to pressure others to believe as I did. Christ had commissioned us simply to be witnesses by our lives and by our words. Only he could draw men to himself, quickening them to faith.

Throughout the week the "work" continued. Betty was very discouraged by the hostility reflected in her sessions. She wondered if her repeated requests for information about Archie were responsible for this.

"If it bothers them to have me mention Archie I won't do it any more," she told Joan. "The Lord knows where he is. Maybe he's even with the Lord. Perhaps I'll just have to be satisfied with that. It will be very hard for the kids if I go back with no definite word about their dad but I know the Lord can help us to live with the uncertainty just as he has helped us the past fourteen years."

Ike was more upset than I had ever seen him after an interview with "Scarface," by far the roughest interrogator of the lot. Scarface banged the table with his fist and demanded that Ike "remove his cloak of disguise and admit to his real espionage activities in Vietnam." When Ike maintained that his village development concerns were not a cloak for other activities the man stalked angrily from the room.

The next day was even worse. Scarface again pressed for a confession of CIA involvement and then gave Ike a preview of plans to "liberate" the Philippines.

"Don't tell *me* the 'domino theory' doesn't work," Ike said to us after the session.

I had sessions with my questioner all week. He continued to be friendly and understanding. I had trouble recalling the names of education and ethnic minority officials we had worked with in the nineteen-sixties. Most of those I did remember were only last names. Because the last name in Vietnamese is the given name this was about as helpful as Mr. Tom, Mr. Dick or Mr. Harry would be in our own culture.

"Could you remember the names of the people you worked with in 1960?" I asked him.

"Of course I could," he said.

"Then you have a better memory than I," I said. "I would recognize these men if I saw them but I didn't know them well enough to remember their names now."

Often communication was difficult because our understanding of a situation was so different. He was convinced that the American Embassy ran things in the South and I tried to explain that the American Embassy had no control over us when we were in South Vietnam. We were subject to Vietnamese authority.

"Who gave you permission to go to Banmethuot when you went there?" he asked.

"No one," I answered, "we just went."

"Aha!" he said. "That proves the Americans were in control."

"Why?" I asked him, puzzled. "The South Vietnamese were also free to move around without papers. Nobody had to get permission to travel in the South."

"If I went to your country," he said, "and I was in New York I would have to get a paper if I wanted to go to San Francisco."

"No you wouldn't," I said. "If you were allowed into the United States as a visitor you could go anywhere you wanted to without asking permission."

He looked unconvinced. "If you came to Hanoi," he said, "and you wanted to visit Hai Phong you would have to get a paper of permission from our government."

"This is your country," I shrugged, "and if those are your rules I as a guest would abide by them. But that is not the way it is in any of the other countries I have visited."

That weekend we passed the seven month anniversary of our detention. In some ways it seemed to us we were no nearer release than we were six months earlier though Mr. Van continued to assure us that his government was working on the problem.

LuAnne developed diarrhea and stomach problems. This was followed by fever, vomiting and sore throat. But this time our resident medic was there with immediate treatment and the condition was quickly brought under control. Thinking back to the situation a few months earlier I realized we had much to be grateful for.

John came back from an interrogation session with a big grin. "You'll never believe what he told me today," he said.

"What?" I asked.

"He said the reason they needed to get all this detailed information about the members of our organization was so that if any of us wanted to come back to Vietnam and work they would know who was really a bona fide member of the group. I actually chuckled a bit as I asked, 'Do you mean you really think we would be allowed to come back to Vietnam?' And he said yes, he thought it was possible.

"At the end of the session he said something that surprised me," John continued. "He said, 'We will remember the Millers and we will remember how you and your wife helped us to understand more clearly your organization and its work.'"

"That's great!" I said. "We must have managed to get something across with all that writing and talking."

John talked with Mr. Van about our desire to assure our families we were alive and well. That same afternoon, October 15, Mr. Van told us he had checked with his superiors and was instructed to let us write and tape letters to our children. This presumably would be broadcast sometime by shortwave radio. LuAnne also wrote a letter to Margie, Gordon and Nate. John and I read our letters into the tape recorder Mr. Van had set up in one of the interrogation rooms but LuAnne declined to read hers.

"Maybe I'll do it another time," she stalled.

"No, LuAnne, this will be the only chance," I told her.

But she couldn't bring herself to talk into the machine. That night when she went to bed she worried about her failure to talk to her brothers and sister.

"They'll think I'm not here," she said, starting to cry.

"They'll know you're here," I told her. "Don't you remember I told them about your birthday party?"

"Yes," she said, by now sobbing heartbrokenly, "but they won't hear me and maybe they'll think I'm not still with you."

"They'll know," I assured her. "Don't worry about it. Besides we don't really know if Margie, Gordie and Nate will ever hear the letters anyway."

That same evening a bus pulled into camp again. Mr. Van told us another trip to places of cultural interest in Hanoi had been planned for the following day. I had mixed feelings about the proposed trip. I wanted to see as much of the country and its people as I could but I wasn't sure I should take LuAnne. Her fever was down but I had kept her in bed almost all day. With my own stomach problems I wasn't sure I could take a day of sightseeing. And I felt somewhat reluctant to expose myself to the "tourist" treatment which would accompany such a trip. It was just too hard to go back to "prisoner" treatment again.

In the morning LuAnne had no fever and seemed to feel fine. Mr. Van was eager to have us all go so we boarded the bus with the rest. Again I felt relief just to be out and to see normal people going about their routine of living and working.

Our first stop was at the Van Mieu (Temple of Literature) in Hanoi. The oldest institution of higher learning in the country, it trained only the most talented students from 1010 to 1789. Engraved stone tablets celebrated the best student from each class. To us it resembled a lovely enclosed park. A girl guide explained its history and showed us through a building where old pottery and ancient dwarf trees were displayed.

Back at the bus children clustered around to ask for something. Puzzled we asked Mr. Van what they wanted. He explained that visitors from Eastern European countries sometimes carried small insignias from their countries which they would give to children.

We next went to the Museum of Art. On the upper floor was a large room displaying artifacts from various ethnic minority groups throughout North and South Vietnam. Looking at the section labelled "Van Kieu" made us feel acutely homesick for our Bru (Van Kieu) friends. Other displays on that level showed art forms from ancient tombs and pagodas. Downstairs were rooms displaying recent contributions. Most of this was revolutionary in nature, depicting aspects of the war or social reform.

We ate lunch in the same simple home where we had eaten before. The front room was barely large enough to hold us all. The camp cook had prepared a typical noon meal. Mr. Van was concerned that Jay was not eating anything.

258

"There is nothing here I can eat," Jay explained. "I figure I am losing about a kilogram a week just because my stomach will not tolerate greasy or highly seasoned food."

Several of us had expressed concern in the past that Jay was unable to eat and was becoming extremely undernourished but not until now did Mr. Van realize the severity of his problem. Now he seemed alarmed.

"I will have the cook make a pan of rice gruel for you each meal from now on," he said.

After lunch we were taken to visit a handicraft shop which specialized in items of silver and gold. Gold could not be sold but items of silver, bone, mother of pearl and other materials were on sale. Mr. Van offered to exchange American currency for us if we wanted to buy anything. We selected several items to take as souvenirs for our families.

As we drove through downtown Hanoi we passed embassies of various foreign countries. "If you see an Australian flag," Peter said quietly from the seat behind us, "get LuAnne away from the window because I am going to jump out."

Our next stop was the Revolutionary Museum. "This is one I'm not looking forward to," I said to John on the way. "We've seen so much about the war in the other museums that I can just imagine what this one will be like."

We went through the upper floor beginning with a room which featured the Declaration of Independence and following through to a room showing the defeat of the French at Dien Bien Phu. Then we went downstairs.

"Well, here we go with the Americans," I thought. But our guide led us down the corridor past a series of doors and entered the last one. This was a display showing the support and congratulations from all over the world for the revolutionary movement in Vietnam.

I was still trying to understand the significance of our not being shown displays castigating American imperialism when we were taken to an adjoining building to view a film.

"We were going to show a film about Dien Bien Phu," an official announced, "but we thought perhaps it would not be appropriate, especially for the women and the child. So we are showing you instead a film about the life and death of Ho Chi Minh entitled 'We Remember Uncle.'"

259

The film was a touching tribute to a charismatic leader. It showed his simple life, his concern for the common people and the easy rapport he had with children. The affection and admiration he commanded was not unknown to us. We had sensed it every time one of the North Vietnamese mentioned Uncle Ho. Portrayed on the film was the overwhelming grief they felt at his death.

After the film was over the official who seemed to have arranged the trip spoke to us breifly. "We hope you have enjoyed the things you have seen today," he said, "and that you have a better understanding of our people and our way of life. We wish we had opportunity to show you more but perhaps some day you will return to visit again and can see more of our country."

"That sounded almost like a swan song," someone remarked as we walked out to get on the bus.

Each of us carried a shoe box. A week or two earlier at Mr. Van's request I had collected footprints of each member in the group. I expected we would be issued a pair of rubber-tire sandals. But today before the film the officer who had accompanied us from South Vietnam had brought in boxes of carefully selected leather dress shoes for us to try on. A tailor had also come to measure us for a new set of clothes.

As I considered these things on the way back to camp I was inclined to be hopeful. But remembering the comedown after the last trip I was unwilling to put too much faith in these signs.

When we got back the camp commander called us into the room next to the office. "Here it comes," I thought uneasily as I accepted a cup of tea and waited to be told why we were assembled.

"Did you have a good trip?" he asked pleasantly. We assured him we had and spent a few minutes describing what we had seen.

"Well, it's almost time for your supper so you probably want to get back to your rooms," he said dismissing us.

"Whew!" Joan said as she walked past the door to our room, "I couldn't even drink my tea for wondering what bombshell he was going to drop."

"You too?" I said. "I had the same feeling."

ELEVEN

Release

Winter was approaching and the weather in Sơn Tây was becoming colder and more rainy. Heavy wool blankets had been issued to each of us and we were thankful for them. But the morning after our Hanoi excursion dawned bright and sunny. I took some of our damp clothes to hang on the line out behind our room. From there I had a clear view of the front gate and the sight I saw made the day seem even brighter. The interrogators and interpreters for whom we had been "working" the last two weeks were walking out the gate! Maybe they were just leaving for the weekend but even so we felt a tremendous lift of spirits.

On Saturday we borrowed paddles and a ball from the guards, and Peter, Ike, John and I played a few games of ping-pong in the building behind our living quarters. The building smelled like a barn because the recently acquired cow, which we referred to as "Bossy the camp lawnmower," often wandered in and left remembrances around the ping-pong table. But the game was fun and good exercise.

"We'll have to do this again," we agreed. But we never did.

That afternoon the medic brought some packets of white powder. Jay, LuAnne and I were being given a worm treatment. He instructed us to take half the powder that evening and half in the morning when we got up. We followed his instructions carefully and all went well until a few hours after taking the second packet. I began to experience an excruciating

261

headache and then numbness around my lips. By 10 A.M. I began vomiting and despite injections to combat nausea I continued to vomit with increasing frequency as the day continued. LuAnne and Jay felt fine!

Lil and the medic both kept frequent check on me and as the night progressed and the vomiting and intense stomach pain showed no sign of letting up the medic was frankly worried.

"I think he's concerned about intestinal blockage," Lil said. "That could be very serious."

Around 11 that night a small ambulance arrived to take me to the military hospital. John was permitted to accompany me and Betty agreed to sleep in our room lest LuAnne awaken and worry.

We'd gone only a mile or two when the engine of the vehicle sputtered and died. The attractive young woman soldier who drove the vehicle got out, took some tools from under the pallet where I way lying and threw up the hood. Our medic held a flashlight while she undertook the repairs. A half hour later she had it running again and we resumed the trip.

At the hospital I was questioned and examined in the early hours of the morning. Then I was put on a cart and rolled out under the stars along a path to another building. I was in too much pain to appreciate the ride or even notice where I was being taken. In a quiet and seemingly deserted building an X-ray technician came out rubbing his eyes sleepily. He wheeled me into another room and proceeded to take some X-rays. As soon as I was back in the empty corridor another technician appeared to take blood from my arm. He also had obviously been aroused from sleep. Neither he nor any of the others appeared resentful of this but went about their work with quiet competence. I was greatly impressed.

The medic wheeled me back to where John was waiting and I was put to bed in a nearly empty ward. The vomiting had subsided. I was given several injections, and by 3 A.M. John and the medic left to return to camp.

The medic returned in the morning bringing me a fried bun to eat. I tried a few bites but was unable to keep them down. Members of the hospital staff gathered to regard me curiously. I hardly felt up to answering the barrage of questions but all seemed friendly. Toward mid-morning an older doctor with an

262

entourage of several younger ones came and spoke to me.

"I don't think your condition is serious," he said , "so we are sending you back to camp. I think you have just experienced a strong reaction to the medicine you took. If you do not improve you will of course be brought back but I think you will improve rapidly."

I returned in the same ambulance with the same young woman driver. This time we made the half-hour trip without incident. John was surprised to see me back so soon. He helped me back into our room where I crawled gratefully onto the hard board bed. The doctor was right. By that afternoon I kept down a small amount of the coconut ice cream Mr. Van bought us as a special treat. And though I was weak for several days my stomach was definitely improving.

Two days after the hospital episode Mr. Van began dropping hints that he expected to have good news for us in a few days. There were other encouraging developments. For over a week now we had been getting immunizations. We were told these were merely routine shots given to everyone in the country but we wondered if they might also indicate preparation for international travel. Then just the day before, Jim Lewis had bounded over to introduce himself and to tell us happily that he was now permitted to talk with us.

He had been captured on the battlefield in Phan Rang six months earlier, we learned, along with three Vietnamese generals. They were taken to Danang and flown directly to Hanoi. The Vietnamese generals had been moved out of this camp the day we arrived. We laughed as Jim recounted his reactions to our arrival.

"I couldn't believe my eyes when I saw this group of Americans walk in with Samsonite suitcases," he recalled. "They looked like a bunch of tourists. And then when I heard one of them say, 'What kind of electricity do they have here? We have a sewing machine,' I really thought I was cracking up. 'Is this some Communist plot to completely demoralize me?' I wondered. 'This used to be a respectable prison!' "

We told him the authorities still seemed to be trying to determine our crime. "That's all right," he said with a rather sheepish grin, "I have enough crimes for all of you. I was just what they were looking for—an employee of the State Department, captured on the battlefield, formerly in Vietnam with Special Forces, and with friends in intelligence work."

"Wow!" I said. "No wonder they have you writing all the time."

"I figure there's no reason not to tell them what they ask," he shrugged, "The war is over now."

Jim told us the camp where we were staying was the scene of the 1970 raid by Special Forces troops to try to rescue American military prisoners of war. "That tree," he said, pointing to one directly in front of our room, "lost its top when a helicopter crashlanded in the courtyard." The raid had been successfully carried off, but the prisoners had all been moved out earlier.

Two other bits of news interested us greatly. Before he was captured Jim had overheard part of a discussion concerning us in the U.S. Embassy in Saigon.

"I didn't pay too much attention to what was said," he confessed, "but I'm fairly certain they knew you were still alive and were being held by the Communists."

About our children he said, "I can tell you for certain they got out of Nha Trang, because I helped evacuate the civilians. After that I don't know."

He had seen a list of people killed when the large plane carrying evacuees crashed but except for two people who had been friends of his he remembered none of the names. "I can't help wondering if our kids were on that plane," I said to John later.

"We can't let our minds dwell on things like that," he said. "We just have to trust that the Lord is working out whatever is best for them just as he is for us."

"Nevertheless I think it's well to remind ourselves that we may be in for some unpleasant surprises when we get out of here," I said.

"I suppose so," he said thoughtfully, "but if we are I'm sure God will give us strength to take them when the time comes."

The next few days we were busy rewriting and taping our requests for release and filling out immigration forms. On Friday, the 24th of October, Mr. Van told us we would probably be released around the end of that month or beginning of the next.

"Will Paul and Jim be released, too?" I asked him.

"I think so," he replied, "but I'm not sure their cases will be

264

finished yet. I would say there is about a 90% chance they will also be released."

Saturday morning the camp commander brought a small flatiron so we could press the "going away clothes" we had received the day before. One of the guards connected it to the bare wires in our room and our bed became the ironing board. The men had received cotton shirts and trousers. The women would wear light khaki trousers and sheer white nylon blouses. These were the clothes for which we'd been measured in Hanoi and I was pleased to see that the order slip which accompanied them was marked "rush."

That afternoon I gave John, Jay and Peter haircuts and was starting on Jim when we were called in to redo our latest request for release. One of the guards took over and sheared off more of Jim's hair than he had wanted cut. They had made it clear all along that they preferred to see the men clean shaven and with very short hair but they always stopped short of ordering this. John could hardly wait to get rid of his beard and mustache which he found itchy and which got in his way when eating. But Peter who had had previous experience shaving off a heavy beard advised him to wait till he had hot water, shaving cream, sharp blades and a good mirror, none of which were readily available here.

Sunday morning we held what we hoped would be our last worship service as a group. Jay and Jim joined us for it. John gave a meditation on the theme "the love of God." I had written out copies of "Love Divine, All Loves Excelling" and "Loved With Everlasting Love" to add to our rather meager collection of hymns. In closing John asked Dick to sing "The Love of God." I felt a very close bond to these people with whom we had shared so much.

Monday morning we were delighted to see Paul arrive back in camp with Mr. Van and Mr. Khoi. We filled him in on our activities and asked him about his experiences. He had, he said, undergone a period of intense interrogation lasting often from morning to night. He had experienced no physical abuse though the threat of it had been used.

"They told me," he said, "that their policy of leniency extended only to people who cooperated with them and if I refused to cooperate I would no longer be entitled to lenient treatment. When I asked them what they meant by leniency they defined this as adequate food and the absence of physical punishment.

"They tried to get me to admit," he went on, "that the missionaries in Banmethuot were an intelligence gathering network which reported to me. They couldn't believe that we never met socially and that I didn't go to your houses or you to mine.

"I gave them a little talk on differences in life styles," he continued with a grin, "and I think that helped them to understand."

Paul said he had also been accused of trying to organize our group to resist cooperating with the North Vietnamese officials.

"They've got to be kidding!" I laughed.

"That's what I thought," Paul agreed. "I told them I didn't think anyone in the world could organize that bunch to do anything. But I had to sign a statement that I wouldn't try to organize you guys to not cooperate with them before they'd let me come back."

That day we gathered in the room next to the office while a visiting military officer addressed us. Here in the North indications of rank were sometimes worn and this man's proclaimed him to be a lieutenant colonel. He informed us that arrangements were being made to turn us over to the United Nations High Commission for Refugees (UNHCR) in a few days. They had agreed, he said, to receive us and see that we got back to we got back to our home countries.

I was amazed to hear him say, "Some of you were involved in service to the minority groups of our country. We want to thank you for your help." This was quite a switch from what we had become accustomed to.

One thing continued to trouble us. They still had not returned to us the papers and manuscripts taken from us. When I had requested to use the Bru manuscripts Mr. Van told me they had been taken to another place to be studied.

"Don't worry about them," he said. "I am 90% sure that everything taken away from you will be returned."

We knew they were going over everything carefully because they questioned us about some of the names and addresses they found in our papers. I wondered what they thought about Mom Miller's pickle recipe I had in my wallet!

On Tuesday the 28th Mr. Van told us our departure from Hanoi was scheduled for Thursday morning, October 30. He brought back to our room the watches and pearl necklace he had taken and asked for the copy of the receipt so he could determine what things were still missing. That was the last we saw of the receipt. Our papers had not yet been brought back, he said.

Joan talked with me that morning in the ladies' washroom. "I don't know what to do," she said. "Betty had chills and fever in the night. I'm sure it's malaria again and she ought to be treated for it. But she doesn't want me to tell the medic. She's afraid they won't let us go if they know."

"On the other hand if she doesn't get treatment right away she may not be able to go," I said, recalling the last attack when she was unable to leave her bed for days.

"I guess I'd better tell him," Joan decided reluctantly, "and hope it doesn't bring a change of plans."

Wednesday morning we were summoned to the meeting room next to the office to receive some parting souvenir gifts from the North Vietnamese government. The women were given Vietnamese hats and woven bamboo purses, combs, perfume and mirrors. The men received plastic flight bags, belts and socks. All of us received soap, toothpaste, toothbrushes, hand towels and handkerchiefs. LuAnne happily put her new treasures in the small black plastic satchel she was given.

"Now I'm an officer, too, Mommy," she said. When I looked puzzled, she explained, "See, I have a black bag."

Mr. Van cautioned us about what we would be allowed to take as souvenirs. We would not be allowed to take any of the clothing we had been issued in the South or anything that would tend to make their country look more poor and primitive than it actually was. We had asked to be allowed to keep the old South Vietnamese army jackets we were wearing since some of us expected to go to places where it was cold. This request was denied. Instead the next day we were given new wool sweaters made in the People's Republic of China.

Mr. Van made it a point to mention that the sweaters were the only things of all the items given to us not produced in his country. It was evident that great care had been taken to secure the very finest quality in everything. Apparently North Vietnamese officialdom was concerned that the country be represented in the best possible way when we returned.

Joan and I helped set up tables in the meeting room for a special noon meal. We had joked about Bossy providing steaks for our going-away dinner and the jokes proved more nearly true than we had imagined. Not steaks but tasty dishes of beef prepared in several ways were served by the camp kitchen that noon. Bottles of beer and extra cigarettes were also provided. Mr. Van was a genial host.

After the siesta hour Mr. Van called us into the men's quarters for a meeting.

"My superiors have informed me that any papers relating to the country or people of Vietnam will not be returned. That i..cludes," he said with an apologetic look toward the beds by the door where the Phillipses and we were sitting, "the Mnong and Bru translation manuscripts and Mr. Phillips' dissertation."

A tremendous weight of disappointment settled on my heart at the news. It was not completely unexpected. We knew from the literature we had been reading that Communism was unalterably opposed to any form of religion and Christianity in particular. Still I had hoped that somehow God would overrule the expected chain of events in answer to our prayers.

"If you have any thoughts about this or anything you wish to say," Mr. Van went on, "I will convey these to my superiors."

"What can we say?" I thought bitterly. "Nothing we say will make any difference at this point." Still I realized we would have to make a protest of some sort. What could we say that would indicate strong feeling without at the same time causing antagonism?

The room was silent. The others in the group, realizing what this meant to the Phillipses and us, looked serious.

"I'm very sorry your government has made this decision," I said. "These papers represent much research and study on the part of Mr. and Mrs. Phillips and ourselves. If your government does not allow us to retain the results of our own research I think this would be regarded rather seriously by linguists and other scholars around the world."

Lil spoke next giving her personal feelings and asking that they reconsider the decision. Dick was silent.

268

Mr. Van stood in the center of the room looking somewhat uncomfortable and taking notes on what was said.

"You have told us that you have complete freedom of religion in your country," John said. "I think it will be hard for anyone to believe this if manuscripts of the Bible are confiscated and not returned by your government."

"I will relay these feelings to my superiors," Mr. Van said gravely.

Back in our room I felt devastated. "I just don't understand it," I said to John. "I really believed God was going to help us keep those manuscripts. You know that verse from Psalm 126 we've been claiming promises 'He that goeth forth and weepeth, bearing precious seed, shall doubtless come again with rejoicing bringing his sheaves with him.' I somehow felt this applied to the manuscripts we had with us. It seemed to me the preservation of those was more important than the preservation of our own lives."

LuAnne came over when she saw the tears coming down my cheeks.

"What's the matter, Mommy?" she asked, looking up at me with a worried expression.

"LuAnne, I feel very badly that they aren't going to let us take the Bru manuscripts with us when we leave," I told her. "The Bru people want so badly to have God's Word and we hoped that some day they would be able to get it."

I left the room to try to find somewhere I could be alone. In the back corner of the wall I found a place hidden from general view by one of the interrogation buildings. I leaned against the guard post support and tried to sort out my tumultuous thoughts.

"Why, God?" I asked.

To the best of my understanding, I felt my motives in praying for the return of the manuscripts had been solely for God's glory and the eternal good of the Bru people. What about all those promises Jesus made about answering prayers which we made in his name and according to his will? How could it not be his will to preserve his own Word?

All the struggles and doubts I had felt before came back to me. Unless God was sovereign, then he wasn't God. If he was sovereign, then no situation either took him by surprise or

269

taxed his ability to achieve his purpose. This took me right back to "square one." Either God was what the Bible said he was or human life was without value or purpose, "a tale told by an idiot, full of sound and fury, signifying nothing."

My decision on that had already been made. I had chosen faith. And faith was not really faith if it existed only in situations where a happy ending was in sight. I remembered telling Lil months earlier that, though we might never see the Bru people again or be able to give them any more translated Scriptures, our years in Vietnam had been well worth the investment. Did I really believe that? The time had come to either "put up or shut up." God could still cause the men who held control of the manuscripts to reverse their decision by tomorrow, but if they did not, I would have to accept it as reflecting his plan and purpose.

I walked back to the room. John was sitting on a stool beside LuAnne's bed reading. I sat down on the bed. LuAnne looked up from where she was playing "store" with her toys.

"Are you still feeling sad about the manuscripts, Mommy?" she asked.

"Yes, honey, I am," I said.

"I thought about telling them I wouldn't leave without the manuscripts," John said seriously, "but I'm not sure that would be a wise decision. Then too there are the kids to consider."

Mr. Van came into the room while we were talking. His look took in my red nose and swollen eyes. "I feel very badly about this," he said to us. "I know what this means to you. But it was not my decision."

"We understand this, Mr. Van," I said.

"This should be a very happy day," he said, "but it is turning out to be a sad one."

After Mr. Van left John said to me, "I've been rereading those verses from Isaiah, and I feel we should just leave the matter in God's hands and wait for him to work out his purpose in this."

I knew the verses to which he referred. Just yesterday he had read me several verses from Isaiah 55 which had impressed him strongly. Perhaps God was even then preparing us for today's announcement. He had read verses 8 through 11 from the Living Bible:

"This plan of mine is not what you would work out, neither
270

are my thoughts the same as yours! For just as the heavens are higher than the earth, so are my ways higher than yours, and my thoughts than yours.

"As the rain and snow come down from heaven and stay upon the ground to water the earth, and cause the grain to grow and to produce seed for the farmer and bread for the hungry, so also is my Word. I send it out and it always produces fruit. It shall accomplish all I want it to, and prosper everywhere I send it."

John and I walked together out behind the building for a time of prayer. Brokenly I acknowledged to God that those manuscripts were his, not ours, and accepted the assurance that he would use them to accomplish whatever he wanted. With acceptance came peace. We returned to our room to finish packing.

That evening the camp officials had planned a farewell party. It was a strange gathering. Even those not directly affected by the afternoon's announcement seemed subdued by it. The camp commander made a speech to which we asked Jay to respond. We excused ourselves to take LuAnne to bed and the others also soon left.

We went to bed early that night exhausted by the emotional strain of the day. I slept soundly until 4 A.M. when light and noise coming from the men's quarters woke me. Unable to sleep any longer they were getting ready to go.

Mr. Van came in around five to inspect our baggage. He hesitated when he saw the little twelve inch broom we had used to sweep our room each day in our suitcase. "You told me I could take it," I reminded him.

"All right," he agreed somewhat reluctantly.

Some items from the suitcase I asked him to give to members of the camp staff who had been particularly kind to us—a set of metal measuring cups to the cook, LuAnne's colored pencils to the medic who had borrowed them on several occasions, a tennis ball to Mr. Van's little daughter Ly, and two tupperware containers to the camp commander.

Breakfast consisted of more of Bossy in the form of beef noodle soup. It was flavorful though somewhat tough but we were too excited to appreciate it. We were eager to be on our way. The camp commander came into our room and gave LuAnne a parting gift—a beautiful carving of a ship done in mother-of-pearl and set

271

on a black carved base. I was greatly touched.

"This is something she will treasure all her life," I told him. "It will help her to remember her friends here."

We were told to take our things to the bus which had arrived in camp the night before. John took "big brown" and headed out the door.

"Where's that sewing machine?" Peter asked, coming into the room. "Let me carry it just one more time!"

As we boarded the bus Mr. Van called Lil and me aside. "I have talked to my superiors about the things you told me yesterday," he said. "They told me that although they are not yet finished studying your papers this does not mean you will never get them back. They will continue to study them and when they have finished you may request that they be returned to you. If they are found to contain nothing harmful to our national security they will be returned to you."

"Couldn't we talk to the men who are responsible for this decision?" I asked him. "Perhaps we could explain to them the contents of the papers."

"I don't think there will be time for that," he said. "There are two government departments involved in this, Immigration and Foreign Affairs."

The bus left camp around 6:15 A.M. Several of the officers accompanied us. The medic joked about going on the plane with us. We felt a sense of mounting excitement not completely unmixed with cautious reserve. Even at this point something might go wrong. Paul and Jim had been particularly careful not to get their hopes up. As the bus made its way through Hanoi and on toward Gia Lam airport, Paul said quietly to Jim, "Would you say our chances of release are about 95% now?"

Mr. Van turned around in his seat and said something to me about the broom I was taking. I could tell he was bothered by this. "I'm taking it to my father, Mr. Van," I explained. "You see, when he visited us in South Vietnam he really liked the Vietnamese brooms. We sent him one from the South for his birthday one time and I thought he would also like to have one from the North."

"Oh," he said in obvious relief, "why didn't you tell me before that was why you wanted it?" I just smiled. I had told
272

him that before but he evidently had not understood.

We arrived at the airport around 7:45 A.M. For an international airport it seemed strangely deserted. No people were coming and going from the terminal and no planes were either taking off or landing. We were taken upstairs to a conference room where we waited. Peter was taken to a separate room where he finally met the Australian ambassador to North Vietnam. That gentleman had been informed of Peter's presence by the Vietnamese government just the day before.

Several Vietnamese officials addressed us. We were not unaware of a strong feeling of uneasiness about what we would say when we got out. We had been asked about this on numerous occasions but they knew from previous experience that people who did not reveal their true feelings to them often spoke very freely on the outside. They had been stung by the critical reports of returning American POWs.

"We do not ask that you paint a rosy picture of conditions here in Vietnam," one official told us, "but only that you give a true report of what you have seen and experienced. If you said that everyone in our country wore clothes and shoes like the ones we have given you, that would be a rosy picture. Most of our people are very poor and cannot afford clothes like these. But if you said that we are incapable of producing things of this quality, that would also be untrue.

"We know we have a long way to go in terms of improving the standard of living in our country. But now that the war is over we expect to make rapid progress. We hope you will come back in a few years. We will take you back to the areas of the South where you lived and worked and let you see the progress we are confident will have been made."

During the morning we saw one plane land. It had the markings of the Royal Air Lao airline. We wondered if this plane brought the UNHCR officials who had come for us. John and Dick were taken to another room to meet with immigration officials to receive the personal papers they had decided to return. There they were told the same thing Mr. Van had told Lil and me about the translated Scriptures and Dick's dissertation.

"How can we make a request for these?" John asked.

"By writing to the Foreign Ministry," he was told, "or by making request to one of our foreign embassies."

"What good will it do them to keep these papers?" I asked Mr. Van. "No one here can even read them."

"Oh we have access to plenty of Bru speakers in the South," he said. "Don't worry," he added, sensing the unspoken concern in my mind, "they won't be destroyed."

We were just finishing some food prepared by the faithful camp cook who had accompanied us even here when the word came to leave. Mr. Khoi took the uneaten portion of a package of cookies and put it in LuAnne's black bag. We followed the others downstairs and through the central waiting room which was now filled with people. Apparently another plane was expected later today.

We entered a long reception room ringed with newsmen. We sat in two facing rows of chairs and were introduced to the officials of the UNHCR who were to receive us, Mr. Alexandre Casella and Mr. and Mrs. Darryl Nyun Han. We listened as representatives of the North Vietnamese government made speeches at the far end of the room. These were translated into French for the benefit of the Swiss Mr. Casella. His reply was then translated into Vietnamese. Behind me I could hear a muted voice translate the proceedings into what sounded to me like a language of Eastern Europe.

On the way to the chartered Royal Air Lao plane a Japanese reporter ran along beside me. "Why did you stay in Saigon when the other Americans left?" he asked.

"We weren't in Saigon," I said, ignoring his further questioning. He tried Dick and John and got no response.

At the side of the plane we said goodbye to Mr. Van and the camp officials. As I climbed the ladder to board the plane Mr. Van said to me, "I feel as though I have failed you and your husband."

"Why do you say that, Mr. Van?" I asked.

"Because of the manuscripts," he replied.

"We appreciate the fact that you are concerned about them," I said to him.

As the plane taxied and took off Paul said to Jim, "I guess it's about 98% sure now."

The Australian ambassador had given Peter several recent

Australian newspapers which we looked at eagerly.

"We will be stopping in Vientiane for refueling," Mr. Casella told us. "Then we will fly to Bangkok."

"Will we be turned over to our embassies there?" someone asked.

"You'll be turned over to yourselves, I guess," he replied.

"I don't know if we can handle all that responsibility," someone joked. It was a heady thought. After almost eight months of being told when to go to bed and get up, where to go, when to eat and what to do or not to do it would seem strange to make decisions like that again.

The graceful Lao stewardess served us trays containing a sandwich, a cupcake, a tangerine and an iced glass of cola. LuAnne surveyed the contents of her tray and remarked, "This is the best meal we've had since we've been prisoners!"

As we got off the plane in Vientiane flashbulbs popped. A reporter put a microphone in front of my face and began to ask questions. We didn't expect to see any familiar faces here and were amazed to spot friends from Vietnam, Luke and Mary Martin and Murray and Linda Hiebert. Their work with the Mennonite Central Committee (MCC) had brought them into contact with us in Vietnam, and Murray and Linda had worked at the Evangelical Clinic in Nha Trang which was adjacent to the school where our children studied.

Linda took my hand. "You don't have to talk to the reporters now if you don't want to," she said gently.

We were led to a private waiting room where members of the Australian, American, Canadian and Philippine diplomatic communities in Laos served us cold drinks and hors d'oeuvres.

But we were more hungry for information than for food. Luke Martin answered the question that pressed most heavily upon us.

"Your children are fine," he said, "and are with Carolyn's parents in New York. I think Gene Fuller from your organization will be meeting you in Bangkok and he can give you more details."

When we were back on the plane again anticipation mounted as we began the two-hour flight to Bangkok. I also felt a little apprehension with the growing realization that we had become a matter of worldwide interest.

"The press will certainly be there to meet you," the UN officials told us. "You can do what you want, of course, but the easiest thing might be to arrange a press conference at the airport where you can meet all the reporters at one time. We will restrict it to fifteen or twenty minutes. You might even want to prepare a statement in advance to read them."

This seemed like a good idea but the preparation of the statement proved problematical. No one statement describing our experience seemed to reflect everyone's feeling. "General Consensus" continued to prove as elusive to this group of individualists as it had for the past eight months. After two proposed statements had been shot down I suggested, "Maybe we should reduce the statement to just thanking the Vietnamese for releasing us and the UNHCR for bringing us out and then let everyone speak for himself."

"That's a good idea," said Peter handing me the paper and pen. "You do it."

"I'll give it a try," I said.

The others approved the short statement I prepared but declined to read it at the press conference. "You read it," they insisted.

When we touched down in Bangkok so much happened so quickly that it was difficult to take it all in. We were met as soon as we got off the plane by the ambassadors to Thailand of our respective countries. These accompanied us on the airport bus to the huge bustling Bangkok International Airport. I saw a large crowd of happy, waving people waiting inside the gate where we were heading. As we got off the bus I saw Betty rush over to embrace her youngest daughter, Gerry, who had flown in from Malaysia. Then we were being greeted by Gene Fuller who had come from the Philippines to meet us.

We went to a private lounge area where only close friends and representatives of our governments and organizations were allowed. Leis of flowers were put around our necks. Gene gave LuAnne a little doll that his daughter, Christa, had sent for her, and one of the C&MA ladies gave us chocolate bars. Gene began to tell us about all that had happened since March 12 to our families and co-workers and what they had done to try to get word about us. We plied him with questions.

Then we were being summoned to another room for the press conference. As I passed the American ambassador on

276

the way out I held out the paper with the statement on it. "This is the statement we prepared to read," I said to him.

He glanced at it briefly. "That's fine," he said. "Whatever you want to say is perfectly all right."

We filed into a large room and sat in chairs which had been placed along one wall. The other sides of the room were ringed with several rows of newsmen. I had never seen so many in my life! LuAnne sat between John and me regarding the scene soberly, still wearing her Hanoi hat and carrying her black bag.

A newsman on the floor to the right reached out a microphone. "What is your name?" he asked LuAnne. She didn't answer.

"That's all right," he went on, "I think I already know. It's LuAnne, isn't it?"

She smiled and flashbulbs popped all around the room.

Mr. Casella announced that we would read a statement and then receive questions.

"This is a very happy day for us all," I began. Recorders whirred and pens moved. The news was flashed via satellite to the U.S. where friends across the country were startled to hear my voice as they drank their breakfast coffee. People we had never even met wept for joy to hear their prayers had been answered.

A reporter asked Betty if she had received any word about her husband. "No," Betty replied, "and this was a great disappointment to me."

"What are your feelings after going through an experience like this?" he continued.

"I love the Lord Jesus more than ever," she said, "and I love the Vietnamese people."

The questioning went on in an orderly fashion until Mr. Casella politely asked the newsmen to let us go. "These people have had a long day," he said, "and they want to have some time with their family and friends."

I was tremendously impressed by the courtesy and kindness of the press representatives. There had been no loaded or high-pressured questions. As we turned to go a man said to Jay and me, "I am from the Australian Broadcasting Commission, Mr. Whitlock's organization, and I would just like to ask if Mr. Whitlock's treatment was similar to yours?"

277

"Yes," Jay told him. "We were together the whole time and our treatment was the same."

"Why don't you talk to Peter," I suggested, only now noticing as I looked for him that he was not with us.

"Mr. Whitlock was whisked away from planeside," he said somewhat bitterly. "We understand he is being flown to Australia tomorrow morning and we will not be allowed to see him."

I was not surprised. Peter told me after talking to the Australian government representative in Vientiane that he would probably not be able to go to Chieng Mai to write out his final project reports before returning to Australia as he had planned.

"I guess I have become somewhat of a *cause célèbre* in the Australian press," he said, "and my presence in Thailand would be somewhat of an embarrassment to the Australian government." Apparently there had been some pointed questions asked by the press about the benefit of having diplomatic relations with a country if this did not result in certain protections for citizens of that country. The Australian government, anxious to improve relations with North Vietnam, did not want anyone to rock the boat.

As we left the airport one reporter ran after me. "Mrs. Miller," he said, "I would like to ask just one more question. Would you ever consider going back to Vietnam?"

"Absolutely," I answered without hesitation. "We would be more than happy to return if we were allowed to."

Gene, John, LuAnne and I rode into Bangkok with two U.S. embassy officials. The heavy traffic, huge billboards, high-rise buildings, lights and noise made me feel we had entered a different world.

"If you'd like to go back to my office," one embassy official said, "I will try to put through a call to the States so you can talk with your family."

The prospect seemed too good to be true. We waited in his office while he worked out the connections and then suddenly, miraculously, my Dad's voice came over the wire.

"Dad!" I said, "it's Carolyn. We're out! Did you know?"

"Honey, that's wonderful," he said. "We heard there was a possibility but we didn't *know* anything."

UNHCR representatives had not been given our names until they had arrived in Hanoi that morning and my parents who had been disappointed by earlier false reports of our release had learned not to get their hopes up. Now it had actually happened and within minutes of our call Pastor Morton Dorsey of the Houghton Wesleyan Church would ring the church bell to let the community know the good news.

Margie, Gordon and Nate were just ready to go to school.

"Margie, this is Daddy," John said. "How are you?"

"Fine," she answered.

"What are you doing?" he asked.

"Getting ready to go to school," she replied.

The conversations were certainly not outstanding in terms of information given or received but just to hear their voices again was sheer joy. LuAnne shook her head when asked if she wanted to talk to them. "You do it," she said.

"It may take us a few days to get there," we told them, "but we'll be there as soon as we can."

TWELVE

Home

"I have plane tickets for you from Bangkok to Buffalo and instructions to accompany you all the way if you need me," Gene told us. He was much relieved to find us in basically sound health. Not knowing what our physical, mental and emotional condition would be he had walked the streets of Bangkok looking for just the right place to take us. He reserved a suite of rooms in a quiet, comfortable hotel near a hospital, a shopping center and the U.S. Consulate where he knew we would have to get new passports. He was ready for any eventuality! Touched by the loving concern of Gene and the other members of the Vietnam Branch who had sent him we hastened to assure him we were well enough to make the trip on our own.

"The feel of freedom can only be properly appreciated," I thought as we approached the brightly-lit hotel entrance, "by one who knows what it is to be without it." There are no words adequate to describe the sense of wonder, gratitude and relief we felt at being free again!

Just to be able to walk down a street mingling freely with the brightly dressed people and being able to make plans about what we would do tomorrow was unspeakably precious. I felt I would like to go up to some of the sedate pedestrians, shake them and say to them, "Don't you realize what you have?" But each of them, engrossed with his own problems, probably took for granted, as I had, the priceless gift of freedom.

The Narai Hotel seemed to us the latest word in luxury. The elevator whisked us up to the tenth floor and we walked down the carpeted hall to our rooms. Gene had brought with him a suitcase of things lovingly donated by our displaced

280

co-workers in the Philippines. They had well anticipated our needs. I could now throw out LuAnne's ragged gray underpants. John was eager to use the shaving cream and razor blades and I could hardly wait to shampoo the sticky film from my hair and don the soft nightgown and colorful robe they had sent.

But first we went to the hotel coffee shop for a late supper. The variety of things offered dazzled us but John eventually settled for a seafood dish and I ordered an omelet. LuAnne had a craving for watermelon which, though not listed on the menu, was surprisingly enough available.

I gave LuAnne a warm tub bath and put her to bed around 10 P.M. John and I stayed up till 1 A.M. talking with Gene and reading the notes, letters and newspaper clippings he had brought. We were amazed at the untiring efforts he and others had made to try to get information about us and effect our return.

John and I crawled into bed tired, comfortable and happy. But we found ourselves unable to fall asleep.

"Maybe the bed is too soft," John said. He took his pillow and blanket and lay down on the carpeted floor. Even that was softer than what we had become accustomed to. I had developed callouses at the base of my spine from sleeping on hard boards.

But it was probably the excitement of the day rather than the softness of the beds that was keeping us awake. It was almost time to get up again before we drifted off for a couple of hours of sleep.

On our way to breakfast the next morning LuAnne ran ahead of us down the hall and into a waiting elevator. Before we could step in with her the automatic door closed. I heard a muffled, frightened voice call once and then she was gone. John started quickly down the stairs, pausing to look at each level. I waited there until the elevator came back empty, got on and went down to the ground floor. A man in the lobby said someone had taken a frightened child back up so I went back to the tenth floor.

"Yes, a man came up with a little girl," a hotel chambermaid said, "but when they found the room locked, they went back down. The little girl was crying."

By now I was quite concerned. I knew we'd catch up to her eventually but I could imagine how terrified she must be. The thing she had feared for eight months had actually happened. She had become separated from us in a strange place, not by design but by the vagaries of modern technology.

Back on the ground floor I checked at the desk and then looked carefully through the coffee shop. John, reporting no success, was about to go up to wait at the tenth floor. Then I spotted her getting off the elevator with a Thai man. At the same moment she saw Gene across the lobby sending a Telex message and started toward him.

I called her and she ran to me. She clung to me as I thanked the gentleman who had helped her. From then on she held tightly to my hand with both of hers each time we used the elevator.

That day we filled out the necessary papers for getting new passports. Our old ones had been turned in to the U.S. Embassy in Saigon and were destroyed when the embassy was evacuated. At the Thai immigration office the Thai officials stamped them with visas making our presence in Thailand legal. There we said goodbye to the rest of the group who had come to be referred to by the press as the "Banmethuot 14."

Peter was presumably already on his way to Australia. Ike and Bogh would leave the next day for the Philippines and Paul would return to the U.S. So would Jim and the Phillipses. Jay would return to Harrisburg via Paris where he was to visit friends en route. Norm and Joan would go to Canada after a few days rest in Hawaii. Betty would go to Malaysia with Gerry though a physical collapse brought on by malaria would delay her for some time.

With freedom came the necessity to make plans. "I know you want to get back to your kids as quickly as possible," Gene told us, "but if you could spare a day or two on your way I know the gang in the Philippines would love to see you. One of the reasons we stayed together as a group after we left Vietnam was so we could pray for you and for the tribal and Vietnamese friends we left behind in Vietnam."

John and I discussed it and decided we'd like to make that our first stop. These people we had worked with over the years were in a very real sense part of our "family," and we had no idea when we might have opportunity to see them again. Gene took care of reservations and sent messages concerning our plans. Still a bit dazzled by our re-entry into the 20th century we were glad to leave everything in his capable hands.

At the hotel that evening Eric Parsons from the Far Eastern Broadcasting Company in Manila interviewed us. "How would you describe your feeling about your release?" he asked us.

"I think it's already been said," I told him, quoting from Psalm 126 from which John and I had taken comfort so many times. "When the Lord turned again the captivity of Zion, we were like them that dream. Then was our mouth filled with laughter, and our tongue with singing: then said they among the nations, The Lord has done great things for them. The Lord has done great things for us: whereof we are glad."

Sunday afternoon we flew from Bangkok to Manila. From the moment we landed we were showered with love and attention. A large group of friends and wellwishers from Wycliffe's Vietnam and Philippine Branches as well as people from other mission organizations greeted us at the airport and went with us to Wycliffe's Manila Headquarters where we answered questions before turning in for the night.

The delicious fish dinner I had eaten on the plane sat uneasily on my stomach which was ill-prepared to handle so much rich food. All night I wrestled with it until along toward morning it came back up.

My stomach was still uneasy and I felt weak and shaky when we left for the airport in the morning. One of the pilots with the Jungle Aviation and Radio Service (JAARS), Wycliffe's air arm, was flying up from the southern island of Mindanao to take us back to the Wycliffe base there. Most of the Vietnam Branch had gone there to continue projects begun in Vietnam. Our three children had finished the school year there before going on to be with their grandparents in May.

Being flown directly from Manila to the Wycliffe base at Nasuli in a new twin-engine plane represented VIP treatment of the first order. "Good grief," I said to John, "you'd think we were important or something!"

Still I was glad not to have to go through the hassle of commercial travel especially feeling as if I were about to fold in the middle. Gene and his wife, Carol, with their two children and the other ex-Vietnamers working in Manila accompanied us.

The plane taxied down the grass airstrip and stopped near the hanger. As we stepped down from the plane we were engulfed by a crowd of our Vietnam co-workers. We laughed and cried and hugged each other for joy! A little way off members of the Philippine Branch, tribal language assistants and Filipino employees and friends stood, not wanting to intrude on the reunion but wanting to share in the happiness for which they too had earnestly prayed.

If we had felt like visiting royalty before, we were now overwhelmed with love. LuAnne clung to me uncertainly, not knowing what to make of all the attention. But before long she had reestablished friendship with the kids who had been like her brothers and sisters in the Children's Home and Wycliffe group homes in Saigon and Nha Trang. The kids lavishly gave her the candy they had saved from Halloween as well as books and toys. Being with them made us even more eager to get back to our other children. I was glad to see LuAnne begin to make cautious entry into the world of children.

"Potato salad!" I exclaimed with pleasure at supper that evening. That was one of the things I had been hungry for during the rice and grease-soup days. But experience had taught me caution and I ate sparingly. We ate first in one home and then another for the day and a half there, sometimes eating together in a group.

Only once during that happy time did we experience sadness. Eva Burton told us that after Banmethuot fell some of our Bru friends had left their village and come through the jungle to make their way to Nha Trang. Eva met them when they came to the Wycliffe center there. They had come, they told her, because the work on the Bru New Testament was not yet finished and they were certain that we would have gotten out of Banmethuot and come to Nha Trang where our children were. When they learned we had not gotten out it was a crushing blow to them. Eva had tape-recorded a message they had sent to Eugenia Johnston Fuller and Pat Bonnell, two Wycliffe missionaries who had worked with us in literacy and medical work among the Bru. As we read a transcript of that tape in our room there in Nasuli we wept.

"I am sorry about Grandfather and Grandmother Miller," one of them said respectfully. "As yet they have not arrived in Nha Trang and I wonder greatly and pray much to God to help them escape safely. As yet we don't have all the Word of God in our language and this will be a terrible loss if the Millers are not returned to finish it. I don't know what to think—if I give way to grief I'll die too but I feel very sad. But I keep praying to God for them. I don't know the road they are on but God does know.

"We don't know where we'll go from here. We ask you to pray for us Bru, Older Sister, especially that God will strengthen those of us who follow him that we will remain faithful to him and always follow his road. And we ask you to pray for the Bru who are now unable to escape. And I ask you to pray continually for the Millers that God will work for them according to his perfect will for life or death."

Still another of our Bru friends sent a special message of love and concern to Margie, Gordie and Nate. And in spite of the feelings of pain and loss we shared with them we knew our lives had been made rich by their love and for this we were grateful. Someday in God's time we would meet again, if not in Vietnam then in "God's Country."

The day and a half passed quickly. We learned the Vietnam Branch had requested to stay together as a group and to seek an expanded ministry throughout other areas of the Southeast Asia mainland. In keeping with this the name of the group had been changed to the Mainland Southeast Asia (MSEA) Branch. Several doors seemed to be opening.

"Come back as soon as you can," they told us as we set off for the return trip to Manila.

We left Manila the next morning, resuming our trip to the U.S. The airline arranged overnight accommodations in Tokyo since the next flight to Seattle would not leave until the following day. I was amused to note that we would stay at the Tokyo Hilton. It was exactly one week since we had left the camp which was part of the complex dubbed by American POWs the "Hanoi Hilton."

The magnificence of the place dazzled us. I felt somewhat intimidated by its elegance—the plush carpets, the chandeliers, the expensive furniture and the well-manicured Japanese garden. "I wonder what Mr. Van would think if he were to come into a place like this?" I said to John. "He'd probably think it a shameless display of capitalistic excess." I was somewhat inclined to agree even while I appreciated the extravagant beauty around me.

The last eight months had given me a new set of eyes for viewing the world. I gratefully accepted the wealth of material benefits available in Thailand, the Philippines and now Japan but with a different attitude. Now I recognized these for what

285

they were—luxuries which made life pleasant but without which life could still be lived and was in fact being lived by much of the world. Looking at the well-dressed people in the hotel lobby I wondered how many of them were grateful for such luxuries as toilet paper, running water and shampoo?

Telephone calls to Japanese and American friends in Tokyo resulted in brief visits with several of them. At the airport we talked with the Rev. Shin Funaki, chairman of Wycliffe's Japanese Council. He too had written letters and made contacts to ask for our return. A reporter from a Japanese religious paper interviewed us, with our friend John Masuda acting as interpreter. All of them told us that many Japanese Christians had prayed for our release.

The trip to Seattle was long and tiring. Backtracking through time zones brought us in at an early morning hour without the benefit of a night's sleep. My sister Mim and her husband, Gene Lemcio, met us at the airport and took us to their home not far from the Seattle Pacific College campus where Gene was teaching.

The two days spent in Seattle were very full. The telephone seemed to ring constantly and several friends came by to visit. Much of the time was spent in conversation with Carey Moore, editor of Wycliffe's *In Other Words* magazine, and Dr. Richard Pittman, Wycliffe's Pacific Area Director. Mim was torn between her desire to listen in on the conversations and the need to supervise the children. Two-year-old Adam had decided Uncle John was his own special friend and whenever they were in the same room his noisy bids for attention completely disregarded tape recorders or adult conversations.

"I think you ought to consider writing about your experiences," Dick Pittman said to us before he left to catch a plane to go back to the Philippines and Indonesia.

When the phone rang about an hour after he had gone and Mim said Dick was calling from the airport we wondered what caused him to call. John came back from the phone a few mintues later with a big smile. "Dick says he thought of a good title for our book," he said. "He thinks we should call it 'Tears In My Ears.'"

We left Seattle Sunday morning, arriving in Chicago with barely enough time to catch a connecting flight to Buffalo. We talked with two of my cousins and their families and some
286

friends from Vietnam as they ran with us from one side of the O'Hare terminal to the other. We settled into the last three seats on the plane minutes before it taxied for take-off.

I have no memory of what the weather was in Buffalo that evening or how we got from the plane to the terminal. But forever stamped on my memory is the moment when our children and then our parents were in our arms. The children seemed to have grown so much since we had seen them last. For them as for LuAnne the difficult eight months had brought greater maturity.

With them we walked to the reception area where a host of friends and relatives waited for us. Half of John's twelve brothers and sisters were there with their families. His youngest sister Kathryn had just flown in from Mexico where she served on the staff of Wycliffe's Jungle Training Camp.

The sixty mile trip from Buffalo to Houghton we made with John's brother Lynn and his wife Barbara. "Your being here tonight is not the only miracle God has brought about," Mom Miller had told me privately. Barbara, suffering from cancer, had very nearly died during the summer, she said. Two months later she would succumb to the disease but that night she was vibrant and full of life. God had given us a reunion unmarred by sadness.

Barb told us what a good time they had shared with our children during the summer when my sister Kathy had brought them down for a visit. Kathy, a sophomore in college, had assumed responsibility for the three children while my parents spent six weeks in Greece working with the general editorial committee of the *New International Version* of the Bible.

Before we reached Houghton Lynn pulled off the road to wait for the other cars of family and friends to catch up. The suppressed excitement of Margie, Gordie and Nate made us suspect that some celebration was planned. This was confirmed when the town fire engine fell in in front of us at the edge of town with lights flashing and siren blowing.

But nothing had prepared us for the scope of the welcome. When we turned off the main highway both sides of the road were lined with smiling, waving, shouting students and townspeople holding flaming torches. In front of our car walked young people carrying huge banners printed with "Welcome Home" and "To God Be the Glory." As we passed through the rows of torches these fell in behind the cavalcade of cars until by the time we reached my parents' home we were engulfed in a sea of blazing torches.

When we stepped from the car the entire group of what seemed to me to be several thousand people began to sing "To God be the glory, great things he hath done."

John lifted LuAnne onto the front of the car and we stood there with our arms around our children. My throat was tight and my knees were shaking but I began to sing with them the beautiful hymn of praise.

"Great things he hath taught us, great things he hath done. . . ," we sang and my heart affirmed the truth of that statement. I would never be the same person I was before this experience. God had opened my eyes to so many things.

". . . and great our rejoicing through Jesus the Son," we continued, my heart feeling it could hardly contain all the joy of that moment.

". . . but purer and higher and greater will be our wonder, our transport when Jesus we see," the third verse concluded.

"God," I thought, "if heaven is any better than this I don't think I will be able to stand it!" Yet at the same moment I realized that the warmth and joy of human love and reunion we were experiencing was but a pale reflection of the glory of divine love and fellowship we would some day experience. In that instant my thoughts went to Hank Blood and Betty Olson who had never come out of the jungles, and other fellow missionaries who had been killed in Vietnam. They had never had a homecoming like the one we were experiencing but they had gone directly to the greater one, bypassing the one on earth. For this they were the richer.

With a full heart I joined in singing the final refrain:

> *Praise the Lord, praise the Lord!*
> *Let the earth hear His voice.*
> *Praise the Lord, praise the Lord!*
> *Let the people rejoice.*
> *O come to the Father through Jesus the Son,*
> *And give Him the glory, great things He hath done!*

288